NATURE AND THE IDEA OF A MAN-MADE WORLD

NATURE AND THE IDEA OF A MAN-MADE WORLD

*A sixteenth-century drawing by Cesare Cesari-
ano of Vitruvius's description of a solar clock.*

NORMAN CROWE

An Investigation

into the Evolutionary Roots

of Form and Order

in the Built Environment

The MIT Press

Cambridge, Massachusetts

London, England

This book was set in Berkeley Book by
Graphic Composition, Inc. and was printed
and bound in the United States of America.

Library of Congress Cataloging-in-
Publication Data
Crowe, Norman.
    Nature and the idea of a man-made
    world : an investigation into the
    evolutionary roots of form and order in
    the built environment / Norman Crowe.
        p.   cm.
    Includes bibliographical references and
index.
    ISBN 0-262-03222-8
    1. Architecture—Environmental
aspects.   2. Man—Influence on
nature.   I. Title.
NA2542.35.C77   1995
720'.47—dc20   94-45594
                                CIP

for my father and brother
and in the memory of my mother

Contents

This book explores the connections between the man-made world and nature as manifested in the things that we build—towns and cities, farms and gardens, our architecture and works of civil engineering—a man-made environment over which we have some direct control. By this approach to architecture and urbanism, the book aims toward a general theory of the human environment in which the built world is seen as a kind of nature unto itself. Like the natural world out of which it is created, the built world operates in response to its own rules, its own means to change and permanence through the interaction of a host of contributing forces. Most important among those interacting forces is our human nature in all its dimensions, including our quest for meaning in the things we create, the fundamental nature of the materials out of which the world we create for ourselves is built, and our idea of nature itself.

The thesis of this book is that when we overlook the long-evolved ways of doing things, we do so at great risk. The modern notion that the urban and architectural world must be reinvented, "free of the inhibiting constraints of the past," presumes that we can, by scientific means, account for all the subtle human factors that traditional processes have accommodated in a long evolutionary descendence of the man-made world—through trial and error, patient refinement, and subtle adjustments in response to the unaccountable human characteristics that are so important to the satisfactory lives of communities and individuals.

The starting point for an inquiry such as this must necessarily turn to the origins of the human attempts at forming permanent settlements. To the primordial world of our Neolithic ancestors, from whom we inherited the idea of urban habitation and the geometries we impose on the landscape of nature, we can trace the geometry of our architecture, our gardens, and town planning, albeit through elaborate chains of transformation. It is from this time in human history, that the imprint of man was beginning to emerge in the landscape of nature, and its most characteristic expression—its artifice expressed in the medium of geometry—revealed a dauntless species out to colonize the earth.

As we have progressively perfected our world, it has moved us farther from the nature that once served as the paradigm for its creation. Vestiges of the past remain nonetheless embodied in the fabric of this world of our own making as well as in our attitudes toward it, and they continue to remind us of our origins. These vestiges are important reflections of our past priorities, but today we often fail to recognize their presence.

Each chapter considers particular circumstances that might be regarded as "natural" in origin and pinpoints their presence in things we usually take for granted. Chapter 1 considers the psychological and practical origins for the practice of building, what amounts to "an alternative nature." Chapter 2 explores the likely historical roots of the man-made world—the first permanent dwellings and settlements—and chapter 3 investigates their relationship to our sense of place and our propensity to distinguish our creations from those of nature through the language of geometry. Chapter 4 investigates our quest for unity and the ancient idea that we are responsible for maintaining a preordained harmony between the world we have created and nature. Chapter 5 traces our responses to the passing of time and discusses the inevitability of change, while chapter 6 considers the opposite, our quest for timelessness in response to "the tyranny of time." Last, chapter 7 looks at the idea of the city as the cumulative expression of our characteristic responses to nature as manifested in what we build.

Although Hegelian logic may conclude that the built environment is in some way natural, such a view is all too often used to justify actions that we know to be counter to humankind's best interests. We cannot presume that the evolution of all our things—be they towns, buildings, instruments of war, or our destructive effect on the natural environment—is the inevitable and unavoidable result of "a natural process." If, however, human intelligence, judgment, and conscious choice are factored into such a formula—as integral components of nature itself—blind determinism is out of the question. In other words, rational choice is itself a part of what we refer to as "human nature" and, thereby, is a constituent part of the man-made environment.

An obvious problem in the pursuit of a topic so broad and subtle as one on the human environment is that it is impossible to categorize some phenomena as belonging only to one area of concern. For instance, the Greek *polis*, a veritable expression of "place" in the form of a city, is described neither in the chapter on the sense of place nor in the chapter on the city but rather in the chapter on harmony and unity. That is because the achievement of the *polis* as a unified expression of the community in harmony with itself and its natural setting provides, in my mind, its most important meaning for us today. Another example concerns the house. It is introduced in relation to the natural sources of geometry as well as to our sense of place. As both source and metaphor it crops up again and again as other characteristics of the built environment are explored.

Some readers may find the discussion of issues from perception psychology to be somewhat shorter than they would expect in a study that acknowledges the importance of the mechanics of human perception in determining the form of the built world, especially the world of towns and cities. However, perception psychology is a subject so complex that it could easily swamp the broader story of all forces working together, particularly the many more subtle forces that are usually unrecognized and therefore more important to explore. Likewise, the approach involves examples from antiquity, from archaeology and history, that seem to be rather isolated instances. The emphasis is on historical examples rather than contemporary ones for two reasons: First, the more remote examples tend to accentuate the commonalties of humankind regardless of place, time, or cultural context; second, the different expressions of those commonalties tend to accent the important role of culture in determining the formal characteristics of the man-made world. The second issue is a main concern of this analysis of interaction between man, nature, and the built environment.

Each reader will come to this subject with his or her own expectations. Those readers whose bias is toward philosophical influences might expect philosophy to be treated more fully than it is. The more science-oriented readers might expect to find the role of science and technology, especially after the mideighteenth century, to receive greater emphasis than it does. Others might find that classical views are explored here in deference to romantic views of nature that arose in the midnineteenth century. Given the breadth of the subject being considered, while at the same time wishing to create a readable work that won't bury the reader in details, I must simply beg forbearance in deference to my objective to present the reader with a sense of the overall sweep of an ongoing dialectic between ourselves, the man-made world, and the world of nature in which we build. Finally, I do not go into detail in my descriptions of theories of architecture and urbanism that were intended by their authors to be regarded as "natural theories of architecture" or "natural theories of urban form." The exception to this is my rather extensive description of the foundation theories of Western classicism in architecture and urbanism. Certain influential modern theories are briefly described; the reader who wishes to pursue them more closely is referred to the original works.

Along with what might be seen by some readers as omissions or an inadequate emphasis in an area, there is the problem of overemphasis in another area to the extent that it might exaggerate that area's importance. Some may find the emphasis on architectural and urban theory of Western classicism to be given too central a position in relation to non-Western traditions. Western classical thought emanating from Greek and Roman antiquity is mainly used here because it has had such a long influence on Western architecture and is, for us, so rich in its history and content. Further, since most readers will be adequately familiar with the historical context, a comprehensive description of its setting is not required. Classical thought in architecture and urbanism serves here as a datum against which other traditions are compared. In the West we tend to see the classicism of Greek and Roman antiquity as *the* classical tradition in architecture and the city rather than one of a number of classical traditions in architecture and the city. An attempt to mitigate this problem, as well as to illuminate different approaches to the same set of problems, is made by comparing certain Japanese, Persian, and Chinese traditions with Western classicism in their respective quests for timelessness. The contrasts and similarities revealed by such comparisons, I believe, highlight the tenacity of those fundamental human propensities for timeless qualities in the form and content of an architectural setting.

A note should be included here about style and language. I have used the term "man-made," for instance, rather than "human-made" or "people-made" both because it remains in common use and especially because I am referring to an ancient notion when I use it as distinguished from the modern idea represented by the more recent "built environment." In every instance of its use "man-made" is intended here without reference to gender. Perhaps the reason that "man-made" remains in common use is that though outmoded, it still connects with our roots and the roots of our language. On the other hand, I have used "humankind" rather than "mankind" because it sounds, at least to my ear, just as good as the more traditional alternative—and I presume most readers will not find it to be pretentious nor too deferential.

It remains to be said whether an investigation such as this is useful, whether it provides information that may change the way in which we think about and operate in the practical world of the present. Today, in our growing concern for the environment, we have focused on protecting nature from industrialization and the expanding human population. We should recognize, however, that our attitude toward nature is inseparable from the way in which we approach our own world—the world of cities, buildings, and works of civil engineering, all of which we accommodate by reconfiguring the natural landscape. The environmental crisis has set upon us because we characteristically take the built world for granted. Nonetheless, there are times when we sense a connection between our attitudes toward nature and toward the world we have created within it. We may be brought up short, for instance, when something so common as an old building or a row of trees threatened by "progress" in the city incites a powerful reaction from the public. It is at such times that we realize there must be other, more fundamental forces at work that provoke such strong reactions. Even architects and planners, and other professionals responsible for guiding the building and maintenance of the built environment, tend to assume that decisions made on the basis of economic criteria by developers or governing bodies are the right ones because economic issues directly affect the well-being of a community. Perhaps our implicit understanding of things is more complex than we assume. Everyone has a world view whether or not he or she realizes it. All too often our attitudes arise from unquestioned assumptions because fundamental understanding is much harder to come by. It is important therefore for everyone—especially architects, planners, and policymakers—to step back now and then from immediate concerns to see things from another perspective, to view them in a much wider context, and to challenge their world view.

Only a century or so ago we were creating places we called "museums of natural history" for the display of the artifacts of "primitive societies," and places known as "galleries of fine arts" and "museums of science and industry" for the artifacts of industrial societies and their immediate predecessors. The implication was that primitive societies are natural and we are not, and that our artifacts are scientific, technological, and artful and theirs are not. But upon reflection we know that the things and places created by all societies result from collective acts performed in a particular cultural setting, always as expressions in one way or another of a collective will. We all share a fundamental inclination toward creativity and a desire to shape our world to suit our ideals and what we perceive to be our needs. It is the intention of this book to reveal something of the evidence of this natural inclination and desire as they manifest themselves in the built world, set as it is—both in actuality and in our minds—in contrast to the world of nature.

Acknowledgments

There were many who either helped to inspire the research that led to this book or whose assistance was important to its completion. First, I want to acknowledge my students whose intelligent inquiry and often fresh insights helped to inspire the direction this inquiry would eventually take. An earlier project that led to this book was concerned with the mechanics of conceptual order in architecture and did not yet involve a focus on the relationship between an understanding of man-made form and our implicit understanding of order in the natural world. That project provided nothing concrete except as it led to this one. Nonetheless, I am grateful to Steve Hurtt and Forrest Wilson who bravely read and provided useful comments on a very rough draft of some of the ideas it explored.

Dennis Doordan's always insightful commentary on drafts of the mature project, both with respect to the writing and the ideas explored, was invaluable. Robert Amico read and commented in depth on a strategic chapter for me, and Arlin Ginsburg encouraged me by his interest in the approach to the material as well as providing valuable critiques and references to additional sources to augment the research. James Seckinger provided the assistance of a legal scholar regarding my analogy between Anglo-American common law and the role of the classical treatise, and Philip Bess read and commented on early references to Aristotelian thought concerning nature, imitation, and the polis. My colleagues Michael Lykoudis and Samir Younés, who were subjected to numerous lunchtime discussions of these ideas, patiently gave me the opportunity to sound out thoughts on a broad range of subjects germane to this research.

There are others who may or may not be aware of their influence on this project. Behind much of the thought that led to this book is an intellectual challenge begun a long time ago at Cornell by Colin Rowe. He will likely detect Rousseau's noble savage hiding somewhere in the shadows here. And even longer ago Richard Smith's course on Japanese architecture at the University of Oregon, and especially our conversations on the subject afterward, helped to inspire this critical part of the study.

At The MIT Press thanks go to Roger Conover for his support; to Dana Andrus, who edited the manuscript, for her expertise and guidance; and to the anonymous reviewers whose commentaries helped immeasurably. Thanks also to Roger Sherwood who provided the valuable series of illustrations of comparative city plans drawn by his students at the University of Southern California;

to James Tice who printed and mailed a critical photograph from his collection that I needed at the last minute; to Wayne Copper for his permission to use some of his fine drawings of city plans; and again to Michael Lykoudis, this time for making available to me his photographs of Greek sites. I am grateful for Linda Messersmith's cheerful and skillful assistance in gathering information through the auspices of the Architecture Library at Notre Dame, and to the Hesburgh Library's Department of Special Collections for their kind permission to publish material from their collection. Notre Dame's School of Architecture alleviated my teaching schedule at a critical point in the process; not only did this provide me with more time to work on the project, but their confidence in the project provided encouragement in itself. I received assistance for a portion of the research from the Graduate School of the University of Notre Dame in the form of a Jessie Jones Travel Stipend, and the illustrations that appear here as drawn by Christopher Placco originated as part of an earlier project conducted under funding from the Graham Foundation for Advancement in the Fine Arts.

Finally, after all the thanks are said, it is important to point out that no one is responsible for any errors, admissions, or ambiguities that might occur on these pages except myself. Such is the nature of the subject that any discussion of it can be neither complete nor conclusively definitive. Therefore I now look forward to a wider discussion which I hope this work effectively stimulates: That is, of course, its ultimate purpose.

NATURE AND THE IDEA OF A MAN-MADE WORLD

1   THE IDEA OF A MAN-MADE WORLD

We enjoy the fruits of the plains and

of the mountains, the rivers and the

lakes are ours, we sow corn, we plant

trees, we fertilize the soil by irriga-

tion, we confine the rivers and

straighten or divert their courses. In

fine, by means of our hands we essay

to create as it were a second world

within the world of nature.

Cicero, *De natura deorum*
(1st century BC)[1]

1.1
View of the medieval town of Bagnorégio, Italy,
on the crest of a prominent hill presiding over its
agricultural hinterlands.

We reveal our presence in the world by creating places—buildings, towns, villages, farms, and cities. They are set either directly or indirectly into the world of nature, and they serve us as a kind of artificial nature, or "second nature," to use Cicero's term for it, one that we are able to control just as the gods of our remote past were seen to control the natural world that lay outside our door. The fundamental sources of all our knowledge, however, still remain rooted in nature. That is to say that nature, as our first environment, was our primordial source of external knowledge and the subject of our speculation about ourselves in relation to all else. By the extension of our imaginations, we created our cosmologies from what we observed firsthand in nature: life and death, the passing of days and the seasons, the geometry of the compass rose, the dome of the sky, and the spatial richness of the earth and the endless variety of living things throughout land and sea. Having once departed Eden by creating a "second nature" all our own, it has been our task to nurture and perfect it ever since—even, it seems, to the detriment of the natural world out of which it was formed.

This book is about the relationship between two realms, the man-made world and the world of nature. Our understanding of each is in relation to the other, the fundamental notion that the artifacts we produce comprise our world as something distinct from nature and that our sense of what is natural is therefore exclusive to the province of nature. As concepts they interact in a dialectical fashion to condition the way we approach nature and what we build.

The research for this book began with a quest into the human compulsion to create architecture rather than simply functional shelter. This tendency is so fundamental that we take it for granted. But compared to other living creatures, we are the only ones who direct our energies toward refining shelter into abodes that might be called works of art. From straightening a picture hanging crooked on the surface of a perfectly rectangular wall to designing the perfectly proportioned architectural facade, we often are compelled to seek perfection in a world of our own making. This observation is not new of course. The first-century BC Roman architect Vitruvius expressed wonder at the recognition that of all living creatures only humans create geometry and "talk philosophy":

> It is said of the Socratic philosopher, Aristippus that, being shipwrecked and cast on the shore of Rhodes and seeing there geometrical figures drawn upon the sand, he cried out to his companions, "let us be of good hope, for I see the traces of man." After making his observation, Aristippus departed for the city of Rhodes and there in its gymnasium talked philosophy.[2]

When did it all begin? Anthropologist Peter J. Wilson looked at evidence from the Neolithic Age—when permanent settlements began to take root in the landscape of nature. He marveled at the rapidity and extent of the transition from a hunter-gatherer's life in nature to one where humans were striving to create their own environments. He looked at these first rude settlements and wondered at the "urban revolution" of the Bronze Age to follow: "If human beings had been content for several hundred thousand years to roam shelterless and with only a minimal technology, why, all of a sudden (historically speaking), should they become seemingly obsessed with architecture, with not just settling down in one fertile place protected from the elements but erecting buildings and cities that contested with nature itself for grandeur?"[3] In a very short time a nomadic wanderer became *homo faber,* "man the maker," and thereby creator of his own place in nature, his own version of the natural world.

As inevitably happens with projects of this sort, initial questions led to others, equally fundamental and germane. An exploration of that human impulse to create artifacts imbued with a certain beauty, distinct from and recognizable within the larger world of nature, led to further questioning why the world of our creation is made to be distinct from the world of nature in the first place. To be sure, this observation is not new. As the quotation at the beginning of this chapter shows, Cicero, writing at about the time of Vitruvius in the first century BC, made a similar observation. Today, however, our immediate impulse is to search for explanations in contemporary science. Chief among these are Darwinian explanations for the human quest for order and perfection in a physical world set aside from nature. But if they are accurate, if "human nature" compels us to create our culture and our own distinct environment in contrast to the natural landscape around us, then can we assume our built world to be a kind of nature as well? Three centuries ago Blaise Pascal puzzled over similar thoughts:

> But what is nature? For is custom not natural? I am much afraid that nature is itself only a first custom, as custom is a second nature.[4]

One question begets another. If we assume that this impulse to create our own environment is natural, can we also assume that our intrinsic evolutionary association with the natural world predetermines, at least to some extent, the way we make an artificial world within the natural one? Then why does our built world so seldom directly reflect its sources in nature, its ultimate paradigm? In other words, if our cities and architecture and our feats of engineering of which those cities are composed are informed by nature, then why do they so rarely manifest nature as their source? Buildings seldom look like caves, or streets like game trails, or gardens like pieces of primeval wilderness.

Of course in the broadest sense we can describe external nature through an intellectual construct of mathematics, geometry, and abstract theory, while sensing that which we know as "natural" in contrast to what is created by humans. Ultimately our understanding of nature configures the way we approach both the environment that we create and the environment in which our creations reside. Thus our quest for understanding what we call "beauty" in architecture and cities must become an inquiry into the intrinsic idea of nature as well.

Historically the idea of our constant search for order in both the man-made world and nature runs counter to the empiricist views, most convincingly argued by John Locke, that our minds are *tabulae rasae* to be filled with sense impressions and cultural information. Immanuel Kant challenged this view by reasserting the Aristotelian position, which asks how could we order our impressions of the world around us if we did not have some innate drive to do so. Kant's view, in contrast to the mind as an empty slate approach, sees the mind as a perpetual searchlight, with natural curiosity as well as a conscious quest for survival supplying the power behind it. It also implies that there must be some system in our minds for storing and subsequently dealing with information, a system that predisposes us to use the information in certain ways.

Darwinian theory tends to support Kant's view (and, by extension, Aristotle's) rather than Locke's. It demonstrates that the search for order in our environment is a mechanism that has evolved to ensure survival within a multifarious and unpredictable world. It is a short step from here to the notion that we are compelled by something we call "human nature" to apply our search for order in nature to that which we create for ourselves: our cultures and the physical world we create for ourselves in the form of towns and buildings. *The man-made world is an alternative nature, so to speak, created by artifice and born as a human reflection of the wonder we find in the natural world—the heavens, the seasons, landscapes and seascapes, plants and animals. The assumption that there is a direct connection between the two worlds at both the subliminal and conscious levels informs the explorations in the chapters that follow.*

Occasionally the idea of nature is an obvious and intentional force directly informing an artifact's design. When it is, the manifest connection between the man-made and the natural environment easily reminds us of their mutual dependence and ultimate interdependence. More often, however, the connection between the artisan's idea of nature and the artifact created is not obvious, sometimes not even to the artisan. The idea of nature may be so intrinsic that its omnipresence fogs our vision of it. It is especially those instances where the connection is obscure, where it is at once subtle and cogent, that are the most vital and interesting and therefore warrant the closest examination.

Search for a Balanced World

The present is always shaped by the past. Today we are immersed in something commonly referred to as "the environmental crisis," stemming from our success in using nature's resources to proliferate our numbers and expand our material wealth. Now that we can more clearly see the results of past and present practices, we have begun to look again for other ways to understand the natural world upon which we ultimately depend. Clearly an exploration into the fundamental connection between ideas relating the built world and nature is appropriate and timely.

Each of us, whether we recognize it or not, acts upon a foundation of some concept of nature. If we want to live in a world that we perceive as balanced, we hold at the back of our minds the notion of an ideal balance between the built world and nature. That balance guides the way we shape our world whether or not we realize it. When some time ago the anthropologist Claude Lévi-Strauss was asked what *he* thought was the ideal balance between man and nature, he responded by suggesting a way anyone might answer that question for him- or herself. Begin, he said, by imagining conditions of extreme dominance of one world over the other. Then ask what condition in your own experience seems to strike a happy balance between these extremes. For Lévi-Strauss, in his many travels one of the most emphatic and unhappy examples of an intolerable domination by man over nature was to be found in India, in a district where every square meter of land not covered by roads or by farmers' humble domiciles was put to the production of food. Judging by the gaunt people and their frail animals, production was barely adequate to sustain them even in the best of times. Except for the sky above, no trace of the natural world was anywhere to be found. Another extreme in his experience was an

Amazonian jungle where he had found people living, it seemed to him, at the caprice of nature. There, he observed, people had little control over their own destiny, living as they were at a dark jungle's whim. Then he searched his experience for the ideal balance that lay between these extremes. The ideal, he concluded, was to be found in his own native France where, in a predominantly agricultural district, towns were dense and compact, taking up as little of the land as they might, yet within them were healthy human communities living in close harmony. In the countryside was a pattern of small fields tended by farmer-owners of the land. At the margins of their fields were hedgerows, thickets, and woodlots that functioned as both windbreaks and as habitat for pheasants, grouse, and other wildlife that might grace their tables from time to time. A geometric pattern of canals combined with meandering streams to water the land, and a cadence of comfortable farmsteads dotted the land to provide convenient access to each family's fields. The scene, in a word, was one of complete *harmony* between the human world and nature.

I have taken the liberty here of elaborating upon the three scenes, beyond what I recall as Lévi-Strauss's more economical description of them, to emphasize the respective qualities of what Cicero referred to as "a second world within the world of nature." What is significant in Lévi-Strauss's comparisons, at least for our purpose, is that he found his ideal world among settings with which he was both comfortable and familiar, there in his beloved homeland. Any objective observer might conclude that his ideal setting was indeed a harmonious one, but obviously for Lévi-Strauss that balance was conditioned both by direct experience and by culturally inculcated values. Cultural values are derived, at least in part, from where they began. That is to say, cultural values evolve and are nurtured in a certain place and they forever bear the stamp, in one way or another, of that place.

Obviously what constitutes an ideal balance between the human world and nature is not the same for everyone everywhere. It is not just a scientific definition but a humanistic imperative. It arises from a personal view of what each of us believes the world to be; of what is nature, the individual, and society; and of what the past and the future are. It is, in a few words, a world view. And what is common among most world views is an idealization of an observable state of balance between the built world and nature, one that evokes that special quality we call *harmony*. If Lévi-Strauss were an American rather than a European, the towns of his harmonious landscape might be less dense, and there would likely have been some land nearby that could be characterized as wilderness, a primeval landscape apparently untouched by the surrounding community of humans. Lévi-Strauss's ideal valley, on the other hand, is entirely under the stewardship of its human inhabitants, every part of it bearing evidence to organization by the hand of man. Our sense of what constitutes a balance between our built world and the natural world is always changing, conditioned as much by personal experience and religious and cultural forces as by coolly objective scientific knowledge.

Expressions of an Ideal Relationship with Nature

One expression of an ideal balance between the built environment and nature can be found in the instance of a house designed for a natural setting. The more profound expression of such a relationship emerges in the work of architects who are sensitive to the imperative of such a balance and who intentionally set this priority before themselves. Two twentieth-century buildings are often compared because they seem to represent diametrically opposed forces in the intellectual argument that seeks to define an appropriate relationship for a work of architecture to its natural setting: the Villa Savoye by Le Corbusier and Fallingwater by Frank Lloyd Wright. It is useful to pause for the moment here to look at these two houses because they illuminate not only the ideals but also the ambiguities that are inherent in the conscious determination of "a correct balance" of human intervention in relation to nature.

The circumstances of each house are similar. Each was designed for an affluent family whose principal residence was an urban one and who wished to establish a nearby country place for entertaining and relaxation, a rural respite from urban living. Savoye is near Paris, France; Fallingwater is near Pittsburgh, Pennsylvania. They were designed and built within about six years of one another in the late 1920s and early 1930s. Beyond these basic circumstances they are very different. Villa Savoye sits in a flat grassy meadow surrounded by trees, while Fallingwater sits deep within a woods on a high, stratified rocky perch over a stream and waterfall. Savoye stands pristine and white in its open setting like a Greek temple, clearly discernable from a distance, seemingly unobstructed and unaffected by the natural order of its site. Fallingwater, on the other hand, is made to appear to fit within nature itself. The trees enfold it; along one side it disappears into an earthen embankment, and its construction replicates the layered sedimentary stone outcroppings of its site. A visitor to either house experiences a very different sequence of events. One approaches Savoye by driving straight up to it, while to reach Fallingwater one takes a winding road through a woods that reveals the house only at the last moment. The entrance to Savoye is also direct, but one enters Fallingwater by crossing a footbridge over the stream and then descending around the house to a cavelike entrance, out of sight until the last moment, set as it is against the hillside.

The interior order of these buildings continues the dialogue that began outside. At Savoye one spirals upward toward the light, into an uncluttered, open living space, thence across an enclosed terrace to a ramp that ascends to the roof where the visitor is presented with an unglazed aperture, in the form of a window, that screens out everything around the house except for a framed view of the sky. At Fallingwater the low, almost hidden door leads the visitor to a well-lit living room that opens out onto balconies. The processional movement continues beyond the living space, as the visitor descends a stair off the principal balcony to a place beneath the building where the stream quietly flows and where the next step, it seems, would plunge one into the water and the rocks below. Savoye presents the visitor with a celestial vision, while Fallingwater returns the visitor to earth. Savoye suggests the light of reason unambiguously perceived, while Fallingwater impresses upon the visitor's senses the mystery of the earth and meanings that lie beyond the bounds of any strictly rational comprehension.

These two works of architecture, one by a Swiss-French architect and the other by an American, appear to have come from opposing positions on the ideal relationship between the man-made and nature. They are obvious expressions of the extremes between two poles of thought: one is most frequently associated with Greco-Roman classicism and continental European traditions in general, and the other with the romantic period and certain Anglo-American

1.2

Villa Savoye at Poissy by Le Corbusier (built in 1929–1931).

a

View from the approach road.

b

The entrance area below the "living platform."

c

A close look up the ramp to the "window" and the roof terrace.

1.3

Edgar J. Kaufmann House "Fallingwater" by Frank Lloyd Wright (built in 1936–1938).

a
View from the approach path.

b
The entrance.

c
Stair and platform over the stream beneath the living room.

traditions that began to emerge in the late eighteenth century. Thus the selection of these particular examples tends to exaggerate the differences between these intellectual traditions, traditions that nonetheless share a common foundation in Western thought. Further each house was expressly designed by its architect as a polemical statement about an ideal relationship with nature based on cultural factors rather than on scientific information about the natural setting. As more or less pure cultural expressions they, however, articulate ideals that have inspired many subsequent building designs.

Despite the differences an important characteristic that these works of architecture hold in common is that they were both created to be seen as clear and unequivocal products of the human hand. Even Fallingwater, which is so elaborately integrated with its natural setting, distinguishes itself from that setting at the same time. Inside it, for instance, a portion of a huge boulder that is part of the natural site emerges ever so slightly through the surface of the living room floor. It was planned that way so that even within the enclosure of the house, one is reminded that its foundation is firmly established in nature, both metaphorically and in fact. The plane of the floor that surrounds the emerging boulder is suitably abstract to be understood as artifice. If it were not, the meaning of the boulder would be lost. In both cases the effect is that of an architecture that strives toward a poetic expression of a particular idea about nature and the place of human creation in it, but which at the same time must clearly distinguish itself from nature.

At the root of any expression of an ideal relationship between the built and natural worlds there must necessarily lie a clear concept of nature itself. It was not by accident that the site selected for Fallingwater was spatially complex, with its woods, its hilly terrain, and the tumbling stream cutting through the earth to form successive terraces out of the sedimentary stone within the earth beneath the house. Villa Savoye, on the other hand, is situated amid a featureless meadow, with the surrounding wood kept far enough away from the house to appear as a distant hedge around the field rather than to be experienced as individual trees or shadowy places. Indeed, if there is to be an expression of an ideal relationship with nature, nature too must be seen in an idealized state.

While these two examples give clear expression to an ideal of the relationship between the built and natural worlds, perhaps nowhere is the idea of nature, as an ideal or as an evocation of its factual presence, more apparent than in the design of gardens. Let us compare, for instance, Central Park in New York City, Vaux-le-Vicomte near Melun, France, and a Japanese *kare-sansui,* or "dry-landscape," garden. Each of these three gardens presents us with a very different expression of the idea of nature in garden design. Central Park appears as if it were a piece of the original natural environment of Manhatten Island, as though it occupied a place that had been set aside to protect it from the advance of streets and buildings when the city began to march northward from the southern tip of the island where it was founded. Actually it was only made to look that way. Central Park was built on essentially agricultural land that had to be modified by the planting of woods, creation of lakes, and even the careful placement of boulders to give it that wonderful primeval presence it has today. Vaux-le-Vicomte, on the other hand, presents us with a completely reordered nature, an idealized world of perfect geometry built of natural materials that have been ordered into one great geometric composition focusing on the house as the center of a truly grand design. Here an otherwise chaotic nature (at least in human terms) has been made to yield to the discipline of a pure idea, while in Central Park a natural condition was re-created through artifice, a trick that cleverly conceals its genesis.

The Japanese *kare-sansui* garden is a product of human intervention that takes direct inspiration from the natural order as well. Here bushes and stones become islands in a sea of sand and moss. The sand is raked daily, each day in a slightly different way, reminding the contemplative visitor of ever-changing patterns on the surface of the sea. The small scale of the garden has the capacity to represent both itself and a larger order of nature at the same time. While Central Park is a convincing replication of the natural order at full scale, and Vaux-le-Vicomte is an elaborate and complete reordering of nature into a mathematically and geometrically perfect creation, the Japanese garden stands out as a metaphor for a primeval world before human intervention. It represents a larger world where the islands of Japan lie at the center, an island world set in an eternal, protecting, and nourishing sea.

1.4

The romantic natural world re-created at Central Park in New York City. A view of the pond at 59th Street in an engraving of c.1870.

1.5

The classical geometry of Vaux-le-Vicomte.

1.6

The metaphorical rock and sand garden of Ryoan-ji in Kyoto.

Each of these gardens represents a remarkably different idea of nature and, by extension, humankind's proper place within it. Each is a product of its own cultural setting and is thereby expressive of much of that setting's religious, philosophical, and mythological history. By intervening in the natural order, each garden becomes a kind of crystallization of a concept of nature. As landscape architect J. B. Jackson reminds us, "the garden was always based on a systematic intervention in the natural order, on the creation of an artificial environment. The weather was modified by protection against wind and sun and frost, water was provided, the soil enriched, and the plant itself was altered in shape and size and time of maturity, and eventually it became the creation of the gardener, unable to survive without his or her care."[5]

The garden is, to use Jackson's words, "based on a systematic intervention in the natural order." With this in mind, there is one more particularly illustrative transcendental expression in the art of the garden to be considered. It is the walled Persian paradise garden, a garden where the intricate interplay between the reality of the natural world and an idealization of it is carried one step further. Placed in the desert, a natural setting that is hostile to human habitation, the paradise garden re-creates a different nature, one that lies at the opposite pole from its desert setting. It is a walled oasis where water splashes, green plants flourish, and the air smells sweetly of plants and flowers cooled by shade and water. This garden has become understandably a metaphor for heaven. It is clearly intended as an expression of perfection and cosmic unity, ordered and composed of selections from the best of what nature has to offer. With a creation of such perfection, no matter that it be man-made or natural, its presence is a reality that has inspired representation in other artifacts. That is to say, the garden is a metaphor for heaven, but its intrinsic perfection inspires a metaphorical response. This response is found in the garden rug, with its colorful and intricate patterns suggesting the paradise garden. Its purpose is to provide comfort, utility, and beauty for a nomadic existence where the real garden must be left behind. While the paradise garden is an idealization of nature's most desirable places on earth in reflection of heaven, the rug is a idealization of the garden. It can be rolled up and carried anywhere. Finally, when this rug with its stylized planting beds becomes a prayer rug upon which a worshiper approaches his God, the circle is complete. Nature, the man-made world, and paradise are joined in a unifying and cosmic spiritual expression of life through

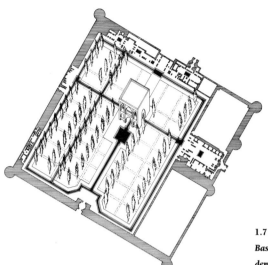

1.7
Basic scheme of the walled Persian paradise garden of Bagh-i Fin in Kashan, Iran.

ritual prayer. Harmony is reached through a combination of ritual and artifice, joining the built world and the natural in an all-enveloping unity.

These places—Villa Savoye, Fallingwater, Central Park, Vaux-le-Vicomte, and the Japanese and Persian gardens—are simply random examples of contrasting views of relationships between the man-made world and nature. They are presented here, without attempting to articulate the complex and profound cultural foundations of each, to simply illustrate something of the range and depth of the idea of a man-made world and its relationship with nature as it emerges from a variety of different cultural settings. Again, as in the example of a personal ideal of a balanced world described by Lévi-Strauss, it is obvious that our idea of nature and what is natural is both culturally conditioned and personal. At its base is something we call *harmony,* a kind of rapprochement between ourselves, and what we build, and nature. Implicit in all of this is a recognition of the presence of two distinct worlds, the natural world with its intricate and delicate balances and the one of our own making, the man-made world, with a complexity of our own making that is sometimes even mysterious in its presence.

Duality of Man and Nature

Seeing the world in this way, as a duality of man and nature, is integral to our culture and normal to our being. Our consciousness encourages us to experience the world as outside ourselves, to separate ourselves from nature and to see it as independent of our acts, even as an adversary to our purposes. To paraphrase Teilhard de Chardin, "The horse, like the man, knows where to put his foot [on the stoney path], but only the man *knows* he knows." It is this self-awareness that separates us from nature and enables us to reflect back on it, leaving open the audacious prospect of creating, in its stead, a world that is a physical expression of our culture.

If we were armed only with our hands and our intellect as means to manipulate nature to suit our desires, we would surely fail. In addition we have an ability to conceptualize in the abstract, a remarkable ability to "image"—to form a mental picture of the way things are and the way we would like them to be. Without what we call "the mind's eye" we could not conceive of a physical world that does not already exist. We are the observers of nature, the beings whose capacity for artifice separates us from nature and joins us to it at the same time. The philosopher Hannah Arendt pointed out the importance of recognizing that our lives are rooted in a world of artifice. In her terms, "we are the *homo faber*": "The man-made world of things, the human artifice erected by *homo faber*, becomes a home for mortal men, whose stability will endure and outlast the ever-changing movement of their lives and actions."[6] Ice Age artisans remembered the beasts that inhabited their world, and they re-created images of them on the walls of caves, imbuing the images with spiritual power beyond simple recognizable representation. Raised to the level of artistic expression, the figures on the walls are made to transcend factual nature by means of that remarkable human capacity to re-create from nature's example— to "imitate nature," an act of the human will that the Greeks called *mimesis*. For us this is the meaning of the figures on the walls of the caves at such places as Lascaux and Altamira: The capacity of *homo faber* to "image" permits him to move from substance to meaning and back again as he establishes his place in the broader realm of nature. In this way we explore nature, not only to satisfy immediate needs of survival but to search for immortality and meaning in it as well.

Our Shifting Idea of Nature

Since the times of the cave paintings important events in history have conditioned the way we have seen ourselves in relation to nature. Once we passed into the Neolithic Age of settlements and agriculture from an existence of wandering hunter-gatherers, our new lives as dwellers in permanent houses and settlements must surely have radically altered our view of nature and even of ourselves in relation to it. Now we could begin to see nature as that which lies outside and beyond the village rather than something of which we are a complete and inextricable part. It became possible to see the natural world as something that we might exploit and control for our own benefit. This paved the way for the ancient Greeks to separate the study of nature from the conduct of religion just as they separated the concept of a soul from the reality of the body. In doing so, they demonstrated that we could build a cosmology independent of the preconceptions of religious dogma. Religious cosmologies became metaphors for what could now be seen as objective realities. In the sixteenth century René Descartes reemphasized the dualistic idea of the separation of mind from nature when he concluded that because our minds are capable of contemplating nature, nature must reside outside our thoughts and is therefore separate from us. This dualism of mind and matter, inherited from both Plato and Aristotle, could now serve scientific objectivity, on the one hand, and religious priorities, on the other. While it gave science the objectivity it required, it provided religion with a substantiation of the existence of God by insisting that only through the intervention of God could there be a link between mind and matter. The freedom of exploration these notions of dualism gave us led across new thresholds that in turn changed or further reinforced the way we looked at nature and our place in nature.

Three thresholds over which modern science crossed that are important in how they changed our conception of ourselves in relation to nature are the Copernican revolution, Newton's predictable clockwork universe, and Darwin's theory of evolution. These three events—one in the sixteenth century, one in the seventeenth, and the third in the nineteenth—radically changed the way we looked at nature and consequently at ourselves. The first of these events placed the sun rather than the earth at the center of the universe, the second depicted the cosmos as regulated with the precision of a fine Swiss clock, and the third tended toward the removal of humankind from the center of God's creation. The first and the last of these three were particularly humbling and of course were met with resistance, anguish, and disbelief because at their base each made us more integral with nature than we had come to believe we were. The one that lay between was reassuring, on the one hand, because it suggested that nature could be objectively understood and even at a certain level made to yield to accurate predictability, though at the same time it made humankind acutely aware of a cosmos that was far more vast and impersonal than had been thought. By implication it suggested that the way to understand nature lay in the abstraction of numbers rather than the humanistic cogencies of comfortable myth.

While these ideas and discoveries eventually brought us back to the realization that we are indeed integral with nature, it also brought us the industrial revolution, which further distanced us from an intimate sense of our own presence in some kind of natural order. We learned to hybridize crops, turn iron ore into automobiles, and change coal into electricity, and this has encouraged us to continue to view the natural world as something to exploit freely and has permitted us to structure our daily lives in ways that further distance us from nature. The lights of cities blot out starry nights, our automobiles and airplanes allow us to traverse the landscape without feeling its presence, and agricultural machines and chemicals make growing food into an essentially mechanical operation. It is ironic that while science has shown us that we are at best minor actors in the broader natural order, our actions lead us in the opposite direction.

Primitive peoples live closer to the natural world and are better than we are at seeing their presence as integral with nature. We are envious of the respect they hold for the natural world. We see their existence to be in harmony with nature because these peoples tend to see their existence as part of a preordained natural order, and not in opposition to or in competition with this order as we so frequently see ourselves to be. Even our preindustrial age ancestors saw themselves as part of "a great chain of being," a kind of continuum with the cosmos, a concept that placed them much closer to nature than our more dualistic emphasis today.[7] For our ancestors, and for those primitive peoples who live, we might say, as completely a part of nature, the man—nature duality is hardly so emphatic as we find it to be. For us, like it or not, the idea of such a distinct duality is unavoidable. It permeates our everyday thought, it is implicit in our philosophies, religions, and legal systems, and it is especially integral with the foundations and conduct of our sciences.

Scientific Objectivity and the Humanist's Critique

Today there is an intense, worldwide concern for the balance between nature and the built world because it has become evident that this once harmonious relationship has gone awry. With the rise of modern science and its objectivity, and the consequent expansion of communication and industrialization, we have become more aware of the interconnectedness of all things in both our world and the world of nature, but this awareness has not yet led us to solutions to environmental problems that plague us. One explanation may be that since the scientific mode of thinking has provided us with such effective analytical tools for understanding the more obvious deterministic side of things, we tend to rely on numbers exclusive of more subtle humanistic evaluations. In other words, our tendency is to even further separate the natural world from the world of our ideals, beliefs, and existential needs, thus exaggerating the man—nature duality that is so much a part of our cultural experience. Archibald MacLeish, in a speech to alumni of Yale described it this way:

> *The old relationship between man and world—a relationship once heavy with myth and intimate with meaning—has been replaced by our new, precise, objective, dispassionate observation of the world. With the result that our understanding of our experience of the world has been curiously mutilated. The world is still there—more there now than ever—bright and sharp and analyzed and explicable. But we ourselves, facing the world, are not there. Our knowledge, that is to say, seems to exist . . . independently of us, or indeed any knower— scientific knowledge stated in its universal scientific laws, its formulas and equations true for all men everywhere and always, not for a single man alone.*[8]

The present-day environmental crisis continues to grow because of our failure to recognize the full extent of our interconnectedness with nature and to deal effectively with it as a public issue. Environmental problems concern not only science and technology but also the ideals, myths, and meaning that we have associated with nature. To date the offered solutions rely on a shift or further refinement in the technologies that are seen to be largely responsible for the environmental problems in the first place. To seek technological solutions to vexing problems has become our characteristic way of approaching problems in general. But, as suggested some time ago by historian Lynn White, Jr., we need a much revised ethic as well.[9] In his essay published in 1967, White argued that new myths and meanings must arise from the old ones to correct where the old ones have failed. That is to say, certain Judeo-Christian teachings that are integral with our culture might be deemphasized, while certain other ones reemphasized to effect a gentle shift in our focus upon the exploitation of nature to one of stewardship over the natural world in recognition of our now extensive power over it. White proposed an approach that would hold a greater potential for success than other more radical approaches in that, he argued, it would not be inconsistent with either our prevailing science or dominant religions but it would deflect their aim without disregarding their roots. In his discussion he enumerated those characteristics of Western science and technology, and their reinforcement in Judeo-Christian tradition, that are antithetical to solving the developing ecologic crisis. He traced the ideological and intellectual roots of our present problems from prehistory through Greek, Latin, and Islamic science and philosophies to Copernicus and Francis Bacon and up to the moment of his writing, which preceded by a decade or so the discovery and substantiation of such significant revelations as the hole in the ozone layer, the warming of the earth, and acid rain. What is significant about his proposal is that it suggests an intellectual framework upon which an effective solution might be built.

Much has been written about the ecological crisis, and it is not my intention here to repeat or elaborate on what has already been said. Just as White and others have looked at the historical roots of our ecological crisis to better understand how we got to where we are, my emphasis will be on the importance of looking at what I refer to as "the idea of a man-made world," to see its impact on places we build and objects we make, and thereby to better understand our place in the world of nature. The world of man and the world of nature are mutually dependent. One defines the other, not unlike the ancient Chinese yin and yang duo. We are nature's gardeners, and just as with any household garden we might attend to, the natural world will not serve us without our constant care.

White was not the only writer to advocate a shift in our system of values to abate the ecological crisis, but his argument was an early and eloquent one. Despite an alleged weakness in overemphasizing the role of religion, his argument has generated discussion that has expanded our thinking about the environment and human culture. For the argument of this book he provides another voice, along with MacLeish's, that calls for viewing factual evidence provided by science and technology in humanistic as well as scientific terms.

Summary and Comments on Method

To a large extent the perspective of this book might be referred to as anthropological. Underlying it are three assumptions: First, there is something we call "human nature" that we all share regardless of culture or historical epoch; second, it is fruitful to generalize from observations of cultural and historical examples in order to shed light on practices of our times; third, the combination of a science and humanities perspective provides the best way to understand culturally imbued acts and artifacts.

The first assumption recognizes that the human mind is guided by culturally conditioned customs, practices, attitudes, and propensities. This view does not preclude natural variations in temperament and disposition; it simply acknowledges that humans share proclivities that vary in outward expression depending on inculcated customs and values.

The second assumption follows from Aristotelian thought. It is part of the anthropological perspective that recognizes that people in different cultures do the same thing in different ways, such as in organizing their cities and architecture, because they share the same natural human proclivities which we call human nature.

The third assumption, also part of the anthropological perspective, seeks a balance of objectivity and subjectivity by combining the factual generalizations of positivistic sciences with the subjective, value-laden truths of the humanities. The intention is to arrive at a more holistic view through the application of an integrated paradigm. Anthropologist James L. Peacock described what he calls "the anthropological lens" in this way: "Emphasis on culture and recognition of the subjective aspect of interpretation link anthropology to the humanities [while] striving for systematization, generalization, and precise observation reflects the inspiration of the sciences."[10] That is not to say that my treatment of issues claims to be entirely consistent in its application with the tenets of anthropology. I am an architect, not an anthropologist. But I have depended on anthropology for a frame of reference that is both logical and consistent.

Much of the discussion in the chapters that follow cuts across cultural boundaries and historical time. Taken together, the examples will afford a kind of story, the story of how we have come to build a world within nature and what that might portend for our future. Most of the examples will be familiar. Each, however, has been selected to reveal something more of the relationship between the idea of nature and the idea of the man-made, and for what it reveals about this relationship and thus about ourselves. Many of the examples were selected *because* they are distant from our common experience. Some may even seem, at first, exotic. But they all reflect our human, often subliminal, attitudes and propensities. Often the more distant example from our everyday experience will enlighten our view of the familiar by its contrast with it.

The late Jacob Bronowski used to say that his aim as a mathematician and philosopher was to reveal "the hidden likeness in diversity."[11] "Science," he said, "is nothing else than the search to discover unity in the wild variety of nature." In saying this, he was inspired by Samuel Coleridge who defined beauty as "unity in variety."[12] Seen in this way, science and beauty are objectives of the same quest. A search for commonalities will pervade this exploration as well. As we explore the idea of our built world set against the backdrop of nature, we will focus on those characteristics that continue to reoccur in various guises, that suggest a special unity of purpose among the myriad artifacts humankind has produced. Although we will look at only a segment of the built world, its architecture will provide us with a basis for understanding the rich and complex creations that humans have constructed within the world of nature.

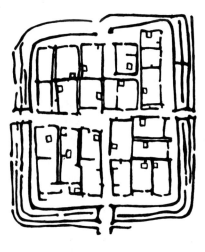

2.1

Fundamental clues to the formation of the idea of a man-made world.

a

Writing and permanent dwelling: Early Chinese ideogram for "shelter" is formed by gable roof shape. Symbols within can form words for "family," "peace," "resting-place," and "ancestral altar"; shown is ideogram for "cold," depicted by man on a mat surrounded by symbols for firewood.

b

Agriculture: Petroglyph from c. 3500–3000 BC, central Germany, indicates domestication of animals and tilling of the soil for planting.

c

Foursquare layout of the prehistoric Karanovo Village in present-day Bulgaria, dated 4700–4500 BC; typical features of many early settlements are the enclosing wall with four gates on the intersecting axes and the separate hearths (small squares within the houses) for each family.

2 GEOMETRY AND THE PRIMACY OF DWELLING

How did a built world, conceptually complete and an entity unto itself, come about in the first place? This is to ask how the first houses and settlements came about, what they were like, how they conditioned the way their inhabitants thought, and what their subsequent effect was on the societies they sheltered. These questions have long been pondered by anthropologists, historians, and others, and theories about them abound.

The first hunter-gatherers to settle and become farmers began to consciously manipulate the natural order to better position themselves in the world around them. Over the millennia our ability to consciously control our individual lives has increased enormously, while our biological makeup has changed very little, if at all. We extended our evolution beyond biology by means of human culture through such achievements as the use of fire, the domestication of animals, the management of crops, and the invention of writing. The first tentative steps toward permanent shelter perhaps included the fabrication of the nomad's tent. The tent, along with the taming of a migratory animal, might well have provided for the first realization that humans could manipulate nature in a permanent way to their advantage, thus leading to the creation of what might be considered a man-made world. The tent meant that the wanderer was assured of shelter no matter where he found himself to be when night fell, and the domesticated animal spared man the hazardous and arduous pursuit across the landscape of nature. Such events led the way to the creation of permanent settlements and the development of architecture, an invention that would become the archetype for myriad means to circumvent the unpredictability of nature. With Eden left behind, a new garden, one permanently positioned in the world of time and space, became the preoccupation of those who chose to wander no more.

Dwelling within fixed and permanent domiciles allowed direct control over the immediate environment through the purposeful rearrangement of nature's materials—wood, stone, and earth—to suit human needs alone. *The domicile and the settlement would become metaphorically a new nature, one that is determined and shaped by the hand of man.* The purpose of the domicile and settlement was to fix certain characteristics among the ever-changing aspects of the natural world and thereby provide a predictable environment. Granaries extended the harvest into the dead of winter, and simple huts protected their inhabitants from the winter cold and summer downpours. The settlement came to be regarded as a bulwark against the uncertainty of a capricious nature. Because the domicile provided an alternative to the natural environment, it was regarded as having certain natural characteristics, "conjured into it," so to speak. These early dwellings, like those of some primitive peoples today, were often imbued with magic and situated according to a strict directional orientation and alignment with the heavens or with an important topographic feature such as a distant mountain or sacred place, or an important feature of the immediate surrounding landscape. In this way dwellings could be integrated with the order of the infinitely larger world outside them. Their roof, in metaphorical terms, was the sky, and their smoke hole the sun. The walls were analogous to the boundaries of the cosmos, while the floor was to the roof as the earth was to the sky. Anthropologist Christine Hugh-Jones has observed similar customs among present-day villagers in South America: ". . . people must transpose the system of the universe with its creative processes onto the concrete systems which they are able to control, or at least change, through practical action."[1]

To expand on the notion that a permanent domicile is regarded as a part of nature, we may consider the situation where the house becomes part of a village rather than something that stands alone in the wilderness. Now the village is in its relationship to the natural world as is the single domicile alone in nature. In this way the house relates to the broader world of nature as a constituent part of the village. And it follows that every family is to the group of families that comprises the village community as every house is to the physical village. Just as the house is a cosmos for the family, the village is a cosmos for the villagers. In traditional societies it is often easy to detect an orderly hierarchy from the individual within a family to the family within the larger community, and that order is mirrored in a parallel hierarchical relationship between the individual house and the physical village of which it is a part. And like the house, traditional villages are often delineated from without—that is, from nature—by surrounding walls, and those walls are in turn pierced by carefully placed gates that, like the door to a lone domicile, connect the village with the world outside it.

But before looking at towns and buildings and their conscious and unconscious relationship to the natural world, it is important to start by looking briefly at the predominant theories that describe how civilized order came about. Then, having obtained a sense of the human communities that made architecture and urban order possible, we will better understand architecture and urbanism in terms of their contrast with the world of nature.

From a Life in Nature to Living in a Setting Shaped by Man

The traditional view of how complex civilized societies came about holds that kinship systems and the quest for material well-being, in concert with the advent of agriculture including the domestication of animals, set the stage for building a civilized order. The natural structure of the biological family provided humankind with a paradigm for progressively larger units of human association such as clans, tribes, city states, and nation states. For instance, in Roman civilization it can be shown that there evolved a continuous ordering of society from the family to the city and the nation and even to the political structure of the empire. Each unit of this order reflected the human family, with the father, the *paterfamilias*, at its head and everyone else with his or her own responsibilities and expectations hierarchically ordered according to custom. The city's magistrates reflected the role of the *paterfamilias* at the level of the city, and so on, with other political and social units tending to follow suit.[2] Aside from the distant Roman example, there are the more familiar examples, both ancient and modern, where the head of a family is literally the head of the state while other members of his or her extended family are in charge of specific territories or subdivisions of the governing apparatus. This is a description of a typical monarchy or sheikdom, of course, where the political structure of a region or a nation is the extension of its controlling aristocracy. And when empires are formed from the expansion of monarchical rule, they usually entail arrangements between ruling families, often formed through intermarriage among the aristocracies of the respective countries, either in lieu of or following on the heels of military conquest.

Along with the observation that early political structures followed the model of the biological family, it is important to note that there had to be some motivation for creating increasingly larger political and social structures in the first place. Larger social and political entities meant greater power to those in charge and a consequent increase in the division of labor, which made the production of goods more efficient and hence enhanced a people's well-being through the accumulation of material goods. This is a view that squares nicely with the empiricist premise that people learn from experience. That is; to believe that there was a conscious quest for ever larger social and political systems, we are not required to hold that there had to be a natural predisposition to seek after such ordering. The advantages of orderly social structures are self-evident. We may simply assume that cool logic demonstrated the advantages, so people invented orderly social structures to solve problems or gain new advantages. Any natural social organization would have provided a paradigm for intellectually ordering a people's experience of the world, likely leading to the classification of things throughout the natural environment. Émile Durkheim recognized this relationship:

> Society was not simply a model which classificatory thought followed; it was [society's] own divisions which served as divisions for the system of classification. The first logical categories were social categories; the first classes of things were classes of men, into which these things were integrated. It was because men were grouped, and thought of themselves in the form of groups, that in their ideas they grouped other things. . . . Moieties were the first genera; clans, the first species.[3]

Still, while the assumption that we build upon natural paradigms might provide a satisfactory explanation for the genesis of social and political structures, could it also explain the physical properties of towns and buildings as reflections of a conscious quest to create a world that appears to us as separate and distinct within its natural setting? A decidedly post-Kant and post-Darwinian view would suggest that the intentional creation of an orderly environment is driven at least in part by a natural or innate desire to effect control over the immediate environment for the obvious purpose of comfort and survival, but it does not explain why that human world is created as something distinct in its natural setting. It simply bolsters the reason for its existence. Durkheim's explanation, then, does not consider the imposition of geometries on nature. There still has to be *something* beyond kinship patterns, agriculture, and animal domestication and the quest for material security to account for what Aristippus (as related by Vitruvius; see chapter 1) concluded when he saw "traces of man" on the shores of Rhodes.

Why is it, we still have to ask, that the physical world of our own making is characterized by the geometries of architecture and ordered settlement patterns while the natural world around us presents itself to us as an enigma of visual complexity? Or is it really so enigmatic for us? We learn to predict the seasons and see order in the heavens and give names to plants, places, and creatures. Perhaps, as previously suggested, our world is actually a reflection of the natural one after all. It is just that the order of nature manifests itself in the man-made world as a kind of abstraction. This abstraction is born of a combination of human intellect and our observation of nature; but nonetheless it is an abstraction—one that we do not easily recognize because it is so implicit in *our* nature.

Setting these questions aside for the moment, it is of interest to speculate on the effect that a geometrically ordered architectural and urban environment, once created, might have had on those inhabitants of the Neolithic Age whose daily lives came to be regulated by a newly built world as opposed to the natural one of their ancestral past. This is to suggest that the order imparted to artifacts, regardless of its source, might serve as a paradigm, influencing the way our early ancestors thought about themselves, how they continued to structure their world, and even how they saw the natural world more and more as lying outside themselves. There must be a dialectical relationship between the order we create and our propensity to seek order in nature. Our innate drive to constantly search for order in nature, to understand the natural world so that we can live more effectively in it, has provided us with a model for constructing our own world with the predictability we have failed to find in nature; the built world has in turn given us a model for further understanding nature, in a dialectical fashion ad infinitum. At the most basic level this is to say that our architecture has provided us with a paradigm for structured thought. "[House plans] are practical symbols mediating between the natural symbols of the body and the environment, transforming the one into the other or creating the link between them. To the extent that this is so, and to the degree they serve to record thought and depict it in a more permanent form, houses make for more extensive and structured thinking about the world than in societies without architecture."[4] In Navajo tradition, for instance, the building of a domicile—that is, a hogan—is considered prerequisite to ordering one's adult life. Accordingly ". . . without a hogan you cannot plan. You can't just go out and plan other things for your future; you have to build a hogan first. Within that, you sit down and begin to plan."[5] In other words, the process of building a hogan and the formal order it imparts, in addition to providing a place to sit while planning the next step, acts as a paradigm for understanding and imparting order henceforth. It is more than just a shelter. Here the domicile is seen as *the* fundamental paradigm for an ordered existence.

Architecture as a Paradigm for Order

A convincing explanation for the dialectic between the built world and nature goes like this: The transition from a nomadic hunter-gatherer society to one that resides in more or less permanent structures located in settlements profoundly changed the way people think, especially about the natural world around them. The hunter-gatherer had accepted the natural world just as it was; he had followed the seasonal migrations of herds and the seasonal ripening of edible fruits, and yielded to the exigencies of nature in much the way other creatures had. If he built shelter, it was temporary, assembled out of limbs, grasses, and leaves of the forest floor; if he fashioned something less temporary, say, a tent of animal skins or of woven fur or plant fibers, it was collapsed and transported with relative ease from one encampment to another. But once the wanderer had chosen to dwell in a fixed place on earth, once his shelter and settlement became permanent, his view of nature changed. Accordingly the settlement provided a distinct "alternative nature," a "second world within the world of nature," as Cicero called it. The agricultural basis for his permanent settlement itself provided an example of effective human intervention in the order of nature. The natural landscape could be interrupted for fields of crops, and animals could be domesticated to serve exclusively human purposes. Plant and animal domestication began sometime between 7,000 and 6,000 BC in the Middle East with the cultivation of grains, and scattered over the globe to Southeast Asia with rice cultivation and later to Mesoamerica with the development of the systematic cultivation of maize. In major areas of the world, "man the hunter and gatherer" became "man the farmer" and before long "man the urban dweller."[6]

Three Houses in Nature

A look at some "primitive" domiciles is in order here to see how the first houses must have related with their natural setting. They will reveal how the structures of nature and early humans would have been inextricably connected. In examining the houses of people who live much closer to nature than ourselves, we generally find these houses to be more finely attuned to the natural world around them than our own houses. In what are sometimes called "low-energy societies," where the consumption of external energy sources such as fuel for heating is low, the domiciles are characteristically efficient in their construction and consumption of energy. To gain a sense for the broad range of effective accommodations that people have been able to make with the world around them, we will compare three disparate domiciles: an Inuit igloo from the arctic north, a Navajo hogan from the American desert southwest, and an indigenous house from tropical Southeast Asia.

Each of these three dwellings is built with maximum efficiency in mind; thus each is sensitively, even delicately, attuned to its setting and the natural characteristics of the climate. But they are all based on the same physical principles. Among those principles are such well-known and important scientifically verifiable phenomena as the facts that warm air rises while cold air sinks, that warm dry air carries away moisture which tends to cool our skin while warm moist air does not unless it is moving fairly fast, that cellular materials are good insulators to the transfer of heat through them while solid, dense materials are not, that heat reflects off shiny light colored surfaces while it is absorbed by dark and dull ones, that moving air promotes cooling while trapped and still air does not, and so on.

Not surprisingly we find the igloo to be a smooth, closed form, trapping inside it the air heated by the bodies of its inhabitants and the tiny flame of their whale-oil lamp. Its long tunnel-like entrance with a wind baffle in front of it places the living area a long way from the winds whistling around the front "door." Its domical shape, as well as responding to tried and true structural principles, presents the least possible surface area to the outside environment for the transfer of heat, while that same shape on the inside tends to reflect heat radiated by the bodies of the occupants and their whale-oil lamp back to them. The floor on which they sit is raised above a cold-air sink to minimize the effect of cold air while maximizing the effect of warmer air around the people. And finally, it is built of water frozen into ice and snow which is readily available and easily cut with bone cutting tools into blocks to be neatly stacked to make walls and a sturdy domical roof. It is a temporary shelter, easily and quickly built, and its smooth, curving, low profile is especially effective against the arctic's high winds and deep cold. Every characteristic of its form and construction, it seems, is a purposeful accommodation to natural forces and materials.

The hogan is built out of the dry desert earth in combination with logs and sticks gathered from the mountains, usually a considerable distance from its immediate setting. Unlike the igloo it is intended as a permanent building from the start. Its thick dark walls absorb the desert sun's daytime warmth and then radiate at least some of that warmth into the interior during cool desert nights. Its east-facing entrance, easily closed against the cold nights with a flap of animal skin or woven cloth, catches the first warming rays of morning sun when the flap is drawn back to welcome the day. And the interior is arranged so that family members normally seat themselves against the warm walls all

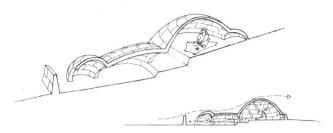

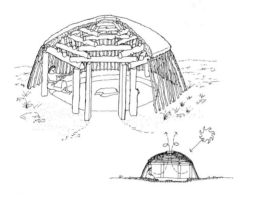

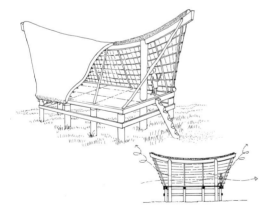

2.2
Domiciles shaped by man in accord with the natural environment.

a
Inuit igloo.

b
Navajo hogan.

c
Tropical house of southeast Asia.

around, with their focus on the center where a small cooking fire burns. This is the hearth, the center of a quiet inner world that closes out the night; above the hearth is the smoke hole that lets the smoke out and during the day admits light to the interior. The smoke hole is a link with the heavens, a constant reminder of the relationship between the world outside and the one within.

Finally, there is the tropical house. It is open, light, and airy. While the hogan is built for bright hot dry days and cool nights and the igloo is set up against the freezing wind with little purposeful distinction between night and day, the tropical house lifts its inhabitants up into the breezes, away from moist earth with its scurrying insects and slithering reptiles. Its large roof provides maximum shade for the elevated living platform and the high ridge allows warm air in the interior to rise high above the inhabitants then vent out the roof's upturned ends. The roof's high, steep profile provides maximum protection against heavy downpours during the rainy season. While the essence of an igloo and a hogan may be seen as "closure," here it is "openness."

Each of these houses came about and was perfected through traditional, evolutionary processes involving trial and error. Once such dwellings were perfected, minor adjustments to compensate for changing conditions around them could be easily made. Indeed modifications to their form or materials can effectively be improvised so long as the changing social requirements or seasonal climatic variations of their respective settings are not too great or too sudden. In this respect these domiciles are like living organisms, able through the ingenuity of their occupants to incrementally adapt to their environment so long as they remain essentially as they were from the beginning, delicately and inextricably connected to the natural world around them. Such is always the nature of tradition-oriented processes. Nature is seen as complex and varied and, more important, as immediate and concrete. It is not nature in the abstract but nature as it is experienced firsthand.

These domiciles may be seen as highly evolved examples of fundamental shelter. Their direct, intricate, and delicate relationships with their environment serve as a constant reminder to those who live in them that there must always be a consummate resonance between what they build and nature. Beyond the basic requirements of shelter, they stand as paradigms of a man-made order constructed in response to a tangible and immediate world of nature.

Primacy of the House

If we try to imagine what the first building and, consequently the first work of architecture, must have been like, we may assume that at least it must have been a house. The idea of a house as the origin of architecture pervades the myths of societies everywhere. Even our names for various nonresidential buildings reflect either their origins as houses or our desire to relate them to mythical origins as houses. From the courthouse to the lighthouse to the houselights in the theater and the houses of Congress and Parliament, our language makes frequent reference back to more humble beginnings for now specialized buildings that have evolved along with the specialized functions they accommodate. Martin Heidegger traced the linguistic sources and transformations of words referring to the places where we dwell to demonstrate the profound importance the very concept of dwelling has on us. He pointed out that language tells us about the nature of a thing. So it follows that the nature of our collective sense of the idea of the house as both a primary source for architecture and a reflection of a fundamental human proclivity can be illustrated etymologically.

Heidegger's account of the linguistic ties that signal the importance of the idea of "house" from our ancestral beginnings begins with a description of the word *buan,* the Old English and High German word for building. It meant "to dwell." Therefore the act of building and the creation of a place to dwell may be seen to have been conceptually synonymous, whereby "to build" would have also meant "to dwell." "To be a human being means to be on the earth as a mortal. It means to dwell."[7] *Bauen* further meant to cherish and protect, to preserve and care for (specifically to till the soil), and to cultivate the vine, as Heidegger has pointed out. "To build" was, in this sense, "to nurture." He went on to conclude that *building* therefore is really *dwelling,* and it is the act of dwelling that makes us what we see ourselves to be: human. Since the fundamental character of dwelling is one of nurturing, the concept of the duality of man and nature as separately distinguishable entities is resolved through this fundamental and continuous act—"the act of dwelling"—which is "building and nurturing." Indeed to build and nurture is to be at peace. The house—that primal expression of building—if seen as symbolic of a broader existential

2.3

Symbolic house forms found in funerary sites.

Top row, left to right:
An example from China, 1500–1027 BC; two examples from Greece, 750–725 BC; and an example from Etruscan civilization, c. 800 BC.

Bottom row, left to right:
A late Neolithic or early Bronze Age example from Kusdeirah in Syria; three examples from Japan, AD 250–550.

view, can represent humanity and peace as well as notions about harmony between the built world and nature.

In recognizing the house as integral with the concept of dwelling, especially as it is reflected in language, it follows that our broader sense of the place where we dwell puts the house at its center. A modern definition of "house" is "a private dwelling." In a sense the house becomes the embodiment of the center of the place where we dwell—our plot of ground, our farm, or our province, county, or "world." The house is often seen as the center of our domain no matter how large that domain may be. Just as the house is at the center of a larger domain, at the center of the house lies the hearth. The hearth has traditionally been both the symbolic and real focus of the lives of those who reside there. And that too is reflected in language: For instance, the Latin word for hearth is *focus*.

Today existential qualities of dwelling and house are more often than not held below a level of conscious awareness, but their influence, whether subtle or overt, is nonetheless a part of us. Gaston Bachelard reflects a common, though often unconscious, fact that the houses in our experience effect the way we understand the rest of our world: "For our house is our corner of the world. As has often been said, it is our first universe, a real cosmos in every sense of the word." He reminds us that "[the house] is the human being's first world. Before he is 'cast into the world' . . . man is laid in the cradle of the house. . . . Life begins well, it begins enclosed, protected, all warm in the bosom of the house."[8]

Another writer who was particularly interested in what our dwellings mean to us is the religion historian Mircea Eliade. Eliade showed that even the modern conception of the role and meaning of a house is a shadow of an earlier one imbued with mystical and religious significance. He went to great lengths to demonstrate through examples how religious beliefs and rituals practiced by primitive peoples have their direct counterparts in practices and attitudes of modern societies, although they are now couched in "more rational," and usually secular, terms. These basic propensities remain because they are natural ones. Some modern counterparts include topping-out ceremonies by construction crews during which a young green sapling is secured to the highest part of the building, house warmings to celebrate a family's move into their new house, and the custom of changing some important part of a newly purchased house to "personalize it" and thereby truly take possession of it, purging it of the presence of its previous inhabitants. More direct descendents include cornerstone laying and groundbreaking ceremonies, the blessing of a newly completed building with prayer and the sprinkling of the threshold with holy water, and the practice of burying historic or sacred artifacts in what is referred to, in modern terms, as a "time capsule" in the foundation.

Eliade saw houses as far from inert artifacts, varieties of "machines for living" but rather as "*the universe that man constructs for himself by imitating the paradigmatic creation of the gods, the cosmogony. Every construction and every inauguration of a new dwelling are in some measure equivalent to a new beginning, a new life. . . .* Even in modern societies, with their high degree of desacralization, the festivity and rejoicing that accompany settling in a new house still preserve the memory of the festival exuberance that, long ago, marked the *incipit vita nova.*"[9] Eliade of course is not alone in these observations. Numerous instances of the establishment of a direct connection between the house and the cosmos have been recorded by anthropologists in the field. In studies of certain Amazon villages, anthropologist Christine Hugh-Jones observed: "People must transpose the system of the universe with its creative processes onto the concrete systems which they are able to control, or at least change, through practical action. To do this they construct their houses to represent the universe."[10]

Like Heidegger, Eliade pointed out that complex public buildings likely descended from humble abodes. Even religious architecture might be seen to have evolved from the more common architecture of dwellings, reflecting earlier notions that imbued houses with sacredness: ". . . religious architecture simply took over and developed the cosmological symbolism already present in the structure of primitive habitations," according to Eliade.[11]

Such an evolution is especially clear when it comes to the Greek temple. The temple—a house of a deity—was usually built to contain an effigy of the deity to which it was dedicated. Its likely a descendant of an ordinary domicile by way of the archaic Mycenean megaron, a sort of large house/palace with a hearth in the center and a smoke hole in the roof above it. The megaron of a king was more or less an enlarged version of the ordinary megaron-house of its time. It served as both the center of government and of religion in archaic Greece, long before nonmonarchial forms of government came to characterize

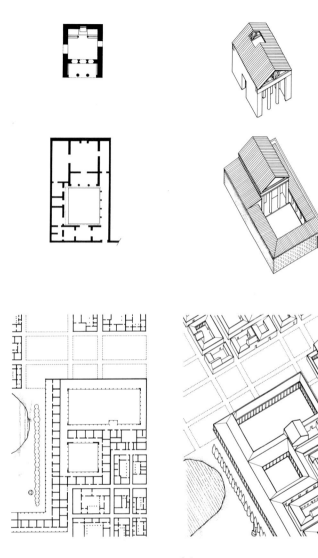

2.4

***The Mediterranean peristyle house as it may
have evolved from the archaic megaron* (top) *to
peristyle city house* (middle) *and integrated in
the Hellenistic Greek city with its agoras enclosed by stoas* (bottom). *In the hierarchy of
spaces the agora served the public the way the
peristyle court served the family.***

Greek city states. In its evolution to a religious temple it gained a peristyle, or continuous colonnade, around its enclosed core. Then the megaron's single room became known as the temple's *cella*. But before the colonnade wrapped itself completely around the temple to become a peristyle, the emerging temple recalled the early megaron of Bronze Age Mycenaean architecture. Besides being somewhat crude in their construction compared with later ones, the first temples were, as we would expect, simpler in their form and less refined in their proportions. Some of these temples, it is believed, had hearths in them, like the residential megaron, along with the cult statue of the deity, as well as colonnaded porches "in antis," like the megaron. The basic prostyle temple, as it is called (a one-room structure like a house with a "front porch" made by simply extending the roof beyond the front wall and supporting it with columns), may be surmised from the surviving ceramic models of houses (or temples) dating somewhere between 750 and 725 BC, shown in illustration 2.3. After this basic, recognizable form for a temple was firmly established, there ensued a series of steps toward greater elaboration and monumentality until the most elaborate and monumental example of the complete peristyle temple was reached. At some point in this process it appears that the wooden house now turned religious temple was made permanent by rebuilding it in stone. The process of making permanent what was previously impermanent will be discussed in chapter 5 where we consider the meaning of the evolutionary sequence of designs of the Greco-Roman temple. For the moment the evolutionary sequence from megaron to temple will stand as just one example of a monumental public building having descended from a house. It provides us with material evidence of the connection between archaic origins and evolved prototypes, just as do linguistic and psychological links such as those described by Eliade, Heidegger, Bachelard, and others.

If we want a more irregular example of religious buildings having descended from houses, there is the example of the Christian church which began as the *domus ecclesia,* ordinary peristyle houses throughout the Empire that provided clandestine shelter for an illegal fledgling religion. If we pursue the evolution of the megaron exclusively as a house, it appears, in effect, to have been turned inside out to produce the urban peristyle house, a ubiquitous domicile throughout the Greek and Roman world from a very early time. Its line of descent might have eventually produced the Roman *insulae,* or urban

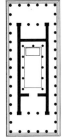

TEMPLES ROMAINS

2.5

The classical temple may have also evolved from the megaron house.

Left:

Two standard Greek and Roman temple forms.

Right:

Some typical Roman temples arranged in order of their increasing complexity, paralleling their likely evolutionary development.

apartment house, which in turn can be seen as the ancestor of the Italian palazzo. But to return to the evolution of religious structures, the *domus ecclesia's* evolution was interrupted when Christianity became legal under Roman law and the institution of the religion was consequently Romanized. In the process of Romanization the house was abandoned and replaced by a modified version of a long-established official governmental building, the basilica. Here is an example of a conscious interruption in the natural descent of a building type for the purpose of interrupting the evolution of the institution it housed—this time in order to exert control over its destiny by deflecting the course of its evolution. Countermovements among the religion's followers have attempted to reinstate the *domus ecclesia* as a means of returning the religion to its roots, and hence to its more fundamental structures and values. In this example the elaborate and successful attempt by a Roman emperor to erase the house as the source of the physical church building and to substitute a building that was part of a different evolution underscores the importance of the continuous linage of a building type in the first place, especially one that is bound to be perceived as highly symbolic from the beginning as is always the case with a religious structure.

Natural Sources for the Geometry of Architecture

Archaeological evidence indicates that an elaborate and often sophisticated geometry characterized the evolving house. Just as geometric decorations adorned clothing, pottery, and other important artifacts produced by very early societies, geometry appears as integral to architectural form very early in the evolution of the house. While geometry was primarily a surface embellishment for pottery and an elaboration of weaving patterns of cloth and baskets, its place in the creation of buildings was fundamental to the determination of a building's overall form. This geometry arose from two natural sources. One may be referred to as *the order of building;* it comes directly from the building process, from the structural characteristics of construction materials. The other is related to the human body and human perception of space. Both of these sources—construction processes and human perception—warrant close ex-

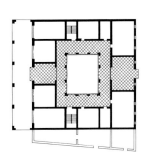

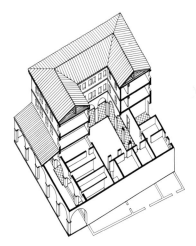

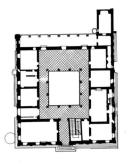

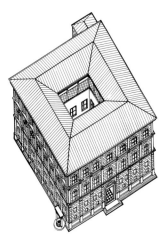

2.6

A late Roman urban apartment block, or insula, from Ostia, the port city of ancient Rome, and the Piccolomini Palace in Pienza, a typical Renaissance palazzo whose architecture is a likely descendant of the insula.

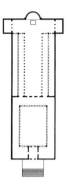

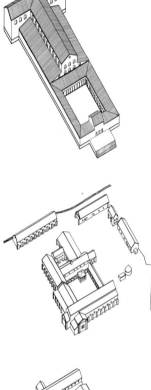

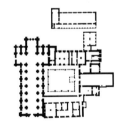

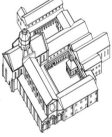

2.7

The probable evolution of the colonnaded/ar-
caded public courtyard from the Hellenistic
agora and Roman forum to the early Christian
basilica forecourt (top) *and the monastery clois-*
ter (middle and bottom).

amination. We will look first at the impact of human perception and body-related geometry on building and then at the more familiar impact of building materials and constructional priorities.

Body, Environment, and Perception

Body- and perception-related geometry is one of those connections to nature expressed in architecture and urbanism that is so implicit that we tend overlook its importance, let alone its very presence. It is obvious, for instance, that doors must be tall enough to walk through, windows positioned to see out of, and seats at the right height for comfort. But beyond these considerations are dimensions that are important to architecture that cannot be so easily described. These are the dimensions that can be traced to our own bodies and our perception of nature in terms of our bodies. Our bodily dimensions link our present experiences in the built environment to our ancestral experience in nature.

Imagine yourself looking out to sea. As you observe the horizon, the line it makes separating earth and sky appears straight, flat and perfectly horizontal. The psychological effect of this horizontality over such a broad extent is calming. Our understanding of it comes from an awareness of our own bodies. In gazing at the horizon, we intuitively feel its horizontality because our bodies are at right angles with it. We are upright while it lies in repose before us. We are intuitively aware of gravity because we walk upright and must maintain our balance while in this rather unstable position, unstable at least as compared with those creatures whose bodies are parallel to the ground because they stand on four legs rather than two. In our perception of things, "upright" is perfectly perpendicular to the horizon. In contrast, if we look, for instance, at the horizon while executing a banked turn in an airplane, the horizon no longer appears horizontal. We *feel* like we are in an up-down relationship because of the centripetal force of the airplane's turn and its effect on the balance apparatus of our inner ear, so the horizon appears to us as tipped. That is because we judge the angle of the horizon from our body's sense of what is vertical. We judge things outside ourselves from a body-related understanding *first,* and an intellectual understanding *second,* not the other way around. It is safe to say that our perception of the world around us is first and foremost in relation to our bodies, even though we prefer to think of our perceptual responses as more objective than that implies. According to Kant:

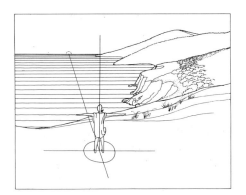

2.8

Existential space. A person looking out to sea is oriented to the landscape by the geometry of his body.

2.9

By relating the world around us to the geometry of our bodies, we reconcile our place in nature.

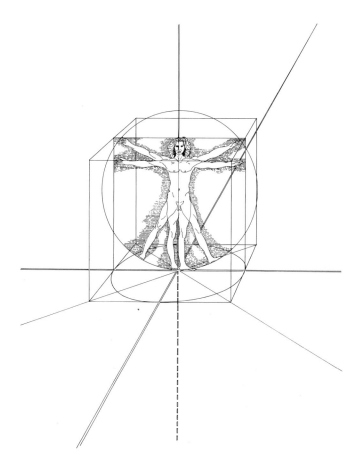

Our geographical knowledge, and even our commonest knowledge of the position of places, would be of no aid to us if we could not, by reference to the sides of our bodies, assign to regions the things so ordered and the whole system of mutually relative positions.[12]

To expand on the situation of gazing at the horizon while standing, our orientation is further keyed into our bodies through an awareness of a horizontal, or "plane-oriented" relationship with the scene before us, as well as with the vertical or perpendicular relationship to it described above. When we stand, we are intuitively aware that our primary orientation to the world is in relation to both our body's symmetry and its frontality. In other words, we are first of all aware of the direction we are facing; and the secondary characteristics of our frontality follow suit. That is, we are secondarily aware of the existence of left, right, and rear with respect to our frontality. Thus our awareness of our bodies in space involves a cartesian, or foursquare, relationship of ourselves to the world around us from the spot where we stand. Although all this may sound basic and obvious, it is very important in understanding how we intuitively structure our three-dimensional physical world of space. We perceive the world from a referential structure of right angle relationships in both the horizontal and vertical planes, *and it is from this natural characteristic of our perception of the world that geometry is born.*

The landscape that stretches before us—namely the natural world of our immediate awareness—forms the tangible basis for our idea of the cosmos which extends from ourselves to far distant places, out of sight but not entirely out of mind. In light of our natural foursquare perception of our environment, it is not surprising, then, that early humankind placed the cruciform stamp on their settlements and their most sacred buildings. Note, for instance, the foursquare layout of the prehistoric village shown in the illustration at the beginning of this chapter. The Egyptian hieroglyph for a city, and the basic symbol for cities across many cultures consisted of a right angle cross inscribed in a square or a circle. The Roman way of laying out a military encampment that would become an imperial town involved a ritualized creation of the right angle crossing of two streets, the *cardo* and the *decumanus,* intersecting at the center of the new encampment. These two streets in turn stretched straight out into the hinterland after passing beyond the line that defines the boundary of the

2.10

Four representations of the town or city. Clockwise, from upper left: Early Chinese ideogram for "village," c. 1300–612 BC; Assyrian bas-relief showing scenes of city life, c. 1600 BC; Egyptian hieroglyph for "city," c. 3110–2884 BC; Icelandic drawing of the "heavenly city of Jerusalem," thirteenth century AD.

castrum, as the encampment was called, and onward to the horizon and beyond, thence to the far reaches of the empire and back to Rome itself. The tie to Rome was all-important to the existence of the *castrum* and the imperial town it would become, and the *cardo* and *decumanus* served along with other reminders throughout the fabric of the settlement to ensure that Rome, while out of sight, was never out of mind.

Besides this foursquare geometry the resonance between an unconscious awareness of our body's dimensions and its relation to space arises from a complex set of perceptions. For instance, we can sense an invisible volume or bubble of space surrounding our bodies, one that shrinks and grows depending on the situation in which we find ourselves. If we sense that someone is standing too close to us, we have a tendency to back away, or when we stand in a crowded elevator car, we all face forward and avoid eye contact as a means to negate the discomfort of standing so close to strangers with whom we are not in conversation. This characteristic of human behavior is, of course, strongly conditioned by cultural circumstances. Northern Europeans find that Mediterranean people stand too close during conversation, and Japanese are annoyed by the American southerners' custom of touching people to make a debater's point while talking, and so on. But the bubble is there for everyone; it is only

2.11

Natural body-related axial forms give stature to the human body by restating its axiality.

a

The campfire whose light fills a dome of space and provides security in the dark of night.

b

A prehistoric dolmen under which a single occupant might huddle for the body-related comfort and feeling of security such "personal" shelter provides.

c

The nomad's canopy which shelters and, by virtue of its tectonic symmetry, gives stature to the occupant's position in space.

d

A great temple's axis which lends stature to the moment in time and space of the person standing there.

53

2.12
Body-related perception illustrated by the way
people stand at nearly equal intervals in a recep-
tion line outside a church.

that its size is dependent on cultural predispositions in relation to the circum-stances of the moment.

As we move through the city or around the inside of a building, it is as though there is a sixth sense in operation, measuring the distance to everything in our peripheral vision and in relation to sounds that return to us off objects and surfaces near and far. We are usually unconscious of the operations of our spatial sense unless we feel threatened, such as when in a constricted space or in an oppressively crowded room, or when we unexpectedly encounter a diz-zying height. But there are the pleasurable spatial experiences as well, such as when we withdraw to a "cozy" corner to curl up with a good book, or as we stride through a grand room with light streaming in from windows high above and the walls glistening with handsome marbles. We find a special kind of pleasure in the sensations these kinds of experiences impart. It stands to rea-son, then, that as we construct an artificial environment to replace the natural

2.13
Figures of saints in niches on the facade of a
church, each in his or her own special body-
related shelter.

one, we seek to reproduce the positive spatial sensations we inherited from an evolutionary descent that took place in the natural world, before we began to supplement nature's world with one of our own making. Our ancestors likely sought the comfort of a fire's circle of light or the relative security of a sturdy tree or a sheltering rock, as they faced an unpredictable world. We have invented architectural and urbanistic equivalents to these and other spatial environments that induce in us pleasurable sensations.

Throughout the ages, architects have capitalized on our natural spatial perception as a way to enhance the experience of a building. Frank Lloyd Wright's oppressively low vestibules, for instance, were contrived to enhance the expansiveness of the honorific spaces to which they lead. Tall spaces can impart a sense of exhilaration or dim spaces that curve out of sight, a sense of mystery. Gothic churches are said to "soar" like the trees of a northern forest, while Romanesque churches provide a sense of protective, impenetrable shelter, like a clean, quiet, and well-ordered cave. The full, round enclosure of the Navajo hogan with its thick walls and layered crosswork ceiling of logs provides a secure, protective enclosure for the family that lives there, just as the Romanesque church did for its parishioners. Statues in niches tweak our sense of body space by inviting us to identify with the figure in the niche for a moment, to sense its place within the protective plane of the wall. And of course there is the ever-present response to the authority and balance of bilateral symmetry, a condition we readily recognize in architecture from our own bilaterally symmetrical bodies as well as those of other creatures that inhabit our world.

Some years back a television commercial for facial tissues cleverly tapped into an elaborate set of natural body-related spatial responses to set the scene for an empathetic response to hearing about the comforting presence of their product. They showed us a young woman with a fierce cold, as was made evident by her red nose, watery eyes, and withdrawn demeanor. She was seated on a kind of padded bench built into a bay window on the landing of a stair in a large house. It was raining outside, the rain streaming down the glass of the bay window. She was bolstered by soft cushions and pillows, and she sat with her knees tucked almost under her chin while she looked out at the rain. Her perch, in the bay window located midway between floors of her house, placed her in a kind of limbo, a world from which realities and responsibilities had been at least temporarily suspended. She was in a place that belonged to neither floor of the house, but from her position she could see the more active spaces on both floors at the base and top of the stairs and, through the windows of the projecting bay, what might be going on outside the house. In some respects she was neither within nor outside the house; instead she was holed up in a warm interior space that was, in effect, outside the enclosing wall. The bay formed a niche in the wall of the stair, a comfortable size for her body to withdraw into. We sensed her desire to be alone in a cozy place while at the same time she could stay in touch with the more active world around her. She had found an architectural element that replicated some primeval shelter that would suit her need to be alone yet feel secure in the world around her. (Of course, beside her was a box of the advertiser's facial tissues, which further complimented her quest for comfort and security.) She had withdrawn from the familiar environment of the more open and active parts of the house just as her ancestors might have withdrawn to a place beneath a protective boulder

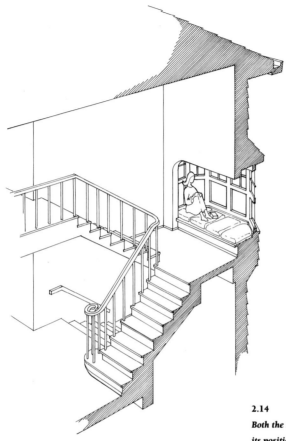

2.14
Both the sheltering niche of a bay window and its position on a stair landing contribute a sense of comfort and security for its occupant.

2.15

Three stages in the refinement of trabeated build-ing practice in traditional Japanese residential architecture.

a

Basic layering of elements with materials in their natural state.

b

Semirefined timber elements.

c

Refined timber elements of trabeated construc-tion. Refinement includes the joinery as well as the squaring and shaping of the members.

from the more open and unpredictable forest or plain around them, to repair for a while before returning to the responsibilities of life.

Frank Lloyd Wright's low vestibules, niches with statues, weighty Romanesque churches, and stairwell window seats suggest just a few of the perceptual characteristics to which architecture can be made to respond. They are indicative of a fundamental search for order that emanates naturally from our body-related spatial perception. This relationship with the environment is fundamental to architecture and, by extension, to urban order. We will return to this subject in a later chapter; now it remains to briefly examine a second source for order and geometry, the order of building.

The Order of Building and the Tectonics of Architecture

The order of building, as it is referred to here, is the more obvious and commonly recognized of the two fundamental sources of geometry in architecture and urbanism. It arises from the natural characteristics of materials of construc-

tion, along with the processes that set those materials into place. In a primitive domicile materials for its construction, such as logs, stones, and earth, are taken directly from nature without much alteration in their physical or chemical compositions. As construction techniques evolved, materials were altered to an increasingly greater extent: Logs were cut into boards, stone into blocks, clay fired into brick and tile, and sand melted into glass. In a modern industrial society, the natural state of some building materials is so changed as to be unrecognizable. Petroleum and grain are transformed into plastics, iron ore and bauxite into steel and aluminum, wood sliced or pealed and then laminated into sheets of plywood. Even though reconstituted, each new material, like the old, possesses natural physical characteristics to which the building process must respond. In this explanation, however, I will keep to building materials that remain close to their natural state.

The two principal forms of construction for architecture are post-and-beam, or trabeation, and bearing-wall construction. Each will be discussed

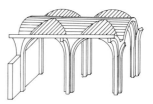

2.16
A series of masonry constructions arranged according to the probable evolution of masonry building practices.

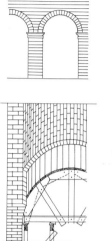

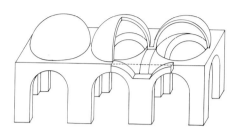

2.17

Some advanced forms of masonry construction.

more fully in chapters 5 and 6 with regard to their potential for poetic expression. Here will be considered their basic tectonics and the way they have conditioned how people think and act.

The trabeation principle was born of wood; it is essentially a post-and-beam frame. Bearing-wall construction arose from the piling of materials such as stone, brick, and earth to make walls. Most high-rise office buildings are elaborations on the simple trabeation principle, and great cathedrals of masonry are elaborations on the bearing-wall principle. The geometric properties of buildings must respond to the materials out of which they are constructed. If a structure is made of mud brick, its walls must be very thick; if the walls are made of a fired clay brick, they can be much thinner. Since mud bricks will easily crush from great weight, increasing the thickness near the base of the walls distributes the weight of bricks over a larger area, but since fired clay bricks are very resistant to crushing, they can be laid in thin layers up to great heights. These characteristics affect the way windows, portals, and other openings are formed, the way the building is roofed, how corners are turned, and so on. In a trabeated structure, on the other hand, the strength of wood beams allows the supporting columns to be spaced far apart. If, however, the trabeation is of stone instead of wood such as in the Greek temple, the columns must be both more massive and spaced closer together to support their stone lintel.

Simple roofs, constructed of wood, are formed by overlaying beams of wood with boards and tiles. In masonry construction, roofs often consist of a series of masonry arches, which create a barrel vault. When the construction consists of wood posts supporting wood girders and beams, the geometry is one of a three-dimensional grid. The major lines of the grid intersect at column positions, and secondary and tertiary lines control the positions of girders or beams and trusses. A similar grid is used for bearing-wall construction, but it must account for the thicknesses of walls in the building plan. Further geometries enter into the organization of bearing-wall buildings to establish the spring lines, apexes, and curvatures of the arches. Pictorial explanations of geometries generated by constructional priorities are easier to grasp than verbal descriptions of them, so it will suffice here to leave it to the accompanying drawings to complete this explanation.

The Nature of Man-made Things

To the builder the geometry of building is not abstract. It is integral to the building form and to the construction process. An argument has been made, recently by architect and theorist Demetri Porphyrios, that the art of architecture and the act of building cannot be separated. What constitutes architecture is in large measure a poetic expression of the constructional priorities that arise from the "natural" evolution of building. Put differently, architecture cannot be reinvented; it must evolve so that, as architect Louis I. Kahn pointed out, "When the work is completed, the beginning must be felt."[13] We will look at this natural evolution of architecture and urban form in chapter 5; for the moment it is important to consider what lies behind the assumption that architecture is at its base "an art of the tectonic."

We often say that natural things such as stones, places in the landscape, creatures, and plants have a character all their own. We tend to impart this metaphorical attitude to the built world as well. When something is seen to be right, we refer to it as "natural." Conversely, when something is badly done or out of place, we say that it is "unnatural." For instance, it may be "unnatural" for a house to look like a fire station or for a fire station to look like a church or for city hall to look like an office building. Anomalies such as these constitute inconsistencies in the *behavior or propriety of place in the overall scheme of things* that we have created. Historically the built world, unlike the natural world, has been subject to human interpretation, cultural determination, and constant change in that the rules that guide its "nature" are not hard and fast like those of Newtonian physics. Nonetheless, standards of propriety have been in operation. Although arguments over what *is* the nature of architecture abound, especially in times of social or technological transition and upheaval, at the base of these arguments is the tacit understanding that the nature of a building must be recognizable. As Porphyrios has noted, the mythical objectification of building is in response to the challenge of building shelter in nature. Through a process of mythical imagination we have evolved time-honored building solutions that have a special physiognomy that looks back to architecture's origins.[14] We further identify parts of buildings as being appropriate or inappropriate to their place just as we judge a building to be natural or unnatural in appearance. Cicero captured the essence of those expectations in a statement about the pedimented roof on a religious temple:

> *It is not for pleasure but out of necessity that our temples have gables. The need of discharging rainwater has suggested their form. And yet, such is the beauty of their form . . . that if one were to build a temple on Mount Olympus—where I am told it never rains—one would still feel obliged to crown it with a pediment.*[15]

The Stamp of Custom and Convention

Winston Churchill once observed, in a now much quoted statement, that we shape our architecture and it in turn shapes us. Usually the effects of the built world on our behavior are too subtle for us to recognize, but over time the experience of this environment may be more profound and extensive than we realize. A comparative example will demonstrate the point.

Consider the respective histories of Japanese and European architecture. Much of the history of Europe was played out in buildings with solid walls of stone, providing rooms of emphatic enclosure: cold, quiet, and inwardly focused. In Japan, by contrast, there evolved a highly sophisticated architecture structured by an open timber frame of posts and crossbeams, that is a trabeated system, disciplined by an orthogonal network of lines. Japanese history was played out within these buildings with their open and flowing interiors, their thin walls of sliding screens, and perimeters open to the landscape. In Japan as in Europe, the humble farm abode, the urban dwelling, and the grand and monumental complexes of rulers and religion followed a respective architectural precedent.[16]

A comparison of traditional Japanese architecture such as the Katsura Imperial Villa with a Mediterranean palace such as the Piccolomini Palace points up the essential differences between these two contrasting approaches to building, as can be seen in illustrations 2.18a and b. From within, the Japanese building is experienced as more or less continuous space, which is punctuated by posts and subdivided where desired by sliding screens, or *shoji*. The interior

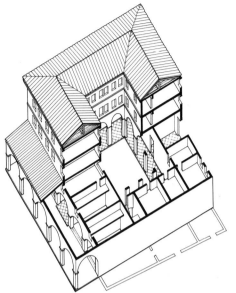

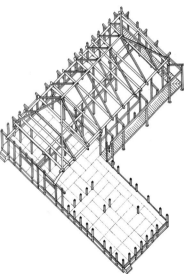

2.18
A Roman bearing-wall masonry building (a)
compared with a Japanese trabeated timber
building (b).

2.19

The landscape as seen from a Japanese engawa, part porch and part interior space, of the Katsura Imperial Villa in Kyoto.

space is, for the most part, open, and with the openness of the *engawa,* a continuous porch at the perimeter of the building, this architecture ensures an awareness of the presence of nature, namely the weather and the surrounding landscape. The Italian palazzo, on the other hand, is sensed from within as a system of discrete volumes, rooms within an unambiguously closed volume. Its architectural space is clearly delimited. The stone walls of the palazzo leave no question as to what are the boundaries of the building in relation to the surrounding landscape. Windows, as in other Western masonry architecture, appear as distinct geometric figures in the building's facades. Seen from within, views of the landscape are framed by these windows. In the Japanese building, by contrast, what serve the function of "windows" are for the most part simply open spaces between the structural elements of its frame, in combination with the changing positions of the panels that slide along the line of the frame separating the *engawa* from the interior. There are distinct differences in other characteristics as well: qualities of light and sound as perceived from within, the durability of materials and resistance to storm, earthquake, and fire, the way they are heated and how they relate to the ground plane, their appearance in the landscape, and so forth. These differences surely generate responses in living patterns and personal behavior as well, with the consequent differences ultimately reflected in broader social customs and cultural values. For instance, the Japanese are able to maintain a sense of personal privacy under conditions which a European or North American would find difficult. The most revealing situation is found in the traditional Japanese public bath where families bathe side by side without appearing to notice each other. They have learned to respect one another's personal privacy under conditions of exceptionally close living in buildings that do not insulate sounds from one room to the next, where wall-less enclosures frequently require partitions of the mind in lieu of real ones. There is no word in the Japanese language that translates directly to the English "privacy." Privacy to the Japanese, it seems, is more commonly a state of mind than a physical reality in the Western sense. Further, subtle expressions of social hierarchy are more elaborate and intricate in the Japanese tradition than in the West. Consider, for instance, the way people greet each other—with the slight bow of the head. This too may be a custom that evolved in recognition of privacy and an individual's dignity and social status in the absence of clearly defined architectural compartmentalization.

Another difference from the West may be found in the sense of space, referred to as *ma* in Japanese. In Japanese art it can be shown that sensing the space between figures is as important as sensing the form of each figure. That is, the ground is given as much importance as the figure. This sensitivity may arise from the importance of sensing the space of a "room" within the openness between posts of the gridded interior of a building. The scene depicted on a Japanese hanging scroll floats on a borderless field, an effect that is very different from that of a framed Western painting. Like the traditional Japanese building the scene on the scroll is open to the space around it, whereas the Western painting is delimited by a frame that may become integral with the composition, just as a view of the outdoors may be delimited by an elaborately framed window in a thick masonry wall.

In Japanese architecture, with its few interior partitions, the posts at the intersections of the beams are the important space-defining elements between the ceiling and floor. Similarly in a Japanese city the intersections of streets are given names, while often the streets themselves remain unnamed; in a European city the reverse is the case. It is not surprising that Japanese literature, especially poetry, concentrates much more on the subtleties of nature than does Western literature, given the open perimeters of its traditional architecture. The Japanese poet looks at and listens to nature up close; he imbibes the sound of insects, the quiet ripple of water over pebbles, the delicate structure of a leaf, or the grace of a dragonfly.[17]

Similar comparisons might be extended to the customs of desert peoples in contrast to the people of the rain forest, the mountains, or the savannah, where the social customs nurtured by one architectural or natural setting contrast with those of a distinctly different setting. Ultimately the built world with its architecture and cities is regarded by us much as we regard nature—as a priori with its own rules and its own laws of change and adaptation. From the more natural world of our ancestors we have evolved socially and culturally in an environment largely created through our own artifice. We have characteristically found our place in the world not through a thorough knowledge of the whole but rather through an intimate knowledge of places within it that are important to our lives. This we undoubtedly share in some way with other creatures of the earth. It is our natural sense of place.

Summary: Dwelling and the Sources of Order

From the earliest times buildings and settlements have reflected the natural world in which they were created. The geometry of early shelters, while borne as abstractions of the human mind, was consciously construed to resonate in harmony with the primacy of nature's order. Domiciles and settlements mediated "between the natural symbols of the body and the environment, transforming the one into the other or creating the link between them."[18] Once established, architecture and settlements served as paradigms for more structured ways of thinking, just as the natural environment had served as the paradigm for the creation of the man-made in the first place.[19] Spatial patterns inherent in the new man-made environment subsequently influenced the evolution of thought and custom. The next chapter will look at another human characteristic that is related to geometry and, especially, the primacy we assign to the act of dwelling and the places where we dwell. It is the sense of place, still another primordial sense that we have reinvested in the world of our own making.

3.1

*A cemetery on the Agean Island of Siphnos. The
wall's enclosure defines a sacred precinct. Access
to the precinct is by a bridge that leads to the
gate in the wall, thereby delimiting the walled
cemetery from the rest of the world.*

3 NATURE AND THE SENSE OF PLACE

Among the natural proclivities with which we are endowed is something often referred to as "a sense of place." It is likely that this special feeling is more responsible for the way in which architecture and urbanism have come about than we generally assume, largely because it is so much a part of us that we simply take it for granted.

At the most fundamental level, however, the sense of place refers to something that we all recognize. A sense of place concerns that need to find a familiar landscape as refuge from the unknown, perhaps from the terrifying prospect of being set adrift in what would otherwise be a dimensionless, time-less, and chaotic world. For a family in Paleolithic times the center of the world might have been a certain cave, near a certain river, within a certain valley. Their place—the cave, the river, and the valley—was for them an important bulwark against chaos. Today the equivalent might be the house, the neighbor-hood, the town, and the familiar landscape beyond: each a kind of circular domain eddying outward in ever-expanding rings of diminishing familiarity. It is the place from which to venture out and, more important, to which to return. We all experience pangs of nostalgia for the homes of our youth. Our word "nostalgia" comes from the Greek *nostos,* which means "to return home."

In its more immediate form a sense of place is responsible for that phenomenon whereby we recognize places we have been without our having to consciously memorize them. In other words, we recognize a place holistically, taking into account all its characteristics—the quality of light, the feel of the air, the constituent elements of rocks, trees, water, the color and smell of the earth, the lay of the land, for instance—without having to enumerate them as we would if we were to describe that same place to someone else. Consider a familiar example from common experience. All of us have had the feeling of coming upon a place by chance and discovering that we had likely been there before but cannot remember when or why we were there. Such a discovery produces an immediate sensation of familiarity—*déjà vu,* we say. It is a reaction without the necessity of a conscious recounting the particular combination of characteristics that jogged our memories. The immediacy of our response arises from our most fundamental understanding of a place; it is an intuitive understanding that is holistic in character and usually quite instantaneous.

That intuitive recognition of places in nature, and consequently in cities, is clearly the product of our capacity for environmental adaptation. It ensures our return to a particular place when we want to, just as the wolf finds her way back to her den after a successful hunt, or a house cat to its owner's house after a night on the town. Further we see each important place in our experience in relation to other places rather than as isolated incidences in a nonhierarchically ordered world. Since we seek to hierarchically order all experience, including the experience of places we know, a particular place of relatively minor importance is said to be a certain distance and direction from another place that is better known or more important. Also, beyond simple recognition of a place and its relative position among other places, we have a tendency to ascribe to it special qualities. We frequently imbue places with human characteristics. A certain place might be said to be sacred or profane, beautiful or ugly, friendly or threatening, filled with forboding or beckoning with promise.

From the last chapter you will recall the body-related geometry with which we orient ourselves in nature. This was especially noted by Kant when he suggested that "our geographical knowledge, and even our commonest knowledge of the position of places," is understood "by reference to the sides of our bodies." Our bodies provide us with a portable reference system to the environment around us, always in relation to the natural foursquare orientation of the human form. Our very understanding of the earth may be seen as based on this natural characteristic of body-related perception: It is the basis for what we refer to as "geography."

Things in the landscape take on meaning for us when we need to give directions to others, remember them, find our way in relation to them. We sense the essential qualities of a landscape before we intellectualize them. Thus their meanings for us often extend well beyond perfunctory recognition. It is a short step from here to the argument that archaic peoples saw what they built as equivalent to features of the natural landscape. They could envision their buildings and settlements in relation to the enclosure of a valley, the demarcation of a cliff, the dominance and objectlike presence of a single hill or mountain or tree. This is reflected in the buildings, monuments, and walls of ancient civilizations everywhere. The pyramids of the Incas, Egyptians, Mesopotamians, and others were undoubtedly expressions of the idea of a sacred and cosmic mountain. But the more subtle expressions of landscape elements are also to be found in less obvious comparisons. At the scale of a house, the floor is a metaphor for the surface of the earth, the ceiling within it for the sky, and so on. The primacy of the landscape in the invention of buildings has been documented with some regularity by anthropologists and historians. While modern occurrences may seem to be farther removed from such traceable origins, our ancestral propensities likely linger in the recesses of our consciousness.

Place and the Formation of Culture

Our responses to places we have experienced are natural insofar as we share the basic apparatus with which we were equipped for survival in nature. These natural responses form a foundation upon which we build our complex, culturally determined feelings about places, and they fill our world with meaning, depth, and richness far beyond the necessary rudiments of pure survival. Speculation about culturally determined understanding of places in the natural and built worlds is sometimes referred to as "place theory." It explores our need to imbue places with qualities that lie well beyond the immediate and practical.

Every civilization, culture, and community puts its own stamp of importance on places within its domain. The nature and character of that stamp arises from the way people experience their world. For instance, early Egyptian civilization saw the world through the experience of an almost perfectly predictable, cyclical nature. Their accurate calendar, the advantage of predicting the seasons for planting and the harvest, the annual life-giving flood of the Nile, and the distribution and storage of the harvest, all contributed to the development of a mathematical prowess arising from a seemingly infinitely cyclical nature in that part of the world they considered to be theirs. That world was characterized by the constancy of the Nile valley, by a closed and finite cosmology, and of course they sought a similar consistency, predictability, and sense of unity and closure in the places they built. We see their immutable pyramids, their sacred mountains in the desert, as embodiments of a quest for static certainty. In marked contrast to the Egyptian sense of nature is the world of their contemporaries the Greeks. The Greek world was the Mediterranean, the Aegean, the Adriatic, and those lands that surround these bodies of water—a world of coastlines and harbors with great distances between and varied lands beyond, some mountainous and forested, others parched and low. The Greeks were merchant traders in this varied landscape where they interacted with peoples who looked, thought, and lived differently than they. Their world was an open system compared to that of the Egyptians. And it stands to reason that if they were to let their curiosity range, it might lead them into philosophical argument that posed opposites, challenged and tested ideas, and welcomed discourse as a means to knowledge. Their idea of nature was a constantly changing one; it accepted the challenge of opposing observations and found coalescence in human reason.[1]

A closer look at ancient Greek civilization shows a resonance in language as well as in custom and artifacts. The Greeks' open and exploratory approach to thought and nature, for instance, is reflected in their word *theoria*. It meant "to experience a place as a whole through feeling, imagination, and memory, together with intellect and the senses."[2] It was a concept that "implied a complex but organic mode of active observation—a perceptual system that included asking questions, listening to stories and local myths, and feeling as well as hearing and seeing. It encouraged an open reception to every kind of emotional, cognitive, symbolic, imaginative, and sensory experience."[3]

The experience of a place by any society over a very long time involves a dialectic between culture and place aimed at a kind of naturally evolved harmony. As a result we humans have always tended toward building a complex relationship with places, both natural and man-made, that we occupy. This attitude, which may sometimes appear to be subconscious (thus natural), finds substance and reinforcement in myth and ritual. For instance, there was the Roman phenomenon of *genius loci*. The Romans believed that certain places manifested spirits. These spirits, or *genius loci*, reflected the uniqueness of a place, distinguishing one place from other places with which it might be confused. They inhabited all places of significance. A spirit would own a place, look after it, and imbue it with sense and meaning. A place's *genius loci* symbolized its generative energy and made it "personal," providing it with a personality, a quality beyond mere fact and "character." The *genius loci*'s consummate duty was to provide a protective presence, thereby animating what would otherwise be an inert, impersonal incident in the landscape, the villa, or the city. The house of a Roman family, for instance, might contain an image of the toga clad *Lar familiaris* standing between two *Penates* in a shrine located near the hearth (which, you will recall, is *focus* in Latin). The *Penetes* guarded the family's food and possessions while, "the *genius* of the *pater,* a guardian spirit, represented the continuity of the family."[4] There were special spirits for gates, thresholds, and even the floor of the house. The house thus animated with spirits was rendered sacred for a family who regarded their domicile as their ancestral abode. Evidence also suggests that the Roman Catholic practice of protective saints of special places grew out of this earlier belief in protective spirits of places.

Of course it is easy to carry to the extreme an argument that posits that custom and culture are derived in large measure from the physical context of a society or civilization. Much of such argument is highly conjectural. There are numerous other factors that necessarily come into play, ones that would either confound or confirm expectations. Nonetheless, the influence of both the natural and the built environment is undeniable in the formation of a people's national and ethnic character. People become a part of their places on earth, and in the best of times and in the most stable circumstances there may be found a true harmony in the relationship of a society with the part of the earth where their cultures developed and flourished over the millennia.

Psychological and Social Importance of "Place"

An intense regard for places like that demonstrated by the Roman respect for the *genius loci* seems to us very distant from the attitudes we now hold. Today the real estate industry encourages us to "trade up" by casting off our present house like an old shoe in exchange for something more impressive and located in a more prestigious neighborhood, or we may regard a select parcel of productive agricultural land as simply awaiting "development" for more lucrative industrial uses that will make it "more productive," meaning that it will produce more income if factories are placed on it rather than crops planted there. In this way we have come to believe the "best" use of land is that which is the most economically productive under present circumstances. Our commercial bent has led us to consider land as commodity rather than resource, and this has fostered the idea that the immediately practical provides the most reliable frame of reference for evaluating both natural and man-made places. In the real world the anticipated return on investment usually outweighs all other considerations in formulating a course of action. But we are nonetheless sometimes nagged by the importance evoked by one place or another that we find we know all too well to regard in such a cold, impersonal way. It is as though the Roman *genius loci* is there, as though its presence and prerogatives would be callously violated if someone were to change things in a way that would deny what has been its long-standing identity. While our more scientific and practical disposition tends to obscure the psychological and spiritual sense of places in deference to a more rigorous analytical understanding, we continue to recognize, if only on a personal and often unspoken level, those special responses that certain places evoke deep within us.

Place theory makes the assumption that understanding the human response to a place is as important as knowing about the place's purely factual characteristics. There are plenty of examples from our common experience to illustrate the point. We may recall, for instance, the spiritual or religious importance of a cemetery with its consecrated earth and attendant memories of family and ancestors. Our recognition of a cemetery as a special place reflects a more ancient response to the sacred qualities that accompany anomalous features of the landscape, what the ancients regarded as sacred mountains, sacred groves, or sacred springs. These are places in nature that distinguish themselves from all else around them in such a way as to make them special rather than just "different." Thus the sense of reverence one might have for the ordered landscape of a cemetery, the chancel of a church, or the *temenos* of a Greek temple (the sacred precinct in which the temple resides) is a natural reaction to a perceived sacredness of special places that evolved from our early life in nature and has been translated by us into the man-made world of the present. The human dimension of meaning that is added to special features of the landscape may become integral with the physical characteristics of a place. For example, the picturesquely gnarled burr oak trees that stood alone in the grasslands of the American midwest served as council places for the meeting of Native American tribal leaders. These trees came to be known as "council oaks" and were thereby regarded as possessing a kind of sacredness, not only because they evoked the image of a lone vigil on the prairie but also because of their accumulated associations with human events. Things in the landscape are often interpreted by us in terms of our lives. When something in the landscape is so prominent that we think it ought to mean something, we sometimes make up events to connect with it—that is, we invent myths about it to justify its presence, to give it a meaningful name and commit it effectively to memory.

Still another reflection of the common reverence for places in the landscape may be recalled by the feeling we experience when coming upon a place where we know a frightening or historic event occurred. For example, Scots in thoughtful reverence continue to visit isolated Glenfannin, where in 1745 the one they affectionately call Bonny Prince Charlie gathered the clans on a low hill at the head of a loch and from there launched the attempt to restore the Stuart monarchy in a brave (albeit foolhardy) march on London; Americans still walk in contemplative reverence across the rural landscape at Gettysburg where, in 1863, a calamitous battle took place in the American Civil War, a bewilderingly tragic episode where Americans killed one another by the thousands. We accord such places special qualities that distinguish them from all else by connecting them to events we consider important to our history, our civilization, or our lives. Whether the event was sad or happy, momentous or subtle, if it is important, then so is the place where it occurred. Were a developer to propose an oil tanker off-loading platform at Scotland's Glenfannin, or were a condominium developer to propose carpeting the fields of America's Gettysburg with housing, there would be more than just public outcry. These places might become battle grounds again! We seem to want to know that such places will remain intact, and when possible, we like to experience them first-hand. A historic event becomes more real if we can experience the actual place where it happened. The place gives substance to the event, and the event significance to the place.

Nonetheless, today it has become increasingly difficult for us to see that sometimes the cradles of lesser events may provide us with places that are important to the memory of who we are and remind us of the important truth that our society at any given moment is still the product of what has gone before. Past and place are inextricable. A place that is important to our past must rise above nostalgia in our consciousness lest it become merely quaint.

"Place" as Concrete versus Abstract

It is the immediate and readily perceivable reality of places that empowers them for us. Their significance to us is both formal and associative. We connect the salient physical characteristic of a place with an event, or events, that we know happened there, or are supposed to have happened there, as a way of making the event(s) concrete and the place meaningful. Anthropologists recount how primitive civilizations gave meaning to the landscape by ascribing mythical events to its more recognizable features. The most prominent hill in the district might be the place where the gods came down to earth to teach the first humans to speak, a deep pool a place where the underworld is accessible to the initiated, a particular valley of heroic stature the province of a race of giants, or a certain boulder a missile thrown there as one god battled another. "Place" is not an abstract term like "environment"; it is specific, personal, and concrete. "Place" is, in effect, a concretization of "environment." People see themselves as having come from "places," not "environments." As E. V. Walter expressed it, "People do not experience abstract space; they experience places. A place is seen, heard, smelled, imagined, loved, hated, feared, revered, enjoyed, or avoided. Abstract space is infinite; in modern thinking it means a framework of possibilities. A place is immediate, concrete, particular, bounded, finite, unique. Abstract space is repetitive and uniform. Abstraction moves away from the fullness of experience."[5]

To put this argument in the context of modern thinking, places tend to become important to our psychological well-being. Just as places are important to us as individuals, they are important to communities of individuals. Certainly the most poignant examples of the psychological importance a place can have may be seen when a town or part of a town is destroyed by a natural disaster such as an earthquake or a storm, or by bulldozers to make way for a real estate development. The grief for the place is not unlike that for the loss of a loved one, and it can be just as profound.

The sense of place, or the assumptions of place theory, "topistics," or what has been called "environmental memory,"[6] are best understood in their infinite variety when seen in relation to places that were designed to fulfill some preordained association with the natural world. Consider again the houses by Frank Lloyd Wright and Le Corbusier described in chapter 1. Each design was preceded by a reflection on the ideal relationship between the architecture and nature, and consequently each building was created partly in response to that conception. Each then became an expression of its setting in the belief that the preexistent natural site became the better for the house having been built there. Beyond the natural ability to recognize familiar places in the landscape, a culturally conditioned sense of place is the basis for our finding meaning in that landscape. Response to site reflected in the design of buildings illustrates how individuals and societies have reconciled their necessary interventions in the natural order. The sense of place is so much a part of all else—body-related orientation in space, memory and meaning, geometry and nature, history and belief—that to pursue its many manifestations here would be to repeat the obvious. I will, however, provide a rather lofty and famous example and then its opposite, a comparably humble circumstance, before departing the subject altogether. The first example is the Pantheon in Rome, a building that has continued to mystify and inspire visitors through the ages, and the second is a small summerhouse on a lake in Finland by the well-known modernist architect Alvar Aalto.

3 NATURE AND THE SENSE OF PLACE

The Pantheon: A Place as a Metaphor for the Cosmos

The Pantheon is one of the oldest buildings in the world to stand still relatively intact. It is an example of a building that was designed to evoke a metaphysical sense of place appropriate to its intended purpose.

"Buildings classify themselves as witnesses fixing the way of life and the moral condition of humanity, age by age," observed the architectural pedagogue and theorist Auguste Choisy in 1899.[7] The Pantheon has remained in its place for nearly two thousand years while everything around it has changed. Its presence has helped preserve the vision of ancient Rome when it was the center of the Roman Empire. Life and society may well have changed considerably around the Pantheon over the years, but the building has never gone unnoticed nor suffered the ignominious loss of dignity that led to the destruction of other buildings. An argument may be made that its intrinsic greatness as a work of architecture has kept it alive for so long. Its many progeny in the form of buildings that it inspired have continued to arise, especially since the Italian Renaissance. Its influence has been enormous, even to the degree that it is likely the most influential building ever built.

The strength of the Pantheon as a work of architecture lies, in part, in the simplicity of its organization. Recall for the moment illustrations 2.8 and 2.9 which represent our perception of the greater landscape in relation to our bodies. We perceive a foursquare relationship to the land because we have a front, back, and two sides, and we stand upright and face forward in the direction of our parallel vision. We have consistently marked our places on the earth as the right-angled intersection of three lines, two horizontal and one vertical: the vertical *axis mundi* passing through the center of the X on the ground where we stand to establish a reference from which all else in physical nature may be judged and measured. The Pantheon may be read as based on illustration 3.3. The axis mundi, the dome of heaven, and the foursquare geometry of space within it determine its plan and interior volume; they form the matrix for both its physical and metaphysical existence.

Keeping this basic geometry in mind, all else about the design of the Pantheon follows logically from it. The substance that gives form to its geometry is a concrete dome and its supporting cylindrical brick wall. The dome is exactly the same diameter and height, from its lip to its top, as the cylinder.

3.2
View of the Pantheon from the Piazza Rotunda
on a quiet morning.

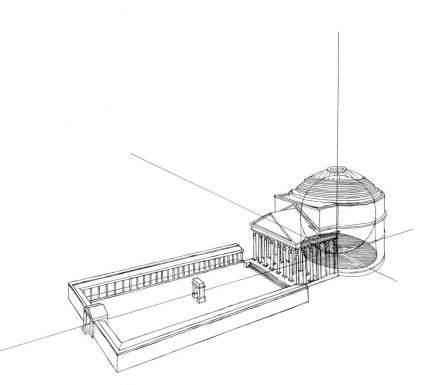

3.3
The forecourt and processional axis of the Pan-
theon as it may have appeared in the first cen-
tury AD. The building's geometry establishes an
axis mundi through the oculus, and its four-
square organization recalls the human body (see
illustrations 2.8 and 2.9).

Thus the dome suggests the top half of a sphere. At the front of the brick cylinder is a portico that marks the entrance and announces the building's function as a temple. The portico and entrance thus establish the main axis of the building, which in turn defines the sequence of entry along a vertical axis that fixes its place at the center of the cylinder by a round opening, known as the oculus, in the apex of the dome.

The best way to understand the sense of place that the Pantheon creates is to describe how it is experienced. To the spectator standing before the building in the noisy piazza, its cylindrical mass rises from behind the portico almost as if it were a feature of a natural landscape. The Pantheon's simple, heavy form, its scarred and weathered surfaces, and the way it seems to dip into the earth compared to the buildings around it, all contribute to that sense of a natural and eternal presence. To enter, one moves down the slope of the piazza, through the forest of giant columns of the portico, then through huge, bronze-clad oak entrance doors and into the vestibule just inside. On the outside wall is a bronze plaque added in 1632, which reads:

PANTHEON

AEDIFICIVM TOTO TERRARVM ORBE

CELEBERRIMVM

[The Pantheon, the most celebrated edifice in the whole world]

Upon entering the vestibule, one experiences a rush of cool air from within. The interior is at first quite dark, at least until one's eyes readjust from the bright sun of the piazza outside. What serves as a vestibule—the transitional space from the portico to the domed rotunda within—is actually the thickness of the cylindrical enclosing wall, which is about 12 meters or nearly 40 feet thick. This contributes to the feeling of the building as a feature of nature. Having passed through this entry, one finds oneself about to enter a large circular space lit only by the sun passing a shaft of light through the oculus in the dome. At the end of this shaft of light is a bright circle of sun falling somewhere on the ceiling, walls, or floor depending on the time of day and time of year of the visit. The brightness of this circle of light (actually it is an ellipse, the shaft interrupted at an oblique angle) is the most prominent feature of the dim interior until the visitor's eyes become accustomed to the level of light within. Standing inside, one is actually in a space formed by a sphere inscribed within a cube, with a round opening to the sky at the very top. If the inner surface of the dome were to be continued and thereby complete the lower hemisphere of the sphere, it would just touch the floor in the center of the circular room.

The dome above, the bright circle of sky at its apex, and the encircling wall that joins the dome at its equator, all contribute to a comfortable sense of cosmic unity. It is easy to see why this building has been called "the temple of the whole world." One might imagine a medieval peasant on a pilgrimage to Rome, when it was a derelict town of about 14,000 people, having come from some distant northern place where the size of a room in a building was limited by the length of wood beams cut from available trees. He would enter the Pantheon and find himself beneath a domical space of 141 feet across its diameter; he would be in the largest free-span interior space in the world.

Once one's eyes have adjusted to the light within, the surfaces of dome, wall, and floor reveal elaborate detail. The floor is a grid of colored squares and

3.4

Views of the interior of the Pantheon.

a

Detail of the so-called equator where the dome meets the circular wall that supports it.

b

Interior view of the "back" wall.

c

The circle of light cast by sunlight passing through the oculus.

3.5

The Pantheon from an architectural treatise by
Antoine Desgodets published in 1682.

a

Front elevation.

b

Longitudinal section.

c

Side elevation.

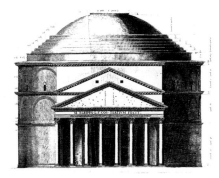

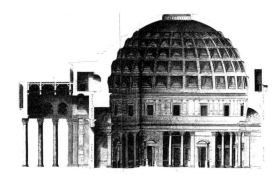

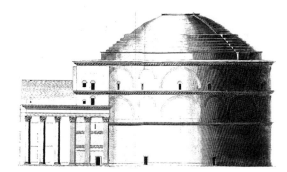

circles set in marble; in the curved wall are niches, aediculae, columns, and surface patterns in granite, marble, and other polished stone, and the ceiling of the dome is articulated by deep coffers that diminish in size as they approach the oculus at the top (for the modern visitor this grid of parallels and meridians is reminiscent of a globe). Everywhere the patterns, colors, and ornament seem to flow together, all muted in a low light and subservient to the unity of their envelope. The geometry, form, and space, the movement of air, the quality of light, and the character of sound within and without come together to produce a unique sense of place. If one adds its history to that knowledge, the experience expands in its richness.

Built under the aegis of the Emperor Hadrian in the first century AD, the Pantheon replaced an earlier temple dedicated to all the gods: thus the name Pantheon. But like most important Roman buildings, it probably symbolized a lot more. From the oculus (which likely descended from the smoke holes of ancient domiciles) to the hemispherical coffered concrete dome (which at one time held a bronze star at the center of each coffer) replicating the dome of heaven, to the encircling wall from which the dome springs (which may have served as a metaphor for the borders of the empire), everything is filled with meaning. Besides the axis mundi which we perceive at the center, the gridded floor pattern around that center may well be symbolic of the *centuriation* of the empire, that is, the practice of surveying the land outward from the center of each newly founded town along the lines of its intersecting *cardo* and *decumanus,* thereby laying claim to the natural landscape by incorporating it into this net of geometry laid down by Rome.[8] The oculus as the singularly most compelling feature of the interior, like the eye of a deity looking down from heaven, animates the interior with that shaft of light that moves with the perfect regularity of the cosmos: The low south sun of winter forces the disk across the lower reaches of the dome, playing with the coffers as they distort the purity of its shape, while in summer it traces beautifully perfect arches across the marble pavements until, late in the day, the disk reaches the vertical surface of the wall where it rapidly climbs until its light is pinched off in the depth of the oculus, leaving a glint on the eastern edge of the opening before it disappears altogether. The cycle of seasons is ever present in the movement of that shaft of light, a perpetual reminder of order and harmony in the universe.

The Pantheon and its setting provide a rich example of the concretization of an idea that relates nature at the scale of the universe to the man-made world. Embodied in its form are expressions that lie at the roots of a civilization. It can speak to us of the wonder of humankind's ingenuity and the wonder of the cosmos at the same time. But its universality harks back to the most ancient domicile, a one-room dwelling with a single entrance, domical covering, and smoke hole at the top: a dwelling repeated throughout time in the Navajo hogan, the Mongolian yurt, and doubtlessly countless other no longer extant examples.

Muuratsalo: Settlement and Founding a Place in Nature

Architect Alvar Aalto built a summerhouse for himself and his wife on a remote lake in his native Finland in 1953. Like Fallingwater and Villa Savoye discussed earlier, this is a summerhouse designed as a place of occasional respite from a predominantly urban life. And like Fallingwater and Villa Savoye it was seen by the architect-owner in an idealized way, as a positive intervention in a remote natural setting. There are no roads to this part of the lake. To reach the house, one takes an hour motorboat ride from the nearest railway station. While the setting is reminiscent of a primeval forest, distant from modern conveniences and serene beside the quiet lake, the house itself reflects the requisite modernist departure from traditional form. However, near the house, but at the edge of the lake, stands a sauna that is very traditional in appearance, in contrast to the modernist house to which it belongs. The house and the sauna, though stylistically disparate, reflect the historical role of the sauna in the settlement of this glaceated land of equal parts lake and terra firma that eventually came to be the nation of Finland.

Finnish tradition has it that the sauna was the first building to be constructed in the wilderness where a family intended to establish a farmstead. The sturdy, thick-walled, well-insulated, but primitive hut was quickly constructed of immediately available materials from the surrounding forest in order to provide a place of refuge while the critical task of clearing the land and planting crops took place during the first spring. When winter came, the tiny but secure hut sheltered the new settlers from wild animals and the extreme cold of the far north. With the coming of the second spring, planting could be accomplished without clearing the land, since that had been done the previous spring; the time was now to begin construction of a proper house with rooms and the requisite privacy for habitation. The primitive hut then became the sauna where one could go to cleanse and refresh oneself after a long day of working the soil. The act of cleansing is a symbolic act of renewal. It is consistent with the primacy of the hut, since cleansing takes place between the sauna and the lake as a symbolic reminder that the humble hut was the first act in creating a human presence here, in primeval nature. As cited by Eliade, instances of founding are often ritualized as acts of creation. The founding of a Roman town, for instance, involved a ritual plowing of a furrow along the line of its walls to open the earth to human habitation and consecrate the place of the town against the profane world around it. The act of cultivating virgin soil during the settlement of Iceland was regarded by Scandinavian colonists as the conversion of chaos into cosmos, thereby repeating the devine act of creation, and for the Spanish and Portuguese conquistadores the setting up of the Cross represented a "new birth," a baptism as a symbolic act of creation.[9]

3.6

Alvar Aalto's summerhouse at Muuratsalo.

a

The courtyard enclosure at the lakefront side of the house as seen from the sauna.

b

Entrance to the sauna seen from the dock.

Aalto's summer place is not a farmstead, nor was it built sequentially according to the old tradition. Still we may presume that it reflects that particular building tradition as a gesture to an ancestral past, consistent with the land and the people who first colonized that land. Even the small wooden dock reiterates the founding theme: It serves to welcome the boat every time it returns. In making sense of a place in nature, one aims to maintain the harmony that was nature's own, before human arrival in that place. Unlike our early ancestors, we cannot so easily believe that a gesture to an age-old custom necessarily has deep meaning, but we still often sense that some gesture is appropriate if our intervention is to be sympathetic to the preexistent qualities of the places where we choose to build.

Summary: Nature and the Sense of Place

The sense of place is a subject that has no bounds. I have described some important characteristics so that it may be easily recognized. In the end, however, the sense of place is integral with all else in the building of a man-made world. It is found in relation to great and sweeping landscapes and dramatic human events, or in the humdrum setting of daily experience, providing meaning to otherwise prosaic places. Heidegger's discussion of the concept of "dwelling" is in fact a discussion of the sense of place, albeit under a different heading. The primacy of the house, as discussed in chapter 2, is in many ways another expression of the sense of place.

Our sense of place provides us with a foundation upon which we have customarily built a great store of culturally related meanings in order to make sense of the natural and the built worlds in which we live. While the evolutionary origins of our sense of place seem remote to us today, they continue to be reflected in ordinary experience. Be it the Pantheon or a courthouse square of the American midwest, a row of warehouses along the waterfront, a now useless fortification at the edge of a European city, or simply a special grove of trees planted by a forgotten ancestor, in each of these places we sense a resonance between the new and the old, between what came before and that which has been added or has evolved. It should not strain credulity to conclude that the social and cultural stability of a community depends in part on satisfying this illusive but important quality of the human condition. The need to find such resonance reflects our common quest for harmony and unity in our environment. In the next chapter we will look at measures taken to reestablish and maintain the harmony of nature and the built world.

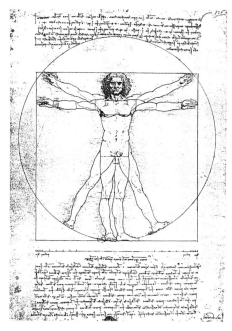

a

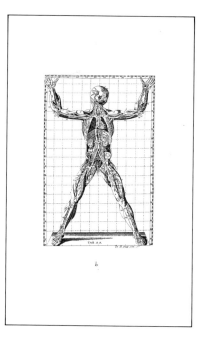

b

4.1

Leonardo da Vinci's "universal man" compared with a drawing from a medical treatise by John Winslow of 1748. Leonardo's drawing is of an idealized human figure superimposed on Platonic geometry, based on a description by Vitruvius. Despite the very different intentions of the two drawings, Leonardo's may be seen to represent the classical, idealized view of man and nature, whereas Winslow's factually accurate cadaver on a nonhierarchical grid may be seen to represent a post-Enlightenment, positivistic view of man and nature.

4 UNITY AND THE IDEA OF HARMONY

Balance, unity, order, integration, resonance, these are words frequently heard today in the explanation of the need to correct damages to the environment brought on by industrialization and urban growth. They are imperatives driven by ideals. Science and engineering address these issues through measures having to do with the calculated preservation of species, prevention of soil erosion, and control over the quality of air, water, and soil, for example, in order to strike a balance between human uses of land and the requirements for necessary natural processes such as photosynthesis and drainage. It is the condition of our time to stress the more active technological means to correcting environmental problems over the ideological roots of the human need to correct environmental imbalances in the first place. That is, we tend to stress the practical over the ideal. It may be said that classical civilization and the rebirth of classical philosophy in the Renaissance tended to idealize the notion of harmony, while post-Enlightenment science has divided it into neat and manageable categories: the disciplines and subdisciplines of science and technology.

To better understand the classical notion of balance between man and nature, we will consider the well-known "universal man," or "Vitruvian man," drawing by Leonardo da Vinci. While this drawing may be familiar to most everyone, its original meaning runs much deeper than the way we have come to think of it. Today it is usually used to symbolize humanism in general, but to the Renaissance architect, as to the Roman architect Vitruvius who described such a figure in his first-century BC treatise, it represented the harmonious relationship between man and nature. It is based on the assumption that the cosmos was established at the onset to be in harmony throughout, and the human body is itself an echo of that divine harmony.

Pythagoras had observed that there is a precise relationship between musical harmony and arithmetic ratios, and it is from that simple observation that he and his followers based their all-inclusive and convincing cosmology. He demonstrated that if two strings, as in a musical instrument, are set to vibrate under identical conditions, the pitch of one will be one octave (*diapason*) above the other if one string is half the length of the other. If their lengths are to one another in a ratio of two to three, the difference in pitch will be a fifth (*diapente*), and if in a ratio of three to four, a fourth (*diatessaron*) and so forth. That is to say, the Greek musical system was based on the progression of 1:2:3:4. Rather than seeing this as an isolated peculiarity of the tonal scale favored by the Greeks, Pythagoras and his followers saw it as a key to understanding the consistency of the cosmos, and as proof that human perception is tuned into the workings of the cosmos as well.

Pythagoras demonstrated that these same relationships operate in the spatial world. For instance, the four cardinal points of the cosmos, crossing at right angles, imply four squares about a center. Through a proof involving a logical series of steps, it can be shown that the right triangles generated by the diagonals of each square, regardless of the ratio of the two adjacent sides to one another, will always yield the length of the longest side, the hypotenuse, by extracting the square root of the sum of the squares on the other two sides. That is what we refer to as the Pythagorean theorem. From this description of the two-dimensional figure one can easily proceed to three-dimensional geometries to demonstrate that the numbers can be progressively related to the third dimension in the same clear, definitive ways that they are related to two-dimensional figures. Thus two-dimensional geometry and the projection of that geometry into the third dimension to create a volume in space are related through the medium of mathematics. With this observation came the conclusion that all phenomena in the perceivable world are related. The Pythagoreans were confident they had uncovered the key to nature. They were convinced that all the regularities in nature are musical, and the movement of the heavens was, for them, "the music of the spheres."

Following Pythagoras's lead, Plato in the *Timaeus* carried the same concept of harmony into squares and cubes of double and triple proportion starting from unity, leading ultimately to geometrical progressions of 1, 2, 4, 8, . . . and 1, 3, 9, 27, . . .[1] Later Vitruvius repeated Pythagoras's argument in his first-century BC treatise on architecture, and Leon Battista Alberti, in his *De re aedificatoria* (1462), carried the concept into the fifteenth century where it became the basis for subsequent theoretical studies in architecture and urban design.

In his treatise Alberti combined the idea that "the same Numbers 'by means of which the Agreement of Sounds affects our Ears with Delight' are the very same which please our Eyes and our Mind"[2] with Vitruvius's description of ideal human proportions to arrive at a theory for proportions in architecture. With the Greek mathematical interpretation of nature now seen as evidence of the wondrous structure of God's creation, the circle and the square became

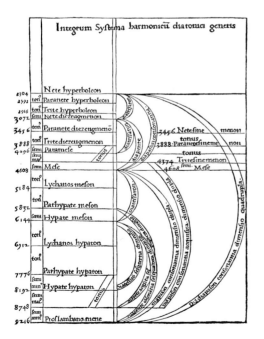

4.2

Harmonic diagram from the 1521 edition of Vitruvius's treatise, **De architectura.**

symbolic of the harmonic relationship of all things, including the presumed consistency between the macrocosm and the microcosm. And it was from Alberti's observation that we are intuitively equipped by nature to recognize both beauty and ugliness, which followed from the Ionian Greek idea that man was created by God as the central creature of the world and from the Judeo-Christian belief that man was created in the image of God. From this it follows that what we in turn create should manifest those cosmic proportions. The male figure inscribed in the circle and the square, as by Leonardo da Vinci, became symbolic of the relationship of man to nature. Thus, to be perceived as beautiful and as a part of nature, buildings should be proportioned according to the human body.

The Structure behind the Myth

Leonardo's drawing of the universal man might strike us today as simply a charming symbol. Nonetheless, for centuries the image represented a very useful approach to architectural design. Take the proportions of the man, for instance. The navel is said to be the center of the composition, while the head, legs, arms, and features are defined as ratios of the body. This construct incorporates such fine points of Vitruvius's argument as, "the face, from the chin to the top of the forehead and the lowest roots of the hair, is a tenth part of the whole height; the open hand from the wrist to the tip of the middle finger is just the same; the head from the chin to the crown is an eighth," and so on.[3] Aside from the obvious problem that not all people are proportioned alike, let us look at what this image accomplishes.

Our intuitive sense of balance arises from our earliest attempts to crawl, stand, and finally walk. As a result we come to judge things outside ourselves in relation to our experience with our bodies. Through the experience of our bodies, we sense such qualities as heaviness, lightness, poise, balance, imbalance, grace, strength, and weakness in other people or animals, and even in inanimate objects. A well-balanced composition, then—be it a building facade, an abstract painting or a scenic photograph—is perceived by us as well-balanced in terms of our direct sensory identification with the elements of the composition under examination *and* human proportions and *their* relative compositional disposition in relation to the overall body. As we mature, we of course learn qualities such as strength and weakness from direct tactile experiences in our environment, such as climbing trees, wrestling with each other, and playing with things that are tough, brittle, heavy, light, and so on—to the point where we are able to form direct associations with many materials and objects. But our initial experience of body-related perception remains with us as an intuitive paradigm from which we judge our environment.

As we learn the qualities of particular objects in our environment, we subconsciously relate them to our first and formative experiences involving our bodies. It stands to reason that we expect a satisfyingly balanced composition of things to be achieved with relative ease if such compositions are themselves based on the human body—on bilateral symmetry, a primary vertical tripartite division (head, torso, and legs), and the characteristic conditions of balance. This intuitive analogical comparison, which is fundamentally a universal kind of subconscious anthropomorphism, underlies the basic structural principle embodied in Leonardo's universal man. The universal man provides us with what can be regarded as natural proportions and a natural compositional arrangement for man-made things such as buildings because our intuitive sense of balance and the tectonics of form arise from body-related perception.

Given the internal logic of the argument, the question must still be asked, How can there be such a thing as an ideally proportioned person, and if there is such a thing how does one recognize it (in him or her) in the first place? This problem was particularly vexing for French architectural theorists of the Enlightenment who wished to find a way to reconcile inherited classical theory with the precision and objectivity of emerging modern science. They compared Vitruvius's descriptions of the correct proportions for the classical orders with those of Roman ruins available to them, and they compared Renaissance examples with each other and with Vitruvius's descriptions. What they discovered was a host of disconcerting variations and inaccuracies in proportional relationships, as well as a remarkable variety in expressed perceptual preferences from one example to another among different observers. While a recognition of the probable role of cultural experience might account for some of the variations in preferences, theorists were still left with far too many inconsistencies to avoid being embarrassed in the light of modern scientific objectivity.

Eventually it was inconsistencies such as these that undermined so many of the tenets of classical architectural theory, leading to the modern movement's attempt to rewrite architectural and urban theory from the beginning by using contemporary science, emerging technologies, and social theory as principal guides and inspiration.

However, those theorists who discredited classical theory were, for the most part, subjecting it to a factual analysis that it was never intended to yield, rather than to see it as essentially analogical and symbolic. For the practicing sixteenth-century architect and the ancient Roman architect long before him, the universal man, according to Vitruvius, represented a paradigm for proportional and compositional consistencies. It was not one person or one archetypal human form that was important but rather the compositional and proportional consistencies that such an example demonstrated. Indeed there were countless versions of the universal man generated by Renaissance theorists; Leonardo's is simply the most popular today, largely due to his superior skill as an artist. Any well-balanced and normally proportioned human form could be seen to provide an effective paradigm, and Vitruvius had demonstrated that very thing. In addition to his description of the universal man, he described how the orders of architecture inherently reflect the character of variously proportioned people. He described the Doric order as evoking the character of a well-muscled man and therefore appropriate to a temple for a powerful male deity, and the Ionic order as a graceful female and therefore appropriate for a temple dedicated to a female deity. It was consistency *within* a given set of compositional and proportional priorities derived from the human body that was being sought after, and *not* the establishment of a fixed formula for design based on some particular human figure.

A somewhat tongue-in-cheek example might illustrate the point. Compare the "ideal" proportions for a ballerina and a sumo wrestler. Neither really fits the proportions of the human body found in Renaissance architectural treatises, but each is as consistent and well balanced as any of many universal man drawings that followed Vitruvius's description or Alberti's recounting of it. (Or at least we can be led to accept the internal logic of the argument, albeit with some difficulty for those of us who are unused to thinking of the sumo wrestler's form as an inherently healthy one.) That is to say, it is the specialized nature of the human form under question that must be taken into consideration before the "right" proportions are established. The sumo wrestler's solidity, weight, and stability, for instance, are appropriate to his calling. His legs are properly proportioned for his heavy body, his arms are thick and rather short as we would expect them to be in relation to the rest of him, and so forth. The ballerina, on the other hand, evinces a lighter and elongated body structure and a taut muscular system, all of which provides her with the ability to move with mysterious weightlessness. We intuitively understand any human body in terms of its proportional relationships; we recognize deformity then as inconsistencies within a given set of proportions. Deformities would, in Alberti's terms, constitute examples of universally recognizable ugliness. In other words, classical architectural theory was saying that buildings should be proportioned as the human body is proportioned, that they should manifest a logic and consistency among all the parts and in relation to the whole and in relation to our customary understanding and consequent expectations. Thus we can have well-proportioned heavy buildings such as those by the American architect H. H. Richardson (whose own body, coincidentally, was near that of a sumo wrestler) or the English architect Sir John Vanbrugh (on whose tombstone is the epitaph: "Lie heavy on him, earth, for he Laid grievous heavy weights on thee"), we can appreciate the comparative lightness of the classical baroque buildings by Giovanni Bernini or German architect Balthasar Neumann, and we can comfortably reconcile the contradictory qualities of stability and soaring freedom in a great Gothic cathedral.

The results of proportioning systems based on the human form and upon geometric axioms of like proportions speak for themselves. The practice of overlaying regulating lines can be applied to buildings from any epoch, style, or culture to analyze compositional priorities and proportional relationships. It involves overlaying a drawing of the facade or plan of a building with a diagram of lines that demonstrate how compositional and proportional consistencies were established. For the classical designer, such harmonic diagramming ensured that all parts of, say, a facade, were related to one another and to the overall composition. The intention was to achieve a unity of composition and a pleasing organization of elements.

From the time of the Renaissance harmonic proportioning was frequently conferred with mysticism. This might be expected, based as it was on

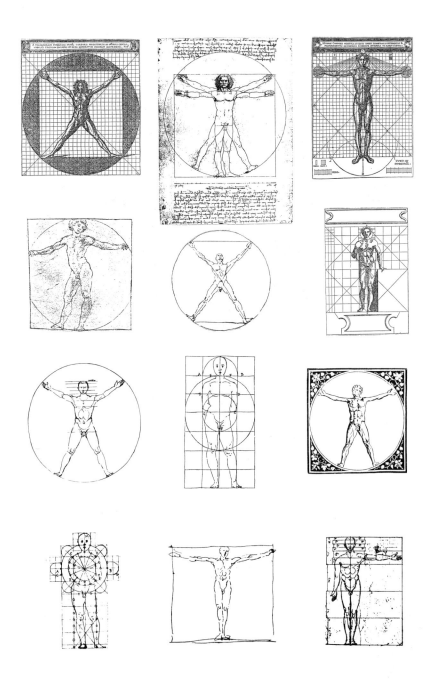

4.3
"Universal man" drawings, inspired by Vitru-vius's description, compared.

a
Cesariano, Leonardo, and Cesariano.

b
Francesco di Giorgio, Albrecht Dürer, and Jean Gevjon.

c
Giuliano da Sangallo, Francesco di Giorgio, and Fra Giovanni Giocondo.

d
Francesco di Giorgio, Dürer, and Sangallo.

4.4
A ballerina and a sumo wrestler suggest the natural logic of basing proportions on the human body.

Pythagorean precepts and Platonic ideals. For early sixteenth-century architects, for instance, harmonic proportioning encouraged the design of central
plan churches in response to the assumed sacred qualities reflected in the geometry of the square and the circle. It was from Plato that the inspiration for the
pure geometry of the circle and square came. For many architects proportional
systems that replicated idealized human proportions had a mystical or sacred
power. From a practical point of view it can be argued that this mystical quality
ensured that the act of designing buildings was not perfunctory. The organization of the elements of a ground plan is a case in point. The harmonic relationship of one part of a ground plan to another can only be observed in a drawing
of the plan, where the whole plan, like the facade of a building, can be seen all
at once. The actual experience of the ground plan while moving through the
rooms and corridors of a complex building takes place in time as a sequence
of perceptual events. These events must be sensed as parts of an overall conceptual framework that is not directly visible. Rudolf Wittkower described the
frame of mind that employed harmonic order to regulate the invisible order of
a ground plan thus: "We must therefore conclude that the harmonic perfection
of the geometrical scheme [of a ground plan] represents an absolute value,
independent of our subjective and transitory perception. And it [can be shown]
that for Alberti—as for other Renaissance artists—this man-created harmony

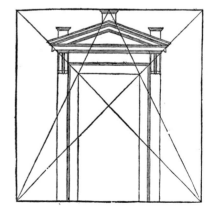

4.5

*The proper portioning for a door and frame de-
rived from human proportions and harmonic geometry as illustrated in Sebastiano Serlio's
treatise on architecture of 1545.*

was a visible echo of a celestial and universally valid harmony."[4] The presence of a coherent organization is still sensed by us in our experience of a building designed in this way. We intuitively recognize a well-ordered plan, even when we cannot tell exactly what orders that plan; we simply perceive a design unity, the source of which may not be immediately apparent.

Harmony, Idealism, and the Quest for Beauty

The use of Pythagorean numbers in building design continued in one guise or another into the nineteenth century, and even into the twentieth century in distantly related forms. Beautiful ideas, regardless of whether they are empirically verifiable, are tenacious. The "music of the spheres" which was held by the Pythagoreans to account for the orbits of the planets, was assumed by Johannes Kepler in the early seventeenth century in his first heliocentric scheme for the universe following on the newly revealed Copernican model. He theorized that the basic order that fixed the distances of the orbits of the planets from the sun was determined by the nesting of five "regular" solids, those referred to by Plato as "the most beautiful of things." In his assumption of regular geometric figures among the planetary orbits Kepler was consistent with the belief in the primacy of regular geometric figures reflecting the order of the cosmos. Eventually Kepler discovered that the shape of the orbits of the planets were actually ellipses rather than the Platonic nesting solids and perfect circles which others before him had assumed, but still his inclination was to follow an aesthetic impulse and search for the presence of primal geometries as the basis of something so fundamental as the structure of the universe. His five nesting regular solids in fact reflect the two-dimensional technique known as *quadrature.* Quadrature was used by medieval masons for proportioning building plans and facades, and for locating and proportioning sundry architectural elements throughout a building. Quadrature involved the 45-degree rotation of nesting squares to produce a series of like-proportioned figures. These figures were used to determine and position the relative sizes of building parts such as the

4.6

Harmonic and compositional analysis of the Pic-
colomini Palace in Pienza designed by Bernardo
Rossellino and begun in 1462.

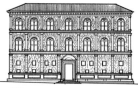

NORTH

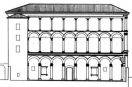

SOUTH

WEST

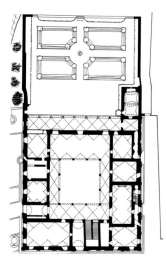

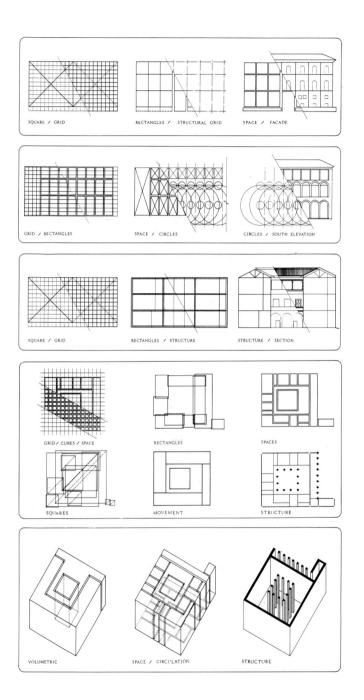

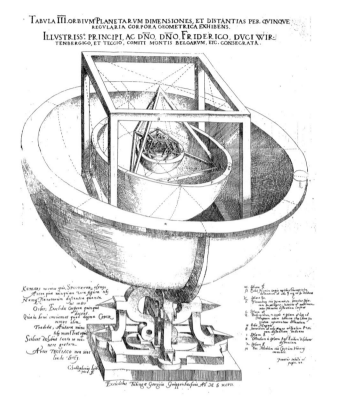

4.7

Kepler's model of the universe from his Myste-
rium Cosmographicum of 1596, a nesting of ge-
ometric figures that account for the orbits of the
planets.

nave piers of a church, to regulate the composition of constituent elements such as a spire or pinnacle, or to generate repetitive carved stone ornament. Such complex, and often mystical, geometries were seen as the key to building design long before the more elaborate and systematic codification of such geometries by architects and town and military planners of the Renaissance.

While this description of compositional and proportioning systems might seem like a digression in the broader discussion of the way we harmonize our buildings with nature, it is important to see what these systems meant to the designers who used them. The idealism inherent in medieval and classical architecture involved a conscious attempt to harmonize buildings with what were seen to be nature's own structural symmetries. Concepts such as the Ionian philosophers' analogy between the workings of the human body with its constituent parts and organs and the implied interconnectedness of an "ensouled" cosmos, or Pythagoras's parallel between musical harmony, geometry, numbers, and the mechanics of the cosmos, all served to ensure an awareness of the interconnectedness of all things, whether man-made or found in nature. To the Renaissance humanists, human perception and the human sense of what is beautiful and what is not are integral to that system.[5] The ancient and the Renaissance notion of beauty was as inseparable from theoretical science and practical engineering as it was from the primal laws that govern the universe. The word "aesthetics" had yet to be coined.

Structural Analysis

It is appropriate to pause yet again before returning to the main discussion and look at the idea of the universal man. An effective framework for understanding complex but apparently unscientific constructs like the universal man—that is, constructs that may appear to be unscientific if viewed at face value as statements about reality—can be found by an approach known as *structural analysis*. The logic behind the universal man—and behind the myth of the primitive hut—lies hidden in the story that conveys its meaning. A story, parable, rule, canon, or myth conveys through time a course of action that assures adherence

to some principle or universal truth. For architecture, the intention to "human-
ize" it is embodied in the myth of the universal man which ensures the engage-
ment of an unconscious understanding of the human body.

Structural analysis began in linguistics and was adapted to the study of
myth and ritual by the French anthropologist Claude Lévi-Strauss and others.[6]
The structural approach reveals a "hidden system of uniformities," as the American anthropologist Alexander Alland, Jr., has descibed it, of which surface realities are only an outward manifestation.[7] Structural analysis has been used by
Lévi-Strauss and others to decode social relationships in order to get at the
roots of a culture. Thus the structural approach is inherently transcultural. In
remote and unrelated cultures a myth, story, parable, canon, or ritual would
likely manifest itself in different ways, but its underlying meaning and intention would be virtually the same, as we have seen, for instance, in our analysis
of the practice of applying to architectural design the principles embodied in
the idea of the universal man.

The Quest for Unity

The single most important objective of a quest for harmony between the man-
made world and nature is the achievement of a unified and all-inclusive existence. If we are to reside harmoniously within that preexistent system, the
sources of nature's unity must be known so that what we build can be designed
in harmony with it. Systems of harmony for describing unity in both the natural and man-made world are not unique to Western classical thought. The ancient Chinese yin and yang, for instance, saw the source of unity in the world
as a graceful balancing of opposites. Chaos and order, fire and water, male and
female, heaven and earth—all of creation was unified through such pairings.
If one of any pair began to dominate its opposite, then the cosmos would tilt
toward imbalance and away from harmony. Thus in planning a building, one
would, first of all, assess the probable consequence of that building on nature's
primordial balances, the fundamental source of unity. In the ancient Greek and
Roman versions, as reflected in Vitruvius's treatise, this act involved a careful

assessment of the relationship of specific sites for buildings to the larger cosmological realm:

> *As the position of the heaven with regard to a given tract on earth leads naturally*
> *to different characteristics, owing to the inclination of the circle of the zodiac and*
> *the course of the sun, it is obvious that designs for houses ought similarly to*
> *conform to the nature of the country and to diversities of climate.*[8]

Many cosmogonies attributed unity in the world as having come from a
single event at the beginning of time. One such belief is that of the ancient
Polynesians who saw all of creation as preceded by the ushering forth of a
primordial soup, the great birth-waters from the womb of creation out of which
all that now exists came to be. The ocean in which their island world floated
beneath the dome of heaven was concrete evidence of the primordial birth-
waters, the primary material of their perceivable universe. The concept of time
is another important part of the idea of unity. Most primitive cultures viewed
time as cyclical and creation as a repetitive event. Unity in a cosmogony lay in
the symmetry of re-creation.[9] Where time is cyclical, events such as the founding of a town or the construction of a temple or of one's own house are seen to
reflect the beginning of time. For the built world to be in harmony with nature,
all of nature's phenomena must be taken into account. Modern science is no
different in this respect. Bronowski's description of science as "nothing else
than the search to discover unity in the wild variety of nature" is not at all
inconsistent in spirit and intent with the mythological cosmogonies and cosmologies of so-called primitive societies. Our primordial birth-water might be
the Big Bang, our primordial substance the atom, our temporal infinity Ein-
stein's relativity, and our yin and yang the tension between mass and energy.
Although modern scientific views of the universe are for the most part impossible for the nonscientist to sense intuitively—as one might sense the meaning
of an ensouled universe, primordial birth-waters, or the tension of opposites—
they are essentially analogical as well. "The wild variety of nature" cannot usually be explained effectively in one whoppingly all-inclusive myth or theory; it
inevitably requires a nesting series of myths or theories to encompass the whole
expansive range of phenomena that comprises nature.

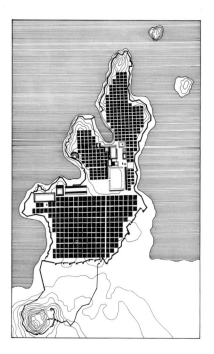

4.8

The physical manifestation of a polis. The Io-
nian Greek city of Miletus after it was rebuilt in
the fifth century BC. The acropolis is at the lower
left-hand corner of the plan; the principal public
spaces are near the center, connecting the two
harbors. The solid black squares represent
blocks of peristyle houses, so each block would
have been dotted with courtyards.

The Polis and the Idea of a Sustainable City

For us average beings making our way in the world, the notion of our unity
with nature is most succinctly expressed in the way the our world is built in
response to its natural setting. That was the observation, you will recall, of
Lévi-Strauss's noted in chapter 1; he urged each of us to explore for ourselves
just what we think the ideal balance between human intervention and nature
ought to be. The ideals of which he spoke are ones that manifest themselves
here and there in the real world of our experience, serving as models for a
conscious relationship between our creations and nature's. Today, unfortu-
nately, it is far easier to find examples to the contrary. The history of the city
nonetheless does reveal one example of a type of city that was effectively guided
in its creation and evolution by an inclusive notion of harmony. It is the ancient
Greek polis. The success of the polis resided in an effective institutionalization
of the idea of unity. The most fundamental expression of the Greek idea of
unity can be found in that setting.

Ancient Greek ideas about the character of nature's unity range from Anaximander's biological analogy to Pythagoras's harmonics, with plenty of secondary and tertiary variations besides, and their language, customs, mythologies, philosophy, and science reflected the importance they placed on the unity of all existence. The Greek habit to see things always as part of larger things provides a case in point. Take the Greek use of the word "character," for example. For the Greeks, "character" referred, first of all, to the mark stamped upon a coin; then, by analogy, it stood for the impress of this or that quality upon a human being. As Edith Hamilton noted, "To us a man's character is that which is peculiarly his own; it distinguishes each one from the rest. To the Greeks it was a man's share in qualities all men partake of; it united each one to the rest." To them, rather than a person's qualities being the most important definition of character, "what was important in a man were precisely the qualities he shared with all mankind."[10] The polis reflected not only the Greek habit of seeing things as parts of larger things but also their idea of the relationship of the man-made world to nature and their sense of one's place in it all.

The polis was the animating idea behind the Greek city-state. It could be seen as affecting Greek literature, science, philosophy, and art. Although its physical embodiment was to be found in the form of the city, the city was only a part of that which was referred to as the polis. The polis was rather a man-made cosmos, whole and complete unto itself, with its own intrinsic order, rules, laws, balances, place, history, and nature. Although the term "polis" would refer to the place where a city resides, together with its hinterland, its essence was every bit as historical and human as it was locational. Some have argued that the historical and human dimensions of the polis were more important than its physical location. In this view the polis was, first of all, comprised of a community of people who resided together in a certain setting, were freely subject to the same polity (the common political structure that binds them together), and were progeny of the same history. Harmony within the human community of the polis was central to the concept of the polis itself: ". . . to live in a *polis,* meant that everything was decided through words and persuasion and not through force and violence."[11] This is not to say that there was no argument—there was plenty of that—but verbal discourse took place in lieu of establishing conformance through force and violence. Central to the concept of the polis was the agreement that the polity binds the community together; each citizen of the polis is aware that he shared a destiny with all other citizens, just as all citizens share in the common history of their polis.

If the physical city was destroyed, as happened to some city-states in times of war, the polis could well remain intact and the physical city would be rebuilt. To quote Heidegger, "The polis is the historical place, the there *in* which, *out of* which, and *for* which history happens. To this place and scene of history belong the gods, the temples, the priests, the festivals, the games, the poets, the thinkers, the ruler, the council of elders, the assembly of the people, the army and the fleet."[12] The hinterland of the polis extended to include an agricultural and natural landscape with the appropriate preexistent natural features of demarcation, such as the foothills of a mountain range, a major river, an escarpment, and the shore-line of the sea. In its growth the polis changed the basic natural features of its site very little. At its center the city was characteristically dense and small, so the countryside was never very far from the city's center. Unity in the physical expression of the polis was embodied primarily in a balanced relationship between the city and its hinterland, and in the existence of permanent reminders of a shared history. That is to say, one of these expressions has to do with an environmental balance and the other with memory. We will look at them here one at a time. First, let us consider the balance between city and its hinterland.

The focus of a Greek city-state is the physical city itself. It was usually established as a port on a bay of the sea in order to facilitate trade with other cities and the city's connection to the rest of the Greek world, which was referred to as "the fatherland." The immediate hinterland supplied the city with agricultural necessities, and the city in turn supplied the countryside with manufactured goods and the products of trade. Now it is easy to see that the city could not grow beyond the ability of its hinterland to supply its need for food, lest it begin to import food and thereby become dependent on agricultural production outside the polis. For this reason it was important that the agricultural hinterland and the city always be in balance. Not only could the population or the area of the physical city not expand uncontrollably, but internal balances within the hinterland had to be carefully maintained, in particular between agricultural land and natural landscape features such as woods for fuel and game, watersheds for abundant fresh water, and natural grazing land for domestic stock and wild game. To ensure that the city not grow beyond the hinterland's ability to coexist with it, population growth was controlled by the founding of new colonies. The colonies subsequently became trading partners of the polis, enhancing both the polis's self-sufficiency and its standing among comparable city-states. (A city-state could function without trade but not without food.) There were other important reasons for controlling the size of the population. The most important was keeping the size of the population relative to the optimum workings of the polity. If a polis were permitted to grow infinitely, the sense of enfranchisement and consequent responsibility of each citizen to the whole would be lost, and the polis would no longer function as intended. Balances between city and hinterland, between population and immediate resources, and between concept and actuality had always to be considered in decisions made by citizens in their councils. These balances worked together to ensure a sustainable existence for the polis, a kind of closed system with its own rules for survival and continuity.

"Let us keep our silent sanctuaries, for in them the eternal perspectives are preserved." That statement was made by Étienne de Sénancour, but it might as well have been by an ancient Greek speaking about his polis. Among the many important physical reminders of the polis's history, the most prominent was the acropolis. This high place where the city was founded was a place of refuge, defensible against outsiders while the city-state built its fleet and army. Once firmly established in this setting, the population of the polis could come down from the heights of the acropolis to establish a town on the harbor, which would be convenient for trade and which could accommodate a network of streets and suitably expansive public squares, the agoras. At this point the acropolis became a place reserved for the city's major temples and commemorative monuments, while often the city's main theater was sculpted into the slopes that led to those venerable heights. The acropolis would serve as a place to which citizens could flee in times of emergency. But as it presided over the city and surrounding countryside, it was a constant reminder of the polis's roots: its heritage of sacrifice and courage. Such a setting must have also served as a reminder of "the fatherland" beyond composed of similar Greek city-states.

The precise place of a city's origin is often the most poignant reminder of its past. The modern city is no exception. Consider Île de la Cité, Paris's founding place. It is an island in the Seine River where stand the city's most historic public monuments. Its centrality at the heart of an expansive city is emphasized by the repetitive ringlike pattern of streets that radiate from it in response to former circular defensive walls built for the city at successive stages of its outward growth. Now these streets appear on a map like ripples from a stone thrown into a quiet pond. The more recent city of Chicago, on the other hand, has it's origin noted with brass markers embedded in the pavement of busy Michigan Avenue, where once stood the walls of Fort Dearborn. The place where the fort stood on the south bank of the Chicago River near where it joins Lake Michigan is recalled on a modern map of the city by the way several diagonal streets cut across the incessant grid. These streets had once been Indian and pioneer trails connecting the important juncture between lake and river with the hinterland to the west. Nonetheless, no modern city can match the power of the ancient Greek acropolis, standing high above the city, to be seen from nearly everywhere in the city, from far out at sea, and, given the limited extent of the city's designated hinterland, from the city's most distant reaches. The acropolis served throughout the whole of its territory as an ever-present reminder of a city's origin and symbolic center.

Below the acropolis was the next level of permanent reminders of the polis's history. Unlike the comparatively aloof monuments on the acropolis, these historic monuments figured into the everyday life of the city's people. Here could be found the city's hearth with its continuously attended symbolic fire. The hearth brought the symbol of the city-state's founding down from the acropolis into the life of the city. It served as the place for important sacrifices and for public ritual meals, and on a grand scale reflected the idea of the family hearth which was the central element of every residence in the city-state. As a community's counterpart to the family hearth, the hearth of the polis reinforced the unity between the citizen, the family, and the community. The importance of the public hearth may be noted in its eminence in the practice of establishing colonies. Whenever some of the citizens would leave to form a new colony, they would take a flame from the city's eternal fire with them in order to light the hearth of their newly established city.

The city's hearth usually stood next to the *prytaneion,* a public assembly hall in which the day-to-day functions of government were conducted by officials known as *prytanes.* This building was one of a pair associated with governance, the other being the *bouleuterion* which housed the council of elders, nobles, or certain officials known as *boule,* depending on the polis's form of government. These buildings, in reflection of their civic function, were strategically placed and had a recognizable character that distinguised them from the city's other architecture, its religious temples, city walls, gates, stoas, commemorative monuments, theaters, and private residences. But like other public architecture that formed the complex fabric of the city, these buildings were conceived to be stately and permanent in appearance, thereby capable of presiding over all else around them. And like the buildings on the acropolis they were conceived to be fixed expressions of the history of the community.

Of equal importance to these buildings were the agoras, large open spaces for public assembly and commerce. Agoras were customarily defined by colonnaded stoas, while appearing as though they were carved out of an expanse of houses. Around them were located public monuments with circulation and gathering spaces. The agora was the place where citizens might meet throughout the day in the regular conduct of their business. Like the hearth, it echoed an important component of the family domicile: the courtyard or peristyle court. The agora served the polis much as the courtyard served the family, as the most public place in a hierarchy of places that extended from the most private rooms of a residence (the often separate men's and women's sleeping quarters), through the most public room (the *andron,* or dining and entertaining room), to the courtyard, then the neighborhood street outside the house's gate, leading first to the neighborhood's own temple precincts, then to the major civic and religious buildings, and finally to the agora. The clarity of this hierarchy of elements of the city contributed to the unity of the polis.

Not far from the edge of the city proper was the *necropolis,* the place of the dead where the polis's heros and common citizens alike were interred. One could trace in the necropolis the natural history of the city; it was a place that recorded "a history of beginnings and ends, of birth and death."[13] The beginnings and ends that bracket the unity of the polis—the acropolis and the necropolis—were the physical fabric of the ancient Greek's understanding of the polis as a cosmos, like nature fulfilling humankind's need for reminders of origins and ends.

The polis remains, however, as one of history's more poignant ironies. While it was responsible for the strength of ancient Greece, it was also a principal source of its downfall. To preserve its all important unity, the polis inhibited the formation of permanent political unions with other city-states, and consequently Greece never evolved an effective federation of cities that might weld themselves into a nation or an empire as Rome did so well. There is of course the exception of the empire of Alexander the Great, which in fact began to crumble only after twelve years. The polis as as an example of an ideal world built in response to nature's harmony remains one of history's great contradictions. Although most Greek city-states eventually became part of the Roman Empire, no longer could each polis be viewed as a relatively independent city-state. Like Romanized cities everywhere, they became incorporated in a vast domain that had Rome at its center.

Scale and the Problem of Unity

The Greek idea of unity traverses the full range of things both natural and man-made, from the macrocosmos to the smallest household objects. Edith Hamilton described the Greek concept of unity in this way: "A house is a very complicated matter considered by itself; plan, decoration, furnishings; each room, indeed, made up of many things; but, if it is considered as part of a block or part of a city, the details sink out of sight. Just as a city in itself is a mass of complexity but is reduced to a few essentials when it is thought of as belonging to a country."[14] Everything is a part of something else, each thing may be considered integral with its context as well as an entity unto itself. Seen in this way, complexity and simplicity in the environment are issues of relative scale.

During the Enlightenment there increasingly developed a tendency to isolate the parts of a subject except as they are related by quantifiable means. Today, however, there is evidence of a new understanding. For instance, more recent studies of complex and expansive ecological systems by biologists have gone against the more limiting approach of examining organisms exclusively in relation to immediate and clearly definable environmental influences. It has been primarily only in the last thirty years or so that the biological sciences have been willing to concentrate upon larger-scale ecosystems, even at the expense of not being able to account for all the diverse factors in operation within them. This may sound a bit like old-fashioned teleology, but it provides a means of encompassing the subtle interaction of unaccountable variables within a complex ecosystem, variables that a requirement of perfect accountability would tend to overlook. From another direction, recent movements in architecture and in urban design and planning have attempted to base design methods and theory as much on the context or setting of the thing designed as on immediate programmatic requirements. In this approach building form is seen to be generated as much by forces that lie outside it as by requirements for functions to be accommodated within. In still another area, engineering students who were once trained to focus with myopic intensity upon clearly defined technological problems are now required in some universities to take classes in philosophy and history of science and technology in order to see their work in the context of history with its societal and value-laden concerns. In a number of other areas such as theoretical mathematics, there is developing a new and somewhat radical way of looking at natural phenomena. This is the movement broadly known as *chaos theory*. It accepts messy diversity in nature as eagerly as more traditional methods searched for signs of predictable regularity. But the more relevant focus for our purposes is that facet of chaos theory referred to as "the fractal geometry of nature." The ancient Greek practice of seeing everything according to its scale and according to its relationship with other things, as manifested in the reality of the polis, can be seen in some of the ideas that lie behind this emerging concept.

"Fractal" is a term coined by Benoit Mandelbrot, the mathematician who first drew together that part of chaos theory.[15] Without going into its origin and diverse applications, it will suffice here to point out that at its roots is an assumption about our visual perception of nature. Mandlebrot refers to a phenomenon, which he calls "scaling," that ties the more abstract chaos theory into our daily experience. Although like Pythagoras and Newton, Mandelbrot's aim is to describe nature with geometry and numbers, his subjects for investigation are rather those that exhibit behavior so unpredictable as to be characterized as chaotic. His search is for an underlying structure in nature that would account for observations that do not yield to traditional mathematical description. Weather patterns, static in radio transmissions, wave action at sea, smoke patterns in the air, solar flares, and the spacing of trees in a forest, for instance, cannot be described with much precision except in terms of averages and probability. Such phenomena can, however, be described as "an intensity of events at selected scales." They range from subjects as large as galaxies to the smallest particle, the atom. Between these extremes—between the observations of the celestial telescope and those of the electron microscope—lies a range of scales. Each reveals a characteristic intensity of occurrence or frequency of change over time or spatial distance.

Interestingly the frequency of events, density, change, or whatever it might be, appears to be relatively constant at any selected scale of reference. A simple example that we can readily relate to our customary perception of things might be a tree. From a certain distance it is perceived as a network of branches supporting a mass of leaves. This will in turn form an outline of distinguishable complexity against the sky. Upon closer observation the outline against the sky can no longer be seen, but visual interest is continued by the configuration of the mass of leaves. Even closer, the mass of leaves will give way to the structure of branchlets and twigs, and the leaves themselves will reveal details of veining as well as their individual shapes. If we were to employ a microscope, the next step in this investigation would continue into the cellular structure of the leaf and stem, and so on. On the other hand, if we had begun at a greater distance from the tree, then the forest, the mountain range, or the continent would be part of the overall picture. By Mandelbrot's hypothesis, this typical scene may be regarded as broadly characteristic of our natural world. The things with which we deal on a daily basis are perceived by us in terms of scale, not unlike the way the Greeks sensed complexity and simplicity in their polis. Since it is natural for us to judge objects in terms of their relative scales and their general context, it does not seem unreasonable to suppose that our visual apparatus, which evolved for our species in primeval times, is naturally attuned to the recognition of a limited range or intensity of detail within a particular set of scales.

The Greek Temple and the Tree

Turning to architecture, Mandelbrot suggests that it likely evolved in a way that would ensure a relatively constant intensity of detail at each scale. Like the example of the tree then, from a distance the colonnaded peristyle and roof of the Greek temple against the sky provide us with enough visual detail to maintain our interest. As we approach the building, its silhouette is replaced in our visual field by such details as the entablature, a series of columns, and other complete elements that comprise the building's overall form. Then the treatment of the surfaces of those elements comes into view, revealing the fluting of columns, the elaboration of their capitals, and so on. A temple is a simple structure—a lintel on which rests a symmetrically pedimented roof supported by a line of closely spaced columns resting on a slightly raised platform and surrounding a single room enclosure. But it can become as complex for us as we want it visually to be. The treatment of the surfaces as well as the shapes of the elements represent a codified system of design that was intended to ensure consistency throughout the different scales of form and detail. Of course Greek architecture was not alone in promoting what Mandlebrot calls scaling. He also points out how the architecture of Frank Lloyd Wright works in much the same way, even though it was not derived from a universally codified approach to design as was classicism.[16] He suggests that the presence of a natural sense of visual detail that relates to scale may well explain why such buildings as prismatic glass skyscrapers soon become boring to many people. This insight might also be considered for our negative reaction to a building or interior that has too much ornament and so appears to us as chaotic. Obviously variations occur from person to person as might be explained by life experiences, dispositional inclinations, and cultural influences (such as the Islamic culture's preference for highly elaborate surface embellishment).

In speaking of fractal geometry in chaos theory as revealing something of how we understand the world, the physicist Gert Eilenberger noted: "Our feeling for beauty is inspired by the harmonious arrangement of order and disorder as it occurs in natural objects—in clouds, trees, mountain ranges, or snow crystals. The shapes of all these are dynamical processes jelled into physical forms, and particular combinations of order and disorder are typical for them."[17] While for some readers the logic of the "chaos argument" will remain uncomfortably loose, as a theory of the universalities of perception and understanding, it describes human perception as it is naturally attuned to the frequency of visual, spatial, and temporal events in the environment. For our probe into the things we have created, it offers yet another lens that reveals our response to nature. Through the phenomenon of scaling we are able to see the unity in nature and in its counterpart, the built environment, and understand this intuitively without the need for abstract theory.

Summary: Unity and the Idea of Harmony

Classical architecture, at least as it was interpreted in the Renaissance, relied on constructs such as Platonic formal ideals and Pythagorean geometry to ensure that it was consistent with nature's order. How did these ideas start? The true origins of what might be called the classical view of architecture are lost in the primeval mists of cultural evolution, likely long before the Neolithic Age, before humankind began to settle into communities. It might have begun with a simple observation of the cosmos, that is, of the perfect regularity of the heavens. Perhaps it was also the observation that the menstrual cycles of most women roughly coincided with the duration of phases of the moon, evidence that humans despite their mortality are tied to things eternal. And they must have observed that when that very human cycle is broken, it usually heralds the birth of a child, a particularly heartening event for creatures who are both self-aware and at the same time conscious of their precarious place in nature's order. Having made such an observation, having discovered this tenuous clue, links to the cosmos could be verified by the magic of numbers. This basic notion of arithmetically verifiable links to the cosmos was fundamental to classical science. But modern science required a significantly different frame of mind in many areas. Modern science, which began to supersede classical science in the eighteenth century, thus gradually undercut the credibility of that earlier system of logic. With respect to architectural theory it has even been argued that the idea of the man-made world in harmony with nature has never overcome "the crisis of modern science."[18] Now architecture and the city are seen to reside in a theoretical realm outside the bounds of nature. It is as though there are two distinct worlds—nature's and ours—and the feeling of unity between them is conspicuously missing, perhaps even lost forever.

To be sure, ideas of harmony and unity are only constructs, mental pictures of how the human world ought to interact with nature. Every age, every civilization, has had its own variation on the concept of harmony and has sought after a sense of unity in the built world, in nature, and in the relationship between the two. The drawings of the universal man, an idea inherited from the ancient Greeks and passed along to Roman and the Renaissance architects, helped to explain this concept. The Greeks' perfection of the polis might be an inspiration to us. It demonstrates that there can be a balanced urban system that, in addition to important social and political considerations, incorporates the physical relationship of the city with the natural world around it.

We will return to the polis and to the idea of settlements and cities in the last chapter. First, there are some aspects of the quest for harmony and unity that must be explored, and they have to do with the passing of time. Time indeed has physical presence because it is in time that things are built, and it is in time that they decay and are remembered or forgotten by the descendents of those who built them.

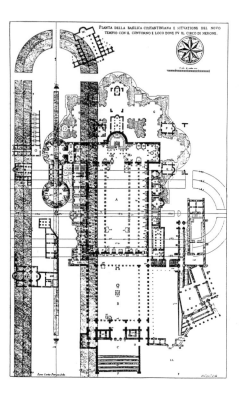

5.1

Composite plan of building activity on the site of St. Peter's Basilica in Rome. The drawing reveals the relative positions of the Roman circus of Nero, the early Christian basilica of Constantine, various shrines, temples, and churches built throughout the ages, and the present-day basilica begun in the fifteenth century. This most recent building, largely from the sixteenth and seventeenth centuries, reflects successive involvement in its design by the architects Giuliano da Sangallo, Sangallo the Younger, Bramante, Raphael, Giacomo della Porta, Carlo Fontana, Carlo Maderna, Giovanni Bernini, and Michelangelo. The meaning and importance of this place in the city ultimately transcends any singular event or building that may "take place" there for its own moment in time.

5 TIME AND THE EVOLUTION OF THINGS

The sense of time like the sense of place arises in the strength of memory, in observations of change in nature—the seasons, the heavens, tides and phases of the moon—in the discovery of fossils of extinct creatures, but especially in an awareness of our own mortality. Because only man, in the words of Teilhard de Chardin, "knows that he knows," we are acutely aware of our fragility, caught as we are within the vastness of all nature. The second-century philosopher-emperor Marcus Aurelius provided this eloquent prospect of time's incessant presence:

> One thing hastens into being, another hastens out of it. Even while a thing is in the act of coming into existence, some part of it has already ceased to be. Flux and change are for ever renewing the fabric of the universe, just as the ceaseless sweep of time is for ever renewing the face of eternity. In such a running river, where there is no firm foothold, what is there for a man to value among all the many things that are racing past him?[1]

Leonardo da Vinci echoed a similar sentiment: "O time, consumer of all things! O envious age! Thou dost destroy all things and devour all things with the hard teeth of years, little by little in a slow death. . . ."[2] When we build—a building, a monument, or a city—we build in time, aware that what we build usually occupies a place where others have built before and that which we build there will eventually be replaced, just as we ourselves have replaced an earlier presence. Awareness of our place in time gives rise to speculations such as these as well as to the practical concerns of immediate realities. Searching for ways to measure time has been an important preoccupation of human societies since they began, its impetus arising in curiosity, foreboding, and the practical problem of survival in a capricious world.

Approaches to measuring time vary according to the needs of who is doing the measuring. The nomadic wanderer must judge the seasons or else risk getting caught too high in the mountains when winter snows begin, the farmer must know the seasons to judge the optimum time to plant, and the seaman must judge the changing stars to determine his boat's place on the globe. But town-dwellers need most of all to know the hours of day, to know when to come together with others to work, pray, or take their meals in common. For each need—the hours of day or seasons of the year—the means to time's measurement is the same. It is the rotation of the earth and its path around the sun.

The first device that told time with more than conjectural accuracy was likely a stick, probably the long slender trunk of a dead tree, its branches gone, its shadow a long straight line on the ground. Someone must have observed that the tip of its shadow traced a graceful curve across the ground as the day progressed. Perhaps in the very distant past an early empiricist, with nothing pressing to do, drew a line along the tip of the shadow to discover the graceful symmetry of the arc from morning to night. Then he or she likely returned at another time of year to show a friend by doing the same thing, only to discover that this time the trace of the arc, although just as graceful and regular as before, did not quite match the first line drawn there while at the same time it was symmetrical with it. The observation was then extended to see if there was a regular pattern to this, in order to find out what happened throughout the seasons.

When is the center of the curving line at its farthest from the base of the tree, and when is it nearest? These are the likely questions to have arisen. Their answers would have revealed the summer and winter solstices, and these two places would serve as reference points for other less obvious points along the

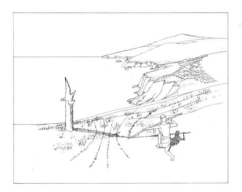

5.2

a

Man in nature establishing his place on earth by means of the geometry perceived by his body in space.

b

Discovering symmetries in the path of the sun and the seasons by marking the progress of the shadow of a "gnoman."

c

The gnoman as an obelisk, casting its shadow on a solar clock and calendar traced onto a building's terrace.

way. Then, when the resulting series of symmetrical arcs (really hyperbolas) were traced upon the ground, the solar calendar was created. Additional lines, or radii, out from the base of the tree to the outermost arc would divide the daylight into even increments to make it a sundial as well. With this early device human beings now had proof that nature's regularity is predictable by relating time and the cosmos to an observable geometry.

A dead tree trunk eventually falls victim to the very time its shadow measures. The next step would have been to erect a permanent marker as the gnoman of a proper sundial. Perhaps it was cut from stone and beautifully carved to reflect its sacred role in describing the wonders of the cosmos. Its shape might have been that of an obelisk, and when placed on a sacred spot, it became a symbolic world axis—an *axis mundi*. Time and place are now part of the same thing. Nature's wonder is all the more immediate for its pulse having been revealed by this first scientific instrument: the simple gnomon of the solar calendar and sundial.

To ancient peoples the sundial held special significance. Its design depended on a knowledge of the movement of the heavens while its gnomon stood at a fixed place on the surface of the earth, thereby relating earthly place to the cosmos through the order of sequential time. On the title page of this book is a sixteenth-century drawing by Cesare Cesariano based on a description in Vitruvius's first-century BC treatise. It was likely a symbolic drawing rather than representative of an actual instrument. It depicts a shadow-casting gnomon at the center of a figure generated by "quadrature," involving 45-degree rotations of a square in relation to the right-angle crossing of the diameters of a circle. The figure is divided into the hours of the day and night, the eight principal winds, and the sixteen parts of the heavens. Beyond telling the time of day, for the ancient Greeks the gnomon symbolized "uprightness," an attribute of human character as well as the normative relationship of the human body to the earth. The Greek word *gnomon,* or "knowing thing," comes from the verb *gignosco,* "I know." Vitruvius noted in his treatise that among all the creatures of the earth only humans stand upright, which permits them to gaze upon the heavens and thus become a link between heaven and earth.[3]

From simple beginnings there descended a succession of solar instruments and calendars for measuring and keeping time, each one an attempt at a further refinement in accuracy or in response to some material need. Especially there ensued a search for related order. Phases of the moon were inscribed between lines of the sun's traces dividing the year into twelve, and the times of each constellation's zenith in the night sky were marked beside the beginnings and ends of the appropriate arcs to register the night's annular rhythms beside those of the day. A Babylonian astronomer discovered that if the flat surface upon which the shadow of the gnomon traces the sun's daily movement, known as "the plane" of the sundial, is warped into a concave half-cylinder, it can be made much more accurate. Someone traced a figure eight in recording the position of the sun at corresponding times of day throughout the year, and this revealed the earth's angled axis in relation to its line of travel around the sun. Then came the astrolabe, a truly practical application of this new knowledge of nature's regularity. It was either a Greek or an Arab invention. In its simplest form it gave a map of the heavens overlaid by a rotating disk whose movable pointer, called an *alidade,* located at its center could be adjusted to correspond to sightings of celestial bodies. With the astrolabe one could determine the time of day from altitudes of the sun and stars if sighted from a known position on earth, or determine the place of the observer if the position of the sun or stars as well as a reference time are known. The astrolabe, like the calendar, was in effect a memory device on which are etched the laws of planetary motion.[4]

A more intricate calendar—and surely the most complex calendar ever designed—was the Pre-Columbian Mesoamerican calendar which we know from the Maya civilization. Twenty sacred signs times 13 form the 260-day *tzolkin,* which cycles in combination with 52 solar years of 18 months of 20 days each, plus 5 "unlucky days" that were added to make things work out right. The 52-year cycle comes from the fact that it takes that long to play out every possible permutation before starting over. Perhaps its greatest appeal to those who counted their days by it was that it provided cycles that suggest a human lifetime, while its complex derivation must have enhanced its credibility. But most important for our purpose, its length suggested that prediction could be based on a considerably greater and more profound sequence of celestial events than that generated by a single rotation of the earth around the sun.

Aristotle tried his hand at calendars as well. He conceived of a calendar whereby the sun, moon, and planets returned to the same relative positions

5.3
Subsequent devices designed to make sense of the positions of the sun and other celestial bodies, as well as the relationship of selected places on earth to time and the cosmos.

Above, left to right:
A "cone of Dionysidorus" sundial of the third century BC; a nineteenth-century "heliochronomometer"; (far right) a multifaced sundial and solar calendar of the eighteenth century and (below) a Syrian astrolabe from c. AD 1230.

5.4
The wondrous workings of the universe associated with God's prowess: A mechanical astronomical clock from 1390 in the transept of Wells Cathedral (above). The sun and a star revolve around the twenty-four-hour dial. A simpler timepiece (below) in the form of a sundial/solar calendar over the entrance to a country church in Cornwall.

every few thousand years, then began all over again to play out the same sequence of events. This calendar could be seen as going beyond the familiar annual cycle of seasons and history to encompass human mortality and confront the terror of infinity. It was time moving forward, with beginnings and endings as seminal demarcations. Plato, by contrast, saw time as the eternal present governed by the incorruptible geometry of the universe—described in Pythagorean cosmic geometry to have always been the infalible intelligence of the Creator without beginning or end. In Aristotle and Plato we have the two opposing views of time, one moving and one fixed.

Time and Place as Related Qualities of Existence

The more elaborate and beautiful the calendars, the more integral they seemed to be with human destiny. Time and one's position on the surface of the earth are revealed as intricately related qualities of existence. The length of a shadow at a given moment on a given day is different from one place to another along a north–south line on earth. With a recognition of the interconnectedness of all things on earth and in the heavens, the Roman architect Vitruvius could instruct architects, when designing a house, to be sensitive not only to their client's requests and to the usual topographic features of the land but also to the house's setting in relation to the heavens. He wrote that houses ought to be sited in relation "to the inclination of the circle of the zodiac and the course of the sun."[5] By this means the house would be suited to its place on earth and in harmony with the heavens, with earthly place and celestial events reconciled. A knowledge of the workings of the heavens places humankind a step closer to the gods. According to Cicero, Archimedes made a mechanical model of the universe that could be manipulated to demonstrate the relative positions of the earth, sun, and planets:

> . . . when Archimedes fastened on a globe the movements of moon, sun, and five wandering [planets], he, just like Plato's god who built the world in the Timaeus, made one revolution of the sphere control several movements utterly unlike in slowness and speed.[6]

Archimedes' model of the universe not only reflects an advancement in scientific knowledge about nature, it verifies the wondrous complexity of the cosmos, permitting humankind to conduct affairs in harmony with nature and the gods who regulate its forces.

Sometime toward the end of the fourteenth century there appeared a new surge of interest in instruments that measure time. Because sun-dependent instruments do not work at night nor beneath a cloudy sky, the next step was to make mechanical devises to replace celestial observations when celestial observations were not possible. The result was the mechanical clock. At first these machines for telling time were relatively simple, but before long the potential for elaborate visual affirmation of the connection between earth-bound human events and celestial ones was too much to resist. "No European community felt able to hold up its head unless in its midst the planets wheeled in cycles and epicycles, while angels trumpeted, cocks crew, and apostles, kings, and prophets marched and countermarched at the booming of the hours."[7] Contraptions such as these soon graced the naves of cathedrals, facades of town halls, and the belfries of churches all over Europe.

Cosmic and practical significance, however, ultimately outweighed the whimsical. In the early Italian Renaissance a painter's perspective drawing theory gave sea charts a grid that could in turn relate features on both land and sea to one another through a matrix of lines spread, as it were, over the earth. With the ability to design instruments to measure time and place with such sophistication and precision, and the possibility of making maps and charts that now positioned places of importance with a new accuracy, far-flung places and events on earth came to be directly related to one another through the medium of time. Thanks to the geometry of the grid, formerly chartless oceans could now join the same conceptual framework as places on the land. The earth became somewhat smaller and a little less frightening, while the heavens became more vast and filled with renewed wonder. Three hundred years later, by the beginning of the Enlightenment, church facades, loggias, gardens, and town squares were newly embellished with a wide variety of solar calendar and sundial designs, tangible symbols of a new scientific prowess.

The Evolution of Things

It may be said that there are two ways to approach the phenomenon of time in the design of artifacts. One has to do with what might be called "natural evolution of artifacts," and the other with the intention to arrest or negate the passage of time. The natural evolution of artifacts, be they functional or decorative, might involve a series of technological inventions. The conjectural history of sundials, solar calendars, mechanical clocks, and navigational instruments described earlier comprises such an evolutionary sequence. Measures intended to negate or arrest the passage of time, on the other hand, would include the translation into stone of a once wooden Greek temple design, the building of a pyramid to stand forever in the desert, or any instance where there is felt the necessity to preserve something that has considerable historic or symbolic importance—such as the original American Declaration of Independence, which is encased behind an ultraviolet screening glass in a sealed frame filled

5.5
The discovery of fire and experimental versions of "the first hut" according to Vitruvius, drawn by Cesariano.

5.6

Interpretations of "the first hut."

Top, left to right:
After Viollet-le-Duc, Claude Perrault, and Walther Hermann.

Bottom, left to right:
After Marc-Antoine Laugier, Francesco Milizia, and Jacques François Blondel.

with an inert gas, guarded by light sensors, and poised on a hydraulic cylinder above a vault into which it can descend if danger threatens. Measures that negate or arrest the passage of time will be considered more fully in chapter 6. In the discussion that follows we will first consider the evolution of artifacts; then we will look at some not so obvious means for dealing with the effects of time.

In any long-term chronological series of a class of objects, one innovation necessarily follows another in a sequence. This assumption places all human creativity in one great continuum, or in George Kubler's words, "Everything made now is either a replica or a variant of something made a little time ago and so on back without break to the first morning of human time."[8] Although at first such a view may not seem to square with the modern notion of invention and discovery (and especially with the romantic image of inventive genius), could anything be said to have come from nothing? Studies of the chronological development of certain artifacts, and associated speculation on the response of innovation to influences along the way, have fascinated artists, historians, anthropologists, scientists, and engineers particularly in this century.[9] Usually the motive is to try to see where we are going by looking at where we have been. At one level comparable sequences may be the same. Developments occur in more or less the same way whether the artifacts have evolved in the crafts tradition or have experienced incremental refinements through advances in science and technology. By using charts reminiscent of ancestral family trees, we can trace sequences of improvements and refinements made to singular classifications of artifacts, subsequently branching off into new inventions which may continue along new branches until those lines of artifacts drop out of use or inspire other inventions, thereby adding branchlets; when we reach the present, we stop and leave the next step in the sequence to our speculation. Long before Darwin's speculations on the natural evolution of biological species, the idea of a kind of natural evolution for human societies and for the artifacts they produce was both common knowledge and considered a fit subject for scholarly research. From Vitruvius and Marcus Aurelius to Immanuel Kant and Giambattista Vico, the idea of social evolution has long been seen as a basis from which to speculate upon the state of contemporary society and the things it makes.

The evolution of things also comprises for humankind an always shifting milieu of memories and meanings. Later, in chapter 6, we will look at the classical notion of "type," an interpretation of the history of things in relation to the timelessness of the ideas that are seen to animate them. "Type" will be treated as the obverse of what we have considered here. For the moment, however, we will return once again to the sundial and solar calendar, which have spawned a long series of progeny for measuring time, and which, besides incorporating improvements over time, were intended to recall time's unfathomable continuum that quietly presides over the creation of things. We will look at how these inventions influenced wholly different artifacts, which took on their own meanings and identities over time.

Invention and Discovery

The observation of the path of the sun traced on the ground by the shadow of a tree would likely have been just one event in a complex celestially inspired cosmology. The regularity of days and nights and the cycle of the seasons have always inspired the religious beliefs of people whose lives are spent in the open air and who are thereby acutely aware of the effects of the seasons on their food supply. Rituals to influence the weather for the production of better crops are among the more obvious attempts to take control of the natural world. Once having discovered that the gods do not always respond to these rituals, some mortals were so bold as to try to understand the natural world through systematic observations in order to find out what they have been doing wrong. In this, science was born. If the shifting shadow of the tree led to the telling of time and the seasons of the year, it likely encouraged the idea that a device could be invented to measure time more accurately.

Occasionally an antecedent continues to manifest itself in the design of subsequent artifacts such that earlier stages in their development are present in the contemporary form. Mechanical clocks, no matter where they emerged, rotate their hands "clockwise," so we say, from left to right across the top of the dial. The obvious reason for this has to do with their descendance from the sundial, whose shadow progresses in that direction because it is determined by the earth's rotation. Likewise in mechanical clocks the distance the hands travel is proportional to the time it takes for them to travel that distance, just as the distance the sundial's shadow travels is proportional to the time *it* takes to trace a complete circle. Sundials and mechanical clocks with hands can be read more quickly and easily by most of us than digital clocks because we readily perceive this direct relationship between time and distance. We understand the circular dial at a glance because we can equate the distance across the segments of the circle that each hand must travel to the time it takes to traverse that distance. Digital clocks, on the other hand, require an additional mental step to adjust to the abstraction of numbers representing time and distance.

Evolution and the Nature of Things

One could easily make too much of a comparison of circular and digital clocks. But this example serves to make a point. The farther something is along a line of descent from its basis in nature, the more abstract it is and therefore the more complex the intellectual processes for understanding it. The computer with which I write these words provides yet another example. Pen and paper are sufficiently related to their predecessors—the stylus and clay tablet and subsequent quill or crayon on papyrus or parchment—for us to immediately sense what is going on. But the computer, its keyboard, its microchips, and a laser printer require a much larger step in our conceptualization of descendances. The circular clock's relationship to nature—as a simplified model of the universe where time and space are played out in circular motions around a point, like the sun, at the precise center—is fairly self-evident. But just as the introduction of the digital clock constitutes an abrupt change in the development of the clock, the word processor constitutes an abrupt break in the descendance of tools for writing. We might say that on the genealogical chart of timepieces and writing implements, the digital clock and the computer would start separate branchs, with courses of descendance all their own.

The real issue for us, however, is towns and buildings that comprise our built environment. The discussion of sundials and digital clocks is intended to demonstrate how an artifact evolves along a line of descent, since the evolution of artifacts such as these is generally easier to understand than the evolutions of complex and culturally interconnected buildings and towns . The notion of

136

an artifact's conceptual distance from its origins in nature will resurface when we look at Western classicism in architecture, especially at the myth of the primitive hut. The phenomenon of conceptual distance is in fact a more serious problem for architecture and urban order than it is for the concept of time in the reading of digital clocks.

Many other artifacts have fascinating family ties with plenty of surprises. Other familiar examples are the printing press—which traces its ancestry back through the wine press, the embossing stamp, and the a jeweler's metallurgical knowledge that made movable metal type possible; and of course the modern computer—whose ascendancy from mechanical clocks branches to automated pipe organs, automated mechanical looms, and gambling devices and then encompasses numerous electrical and electronic inventions such as the vacuum tube, transistor, and microchip. Although along time's continuum unexpected connections may result in what appear to be unrelated artifacts, time lines can lead us back to mutual origins somewhere, until all the artifacts converge on one or two fundamental discoveries. In this respect the Neolithic Revolution's development of geometry—that first realization of the order of the landscape in relation to the human body which manifested itself in the design of domiciles and settlements—may be seen as the mother of all arts and sciences. Tonal music, perspective painting, architecture, land surveying, mechanics, ballistics, formal gardens, and town planning, among other things, are the likely descendants of Neolithic paradigms. The discovery of geometry provided the basis and inspiration for a long line of inventions upon which we continue to build today. Long before any mathematical logic a primitive people were able to see and interpret a geometric order in the cosmos, one that could be imitated to ensure a built environment that is coherent with the unity and order found in nature. In *The Constitutions of Masonry,* written around the year 1400, someone wrote:

> *Don't marvel that all science lives only by the science of geometry. . . . There is no tool to work with that has no proportion. And proportion is measures and the tool or the instrument is earth. And geometry is . . . the measure of earth, wherefore I may say that all men live by geometry. . . . You shall understand that among all the crafts of the world . . . masonry has the most notability and most part of its science is geometry.*[10]

Seeking Meaning in Time

The inevitability of change may be seen from the positive point of view of the natural evolution of invention, or from the cheerless perspective that all things in time decay. So that ideas and experience would not be forgotten, our ancestors invented the epic poem; to perpetuate the poem, there was the bardic tradition. Then, to compensate for the bard's human frailties of imperfect memory and mortality (along with a need to keep records of the harvest—a task insufficiently interesting for the bard to bother to pursue), our ancestors invented writing. It has also been an explicit requirement of the world of towns and buildings that it manifest memories that will help hold the community together and express the relative importance of one thing over the other. The Pantheon reminds us of past ideals and sensibilities. For the same reasons we will refuse to allow an old courthouse on the town square to be torn down, even though it no longer efficiently serves the needs of the county's courts. As important vestiges of our past, our historic buildings tie us to our real and imagined roots and become, as Italian architect Aldo Rossi puts it, "a part of the past still being experienced."[11] Sometimes when we build anew, we feel compelled to consciously preserve the past. Cicero said that temples ought to always have pediments because that is how they were built in the first place and it is an important part of how we identify them as temples. Louis Kahn said that a building should remind us of "its beginning," that is, it should manifest its ancestry in its present visage.

Our need to sense the past in the present can perhaps be seen best in things that themselves are incidental. Consider the origins of neckties, cuff buttons, and the collars on men's suits and coats. The necktie is likely the descendent of a scarf worn around the neck to keep out the cold, but it now serves to add a dash of color to a man's attire; cuff buttons are purely decorative on most jackets and coats, no longer functioning to fasten the sleeves; and collars were once meant to be turned up against the cold, but today on men's dress suits they provide only a touch of style. Today in most cultures men wear more conservative clothing than women, but even among women's clothing there are remnants of formerly practical things such as collars that cannot be turned up against the cold or pleats and ruffles recalled in printed fabrics. Such vestigial elements are mostly found on clothing that is ceremonious, designed to be worn on special occasions; work clothing must generally emphasize the practical with less concern for appearance.

Vestiges of time also abound in agricultural practices, in urban settlement patterns, in the siting of buildings, in the layout of gardens, and in the content of refuse dumps. All may yield information on how we once saw ourselves in relation to time and our environment. Occasionally, however, it is the reverse of this evolution that we want: Not so much to know where something came from and how it evolved, but to be able to consciously control its evolutionary process as it proceeds through time from a point in a history we already know and believe we understand. This has especially been the case with architecture. For instance, an important civic edifice is often made to manifest a memory of a culture's history in its facade. Like a formal outer garment, it is called upon to reflect importance and assert this through the retention of commendatory vestiges of the past such as classical columns, entablatures, and moldings, inscriptions of heroic statements by former orators, or recognizable symbols of past glories.

Imitation and an Evolution for Architecture

Western classicism in architecture presents us with an elaborate and beautiful means with which to control the design of buildings against the passage of time. By tying the present to the past, it ensures that the beginning will always be felt no matter how sophisticated and complex the work is in comparison to its predecessors. If we look more closely at the logic and structure of classical architecture the way we did in our discussion of the clock's origin, we will find that it touches on many sensibilities that are fundamental to the structure of the man-made world.

Of course there is no reliable way to determine what a building's earliest predecessors were. This was clearly less of a problem for the ancient Greeks than it is for architects today. The Greeks' idea of history extended back through documented events into mythological times without a break.[12] The evolution of Western classical architecture is customarily described as extending back through a historical past, thence to mythologies about the first building, the crude hut. The charming story about such a first building came to us from the Roman architect Vitruvius. He quoted Greek sources and then layered them with Roman ideas, as well as some of his own interpretations, to produce a complete and logically consistent pedigree for architecture.

Vitruvius's story begins with a description of how men of old "were born like the wild beasts, in woods, caves, and groves." Then he goes on to explain how these men of old discovered fire, and how the warmth of it encouraged them to gather around it. The fire, he claims, drew them together around it for warmth, so with this recognition of the advantages inherent in cooperative effort, they invented human society. Further, he says, they came to see their own actions and newly created social organization as distinguishing them from the rest of nature's creatures. And they took pride, he said, in the discovery that they were "gifted beyond the other animals in not being obliged to walk with faces to the ground, but upright and gazing upon the splendour of the starry firmament." Along with this recognition that they could be inspired by contemplating the heavens, they discovered they could "do with ease whatever they chose with their hands and fingers," and "they began in that first assembly to construct shelters." Clearly these early people caught on very quickly. Vitruvius allows, however, that they did not at first make the connection between their gazing at the wonder of the starry night sky and their new-found capacity to create shelters for their own comfort and convenience. Instead, he said, they began by imitating "the nests of swallows and the way they built." But by and by "they constructed better and better kinds of huts as time went on." The natural human proclivities that he assumed had fostered their experimental frame of mind were important to Vitruvius:

> And since [these men of old] were of an imitative and teachable nature, they would daily point out to each other the results of their building, boasting of the novelties in it; and thus, with their natural gifts sharpened by emulation, their standards improved daily. At first they set up forked stakes connected by twigs and covered these walls with mud. Others made walls of lumps of dried mud, covering them with reeds and leaves to keep out the rain and the heat. Finding that such roofs could not stand the rain during the storms of winter, they built them with peaks daubed with mud, the roofs sloping and projecting so as to carry off the rain water. (my emphasis)[13]

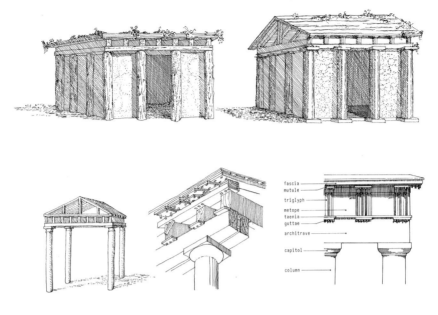

5.7

Evolution of the first hut into the basis for architecture.

Top:

Two stages of the primitive hut evolving into the Doric order after drawings by William Chambers based on the description by Vitruvius.

Bottom, left to right:

An early form of architecture after a drawing by Charles Delagardette, a fully evolved timber form of the Doric temple as suggested by Auguste Choisy, and the now symbolic, constituent parts of the masonry Doric temple (with their names) by William Chambers.

As Vitruvius implies, architecture likely developed through a combination of trial and error, human logic, cooperative effort, and discoveries of the innate characteristics of natural materials as applied to the problems of building. What is important in this is that Vitruvius is not just describing how architecture had likely come about in some prehistoric epoch, he is providing a basis for the design of architecture in the present. Because "their natural gifts [were] sharpened by emulation, their standards improved daily," he said. In other words, the myth shows us that the basis of invention is imitation. It tells us that imitation is natural to humans, and it is progressive—unlike copying which is what other creatures do when they build their nests or dig their burrows. In this Vitruvius was simply exercising Aristotelian aesthetic principles. For Aristotle, imitation (*mimesis* in Greek) is the natural human ability to envision things as they ought to be, as a modified version of the way they are. Because "nature" for Aristotle referred not to the things around us but rather to "the active forces of the universe," the frequently quoted statement by Aristotle that "man imitates nature" in the act of artistic creativity means that man is the only creature who, like the gods, has the capacity for true creativity. It does not mean what it sounds like in our language, that man replicates things as they are found to be in nature. Vitruvius therefore is saying that *mimesis* is natural to man, that it involves learning from things as they are found to be and then building upon that knowledge to make things "as they ought to be."[14]

In the next passage Vitruvius tells us that even in his time one could find examples of various stages of evolving building practices. They were taking place in lands occupied by what he called "foreign tribes." He compares two such "tribes," one that lives in a place with "forests in plenty" and has therefore evolved techniques of building based on wood, and another that lives in a place where timber is scarce and has therefore developed ways of using timber very economically and yet is able to produce buildings that make "their winters very warm and their summers very cool" owing to a practice of molding earth over a framework of light timber construction[15] (something like the traditional Navajo hogan described in chapter 2).

On the origin of building Vitruvius makes several important points: first, that building practices evolved over time and their evolution was assisted by the formation of human societies where people conversed with one another to solve mutual problems; second (or perhaps this should be listed first) that societies were formed by people coming together around a fire, suggesting the sacred quality of the hearth and the smoke hole in the roof above it present in Vitruvius's own time (recall from chapter 4 that the hearth, known in Latin as *focus*, symbolized comradeship, fraternity, family, and even political unity for the Roman citizen); third, that progress was possible because people were teachable through their ability to imitate; and fourth, that good building practices responded to available native materials and local climatic circumstances. He is instructing us in an architecture based on the logic of materials, thoughtful response to climate, and sensible construction practices arrived at through emulation and experimentation: "For this book [Book II of his *Ten Books on Architecture*] . . . treats of the origin of the building art, how it was fostered, and how it made progress, step by step, until it reached its present perfection."[16]

On the art of architecture Vitruvius discusses the orders of architecture and their sources. Here he describes a mythical early hut, the precursor of the Greek temple, consisting of a columnar structure of evenly spaced round tree trunks supporting squared timbers that hold up a symmetrical sloping roof. Each wooden part of this lowly hut, he explains, can be traced to a function in an even earlier primitive stage in the sequential development of a coherent and unified assembly of structural beams, rafters, crossbeams, and so on. He then names the various corresponding parts of a fully evolved marble and stone temple and shows the functional antecedents for familiar ornaments and details in the primitive wooden hut. His explanation suggests that if a detail or ornament cannot be traced to a source and its subsequent evolution, it does not belong there:

> Hence the ancients held that what could not happen in the original would have no valid reason for existence in the copy. For in all their works they proceeded on definite principles of fitness and in ways derived from the truth of Nature.[17]

Thus the ultimate test of validity for a work of architecture is for it to be true to nature, and that may be obtained by the designer who follows the appropriate precedents with care and understanding.[18] There is no place in this architecture for the arbitrary. But there *is* room for personal expression provided that it is held within the context of what were considered to be classical architecture's unassailable universalities.

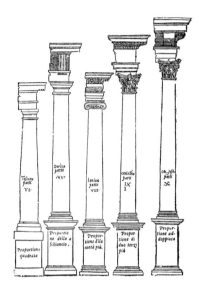

5.8

The orders of architecture.

Top:

*Serlio's sixteenth-century treatise began the prac-
tice of employing the orders as a primary means
to the design of buildings.*

Bottom:

*A more refined drawing of the orders appears in
Chamber's eighteenth-century treatise.*

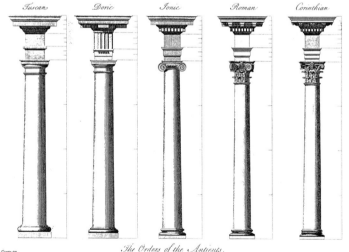

The Orders of the Antients.

The Orders of Architecture

We will now proceed to look at how some building elements evolved to get a sense of what Vitruvius meant when he said that each building must be validated by nature and history. Among the four fundamental orders that Vitruvius described, the order known as Doric is often used to demonstrate how the logic of the classical system works. In the primitive hut that is seen as the precursor of the Doric order, round columns roughly hewn from the trunks of trees support squared wooden beams on all four sides, and over them are laid roof rafters and ceiling beams. In the stone temple this beam assembly resting on the columns is replaced by the entablature, which has three corresponding parts: the architrave (the main beam in the wooden hut), the frieze of triglyphs and metopes (respectively, the ends of the ceiling beams and the open spaces between them), and the cornice (the extension of the roof rafters beyond the structural assembly). In the temple then, the structural members of the crude precedent have become stylized, and they will be further embellished as the temple evolves. The blank panels in the frieze, for instance, will invite repetitive decorative motifs. Other refinements will include the stylized block at the top of the column to adjust its height to the level of the entablature, a swelling of the column shaft, known as *entasis,* to express its task of supporting a great weight, and bands around the top of the column to strengthen its sense of completion. Each addition was seen to have had a practical reason for existing in the earlier wooden building, so every element of the stone temple was a reflection of a former tectonic element.

Implicit in this logic for determining the appropriate expression of an architectural work is the intention to control a building's design so that it appears consistent with its presumed predecessor. There is more to organizing the parts of a building and to modifying their character to suit individual taste and differences than has been recounted here, but this explanation of a Doric entablature and its characteristic column will suffice to provide a picture of the fundamental structure of the system. We will return to Western classicism and the role of the primitive hut later, when we consider what were regarded as the timeless qualities of architecture.

The story of architecture as related by Vitruvius, part mythical and part real, articulated a coherent set of principles that any thoughtful architect could remember, interpret, and follow. But like all such principles derived from human reason, this one is open to argument. Some scholars believe that the main reason for Vitruvius's writing was that he wished to reaffirm traditional principles of design, which he judged as being too often disregarded or misunderstood by many of his contemporaries. His cause was taken up again in the early Renaissance, then reinterpreted and given new life in the seventeenth and eighteenth centuries. Today it is valued for what it tells us about architecture and the city's civilizing resonance with culture and society. The Renaissance focus on the orders of classical architecture was *the* turning point for both understanding and re-creating that architecture. The classical system provided the Renaissance architect with the incisiveness required to accomplish proportioning, embellishment, and organization. But by the eighteenth century the system of orders began to be seen by a few theorists as a narrow dogma based on mythical precedent without the authority of objective, scientific proof. In more recent times the orders of classical architecture are again being seen in a more positive light, one that rejects the tacitly literal interpretation of Vitruvius's description which ultimately resulted in the Enlightenment's and post-Enlightenment's rejection of the idea of the orders of architecture altogether. According to contemporary historian and theorist Joseph Rykwert, "To understand the orders aright, it seems to me you must think of them as linguistic elements—not of a precise, clipped kind, but as distilled, poetic allusions, having the force of proverbs, or familiar quotations."[19]

The Analogy of Language

The evolution of an architecture may be further compared to the evolution of language. Just as a language is inextricably related to its own past, so must be architecture if it is to be effective and meaningful, and just as language changes incrementally (or as we say, "naturally") along with the society that uses it, so does an architecture. Syntax, grammar, and the vocabulary of a language continue to evolve in an organic way because the language of which they are a part must continue to evolve so long as it is spoken. By analogy, then, architecture will continue to evolve so long as buildings continue to be erected. Western classicism provides an example of a system of logic for recognizing that visually important details of an architecture are traceable to earlier structural forms. As in literature, the knowledge of antecedents in a work of architecture provides artistic resonance. It establishes connections across time to other settings and events that enrich the present work.

An analogy between architecture and language can also be drawn for the idea of style and expression. Vitruvius described architecture as having four orders, or styles: Doric, Tuscan, Ionic, and Corinthian. In the Italian Renaissance there was added a Composite order, which was found among the ruins of Roman buildings. These orders may be said to be analogous to a style of writing. Each order is characterized by a certain entablature and column assembly that forms a common grammar. I have not described the grammar here, but it will suffice for the moment to say that the grammar of classical architecture determines how all the components can be combined, how they can be modified without losing consistency and logic, and how they can be related to one another from the scale of a part, to the scale of the whole building, to the scale of an urban setting.

Like language, the elaborate code of architecture known as Western classical architecture, had its regional variations and recognizable forms of individual expression. Its rules incorporated a means to systematic change and evolution over time. And the process of change itself was dynamic, always open to challenge, which ensured the code's continuity with the society of which it is a part.

Natural Theories of Architecture

Since the early Renaissance numerous theories of architecture based on evolutionary principles have been inspired by Vitruvius's writing. In the nineteenth century the German architect Gottfried Semper described a fundamental and detailed evolution for architecture that began with the nomadic tent of knotted fabric. He then suggested logical stages of its evolution that could be verified by contemporary archaeology and anthropology. His theory focused on the development of the so-called primary elements of architecture—walls, floor, ceiling, and roof—as they might have progressed through history. Like Vitruvius, Semper emphasized in his theory the tectonic qualities of architecture as its true basis.

A near contemporary of Semper's, the French architect and engineer Eugène-Emmanuel Viollet-le-Duc studied historical examples and compared the structural characteristics of past architecture with the emerging technologies of his time. He illustrated his points with detailed drawings of how medieval, classical, and Byzantine buildings were constructed. In these drawings he showed the critical technological developments in each epoch and drew some theoretical conclusions. If Gothic architects, for instance, had been given the technology of cast iron construction, he demonstrated what they would have done with it. Viollet-le-Duc's view of the evolution of design in terms of a history of technology, albeit with a preference for the Gothic style of France, provided a requisite logic to what might otherwise appear as an erratically eclectic architectural expression. He emphasized the consistency of rigorous structural priorities as seen from the perspective of their evolution.

In the early twentieth century the English architectural theorist W. R. Lethaby developed a natural theory of architecture based in part on the evolution of magic and religion. He showed that this very human need was expressed most clearly in the architecture of antiquity and appeared to have continued to guide the development of architecture into the twentieth century. He demonstrated that to some extent the increasing formal complexity in architecture was parallel to the increasing complexity and sophistication of cosmological systems. His theoretical conclusions recommended a return to the conscious and careful linking of architecture with other nonformal/spatial systems of thought in order to restore architecture to its former consistency and depth of meaning.

The Enlightenment inspired numerous other theoretical treatises on architecture that sought to reconcile architectural theory with the emerging theory in the natural sciences. Although the theory of evolution in biology had yet to be written, a carefully reasoned argument for an evolution in architecture based on the primitive hut emerged in the work of Marc-Antoine Laugier, a French Jesuit priest whose controversial *Essai sur l'architecture* was published in 1753. He reasoned that the primitive hut pointed the way to a truly natural architecture, in contraposition to the extravagant Baroque and rococo of his

5.9

Cast-iron is combined with traditional masonry construction by Viollet-le-Duc, in his Dis- **courses on Architecture,** ***to demonstrate the "natural" transition possible in architectural expression with this technology.***

time, and he sought to purify contemporary architecture of extraneous "unnatural influences" by returning to the hut. Laugier thus rebuilt architectural theory through a largely conjectural step-by-step account of the evolutionary development of the orders of architecture. His writings coincided with the essays of Jean-Jacques Rousseau, both in time and in spirit, in that each aimed at purging Western culture of accumulated artificiality and urged the return to a more natural way of life.

Charles Darwin's speculations about the natural world and biological evolution likely influenced nineteenth-century architectural theorists. Gottfried Semper was quite explicit in his debt to Darwin: For him building styles developed "according to the laws of natural breeding, of transmission and adoption. Thus the development is similar to the evolutions in the province of organic creation."[20] And likewise is Viollet-le-Duc in his view of medieval architecture as an organism that "develops and progresses as nature does in the creation of beings; starting from a very simple principle which it then modifies, which it perfects, which it makes more complicated, but without ever destroying the original essence."[21]

The idea of redirecting the principles embodied in the primitive hut in a synthesis consistent with modern scientific views can be read into the words of science philosopher Karl Popper: "Darwin's theory of natural selection showed that it is *in principle possible to reduce teleology to causation by explaining, in purely physical terms, the existence of design and purpose in the world*."[22] Although Popper was not speaking of architecture or the primitive hut, his words are nonetheless appropriate in describing recent theories about architecture and the built environment that reflect Vitruvius's primitive hut while engaging Darwin's theory of evolution.

Each of these historical attempts to formulate a new theory of architecture submitted to a belief in the achievement of a harmonious relationship between natural forces and human nature. In that equation the effects of natural forces are easy to recognize, while those of human nature are much more subtle. One easily recognizable and easily isolated influence of human nature on building tradition, however, concerns the use of fenestration systems—windows and their characteristic organization across the facades of buildings—in highrise construction. In the persistence of tradition here, we may surmise our natural sense of tradition to be operating in a relatively unself-conscious manner to condition building design.

The distinct advantage of the cast-iron or the later steel framing system was that it allowed the construction of very tall buildings without the ever-thicker walls of masonry to support additional floors. When the first cast-iron frame buildings were built, they continued to look like bearing-wall buildings regardless of their height. This is not surprising given that the architecture that was universally accepted in the late-nineteenth century was derived from the masonry building tradition. The first cast-iron frames were therefore hidden within relatively thin envelopes of brick or stone cladding that were pierced by vertical windows spaced across the wall as though they could be no larger nor closer together without weakening the wall, and thereby the support for the floors and roof. If one were to arrange a succession of North American highrise buildings side by side in the order of their construction from the earliest "skyscraper," namely the Tribune Building in New York of around 1873, to the steel and glass towers in Chicago by Ludwig Mies van der Rohe of the 1950s, one would see a steady progression from the look of pure bearing-wall to a pure expression of unconcealed frame construction. In other words, the first building would appear to be of heavy masonry construction, and each successive building would look much like the one before it, but its windows would be slightly larger and closer together. Eventually the lineup of buildings would pass through a stage where it is unclear whether the facade is composed of figural windows or whether it has a masonry frame with the interstices of the frame closed off with glazing. That is to say, the lineup of buildings would progress by almost imperceptible steps from a facade where the windows are figural to one where the surface between the windows, now only slightly broader than the frame members, is the figural element, and "windows" are no longer in evidence.

Keeping in mind that it would have been theoretically possible for the first tall commercial buildings of frame construction to be built as virtually exposed frames with glazed interstices much like the skeletal high-rise buildings of the 1950s and after (as were greenhouses or "glasshouses" of the period, inspired by the Crystal Palace in London), it is evident that our willingness to accept radical changes in the idea of what constitutes architecture has a very strong inertia built into it. What is of special interest in the case of the high-rise frame and figural window is that after the pure frames of the 1950s the sequence appears to have reversed itself. Most tall commercial buildings designed and built in recent years have returned to a place in the evolution of high-rise facades where the opaque wall-with-windows visual effect is more normative. If the present situation remains relatively stable, discounting emerging concerns for energy conservation, I suspect it is because the pure frame is so limited in its potential for varied artistic expression that we have found it necessary to return to an architectural expression that offers a greater variety of expressive options. In addition the wall-with-windows facade easily yields to a human sense of scale, given that the vertically proportioned window, once of structural necessity, readily relates to the proportions of the human body and provides a recognizable feature that we intuitively use to judge a building's size and scale.

Summary: Time and the Evolution of Things

All art begins in memory. In our art and in our ideals we seek both to recall the past and to make it a tangible part of the present. At the most fundamental level we intuitively understand what we see around us, and only secondarily do we make rational and analytic judgments. We measure time by sensing eternal celestial rhythms—day and night, and the changing seasons—in contrast to our own mortality. We recognize change as a natural condition of our world, and we seek to reconcile that with what we do, including what we build. Clocks tell us the time of day, old buildings remind us of earlier times, peeling paint confirms the impermanence of all things, and we build museums to preserve the evidence of former times so that we may learn from the accomplishments of our predecessors.

The idea of the primitive hut offered a paradigm for understanding how social evolution operates, how the evolution of artifacts progresses in relation to the societies that create those artifacts, the importance of retaining a structure of familiarity among things that must serve both cultural and technological objectives, and the necessity to allow for change that will respect the intrinsic sense of a place and will selectively accommodate newly established needs, wishes, and emerging technological priorities.

Like language, an architecture must be consistent with its past for it to live in the present. There were modernists who tried to invent a new primitive hut that would be consistent with the twentieth-century notion of a society reinventing itself, when change had become so accelerated that the past could be forgotten else it encumber the future. Le Corbusier's Maison Domino project was intended to replace the classical primitive hut with an archetype born of the latest ferroconcrete (steel-reinforced concrete) building technology. It was to herald a new architecture, for so different did he regard the present from the past that the use of historic archetypes was irrelevant. Le Corbusier's influence, along with that of many other modernists, tended to encourage the reduction of architecture to a more limited range of structural or functional expressions, and to singular ideas such as universal space, the purity of an abstract diagram, or the reliability of exclusively economic accountability. All of these ideas effectively squeezed out any ties with the past except those that would support the singular personal perspective of the designer. The overriding motive was to purify the man-made world—to make it more intelligible by purging it of the clutter of the past, a clutter that had appeared to be out of control. This, it was reasoned, would celebrate the pure and intelligible essences of man-made things and would help simplify our lives, which were increasingly being subjected to the complexities of a burgeoning industrial world and the bureaucratic machinery of modern government.

As with any purification attempt, some of the theoretical and practical measures that sought to reform architecture and the city were instructive and even beneficial. But their impact on the city was to further fragment rather than unify the experience of urban living. Put more poignantly by Kubler, "Purists exist by rejecting history and by returning to the imagined primary forms of matter, feeling, and thought. . . . By rejecting history, the purist denies the fullness of things."[23]

Human history could be told as a story about the way we have regarded the passing of time, how we have recognized our own mortality, and how we have dealt with change. Likely the most dramatic part of the story would be the realization that all things, our built world included, may be seen as temporal events. As Loren Eisley expressed it, "Since the first human eye saw a leaf in Devonian sandstone and a puzzled finger reached to touch it, sadness has lain over the heart of man. By this tenuous thread of living protoplasm, stretching backward into time, we are linked forever to lost beaches whose sands have long since hardened into stone."[24] Nothing can logically be said to be permanent. Still we must seek to make as permanent as possible that which we value most. This is the topic of the next chapter.

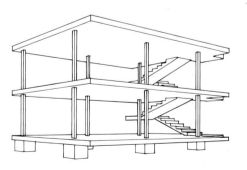

5.10

The "Dom-ino" paradigm by Le Corbusier, who by this 1914 drawing attempted a re-invention of the primitive hut in order to mark the beginning of a new age of architecture based on emerging steel and concrete technology.

6.1

*The church of St. Front, Périgueux. Such time-
less buildings as temples and churches, built as
reliable anchors in times of uncertainty, compare
with the natural features of the earth. At Périgueux both the solid presence of the stone vaults
(bottom left) and the clear Platonic geometry of
the plan, arrived at through the medieval geometric technique known as quadrature (bottom
right), reflect the quest for timelessness.*

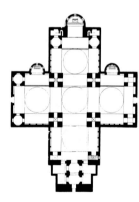

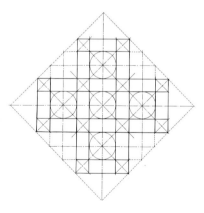

6 TIMELESSNESS AND THE IDEA OF THE CLASSICAL

The desire to render permanent that which we create is to seek timelessness and monumentality. We sense timelessness in the elements of the natural land-scape—the sea and its tides, the mountains and the permanent line they etch against the sky. The natural landscape provides reliable anchors in a world of human mortality. The changing seasons and the river's unpredictable floods are played against the immutable presence of the earth to suggest a balance in all nature, regardless of the fortunes of human affairs. In a balanced world, timelessness and temporality must themselves reside in equilibrium. That is the lesson we learn from nature, and we want to manifest it in the world we build as well.

In the extreme it can be said that there are two ways of looking at time in relation to the physical world. One sees, as discussed in the last chapter, the inevitability of change and looks for ways to deal with it. The other considers permanent values and immutable knowledge and may entirely disregard the temporal. This second way of looking at time sometimes dismisses the tempo-ral as ephemeral, even as unimportant or outright illusory. Societies that em-phasize the timeless over the temporal may be characterized as static, such as ancient Hindu or Egyptian under the Pharaohs, while those that emphasize temporality and change may be thought of as dynamic, such as our present-day society. The ideal balance between timeless and temporal qualities of a society's architecture is largely determined by cultural forces. It is always important that there be some balance between timelessness and temporality because without it the social fabric begins to unravel.

In the West the duality between the timeless and the temporal is characteristically illustrated by contrasting arguments regarding the idea of nature by Plato and Aristotle. Plato preferred to view perceptible nature as irrelevant to the task of understanding nature's essence. For him the laws that govern the natural world were abstract, apprehended only through reason. A Platonic philosopher would see little relevance in a study of the flux in human history because it would likely only illustrate degenerate forms, now descended from the perfect ones that preceded them. Plato tells us in the *Timaeus* that "[God] resolved to have a moving image of eternity, and when he set in order the heaven, he made this image eternal but moving according to number, while eternity itself rests in unity; and this image we call time. . . . The sun and moon and five other stars, which are called the planets, were created by him in order to distinguish and preserve the numbers of time."[1] Plato's student Aristotle, on the other hand, insisted that understanding the natural order of things requires dealing, first of all, with the behavior and properties of the tangible stuff of the universe rather than with intellectual forms. Change, for Aristotle, was organic, an integral part of the overall plan and not an inferior descendent of abstract ideals. He saw timelessness *within* the temporal. As change on earth mimicked the cyclical rhythms of the heavens, even the rise and fall of civilizations might be explained as conforming in some way to immutable celestial rhythms. Nature, for Aristotle, was both the perceivable physical world and the active force of the universe that manifests itself in the principles that govern the cosmos, human beings, and all that humans create. In this way he reconciled the timeless and the temporal in a single concept. Through reason we recognize timelessness in physical things that decay because their meaning does not decay. Christianity took inspiration from both Plato and Aristotle. But while the question of the importance of the timeless over the temporal pervades Greek philosophy, for Christians the overriding force lay in the resurrection of Christ which demonstrated that the timeless world lay beyond the temporal. This separation of the timeless from the here-and-now further emphasized the separation of humankind from the organic world of nature in deference to "an eternal beyond," another reinforcement to an evolving duality between humanity and nature. Still the argument for reconciling the temporal with the timeless, which has been played out again and again in every culture and epoch, began long before Plato and Aristotle lived, and it continues to reverberate in abstract concepts of time in modern theoretical physics and in the beliefs with which we approach what we build today.

The Idea of the Classical

We use the term "classic" to refer to artifacts, ideas, values, rituals, and customs that we prefer to regard as timeless. A certain dress, simple and elegant, is said to be "a classic" because it is never out of fashion. The word comes from Latin and once referred to the classes of Roman society, which of course were fixed into distinct hierarchies. Before the end of the second century AD the term was used to refer to things or people as "aristocratic," similar to our vernacular expression that a person "has class." It is from the humanist writers of the Renaissance that we get the use of the word classic to denote both permanent values and the inheritance of Greek and Roman antiquity, which were thought of by them as more or less synonymous.

We refer to certain music as "classical" because its structure can be repeated in any age without necessarily referring back to the time of its creation. A particular performance of that music might reflect a currently popular way of performing a composer's work, but the music itself is timeless. It simply awaits each age's and a performer's personal interpretation of its meaning and expression. In this way music's temporal and timeless natures are reconciled in what might be seen as consistent in spirit with Aristotle's reconciliation of organic temporality and timelessness in cosmic nature. "Popular" music in contrast to classical is considered impermanent; the short life of a pop tune is regarded as appropriate to *its* intrinsic nature. It takes both kinds of music—and the variations on each that lie between these two poles—to make a well-furnished world of music.[2]

So it is with architecture. Variations on a theme, adaptations, permutations, innovations, and the like, reflect the same artistic principles. There is the acceptance—or recognition—of the archetype upon which the variant is based. This recognition of the connection is not necessarily a conscious act. When we hear a tune we like, we intuitively recognize the type of music from which it comes; hence we approach it with a ready frame of reference. The same is true for a work of architecture. We judge a new building in relation to that with which we are familiar, whether we are conscious of doing so or not. Familiarity of some sort is a necessary prerequisite to what is referred to as "beauty." In painting, for instance, we recognize the work of one artist as belonging to a formal aesthetic system that identifies him or her as a member of a particular school or cultural milieu. We often refer to this presence of a recognizable aesthetic system as a "style"—that is, a coherent system of conventions that gives the work of art a sense of unity while at the same time providing us with a way to relate it to other works of art with which we are already familiar, and which are therefore intuitively recognized as its natural relatives or ancestors.

In observing the basic characteristics that distinguish one school or cultural expression from another, we can see that there are implicit rules that guide each work, and that within these rules each expression may operate to its maximum creative potential without losing the connection with its typological basis. Rules that guide categories of art are seldom written down. Their application is implicit in the nature of artistic expression. It is only when we wish to generate new progeny from a complex art form such as architecture that we have a need to deduce rules that may guide the creation of the new. That is to say, we deduce rules from a basic type to ensure that subsequent works are crafted in ways that are consistent with the artistic priorities of that generative type.

In our preliterate past the role of art was likely much more important in reinforcing social and cultural ties than it is for us today. Before written language, art forms reinforced cultural identity through the use of certain accepted expressions in a given society. For primitive peoples art became a way of giving substance to prophecy and belief. According to anthropologist Alexander Alland, art in these societies was "an emotionally charged and culturally central storage device for complex sets of conscious and unconscious information."[3] Such information made tangible could be easily retrieved and also transformed, provided that the original form was still recognizable. As Alland put it, "Transformation is something that is likely to occur by accident, but it is also likely to be part of the aesthetic game in which playing with form is a major element. Transformation without significant changes in over-all structure keeps the game exciting at the same time as essential information is guarded."[4] Aesthetic perception is allied directly with another natural characteristic of human behavior: play. Alland has dedicated his life's work to the study of what he calls "the aesthetic response" from the perspective of anthropology. He, like many others, has observed that we are disposed to approach art as we do a game, as something to be conducted within the constraints of agreed-upon rules. The freedom that rules for art allow "is linked to such cultural factors as the purpose for which works of art are produced (icons, for example, tend to remain very stable), the role of the individual artist in society, and the set of formal rules that surround artistic production."[5] He traces play and gaming behavior in animals, as well as aspects of their concern for order and environmental coding, and concludes that these are all related behavioral characteristics. If he is accurate in his observations, as I am confident he is, then art—and the natural aesthetic response and subsequent rules that guide its creation—evolved as a means for humans to reinforce cultural identity, to help maintain effective and durable social and cultural groups.

The apparent relationship between gaming and the rules that govern forms of art or classifications of aesthetic expressions involves perceiving a kind of symmetry—or unity—in the game or work of art. Lévi-Strauss observed among the peoples of Gahuku-Gama of New Guinea a link between games with rules and ritual: "Ritual, which is also 'played,' is on the other hand, like a favoured instance of a game, remembered from among the possible ones because it is the only one which results in a particular type of equilibrium between the two sides."[6] That is to say, the performance of ritual, the playing of games, and the creation of works of art are, at some level, related. The game must be resolved to the mutual agreement (if not the satisfaction) of all; there must be no ambiguity as to who won because the game itself must be a kind of *temenos,* a unity that separates it out from all other games and from other ongoing aspects of life around it. This is a unity of composition and finality of intent, which is not dissimilar to the principles guiding a work of art, be it a painting, a ritual mask, a costume, a tattoo, or a work of architecture.

The rules in classical architecture are not inflexible. They are not intended to prohibit what Alland calls "transformation," but rather they ensure that the architectural creation remains connected with its past—and consequently with the society that has evolved with it. Transformation—as well as invention, imitation, and innovation—must occur within a framework of pre-established rules in much the way play and gaming must operate within their own rules. For Western classical architecture Vitruvius's universal man and myth of the primitive hut help provide the primary theoretical structure for those rules, but the rules themselves are far more explicit. A quick review of the more important rules is in order so that we may grasp their effects and their meanings. After considering these rules, we will look at several non-Western examples to get a sense for the commonalities of classical architecture.

Western Classical Architecture: The Rules

Type, Archetypes, and Models

You will recall the discussion in chapter 4 on our expectations that a certain building be recognizable for what it is—that a house look like a house, a library like a library, a courthouse like a courthouse, and so on. This proclivity for satisfying basic expectations about the nature of a thing can be found in our recognition of any useful item: an ax or a water pitcher, an automobile or an airplane. It likely arises from our intrinsic need to recognize and assign meaning to useful or important things in nature, such as edible plants or dangerous animals, and to recognize and give meaning to constituent elements of the landscape around us: mountains and hills, cliffs and canyons. Obviously our expectations for a big city courthouse are different than for a courthouse in a small town of a sparsely populated rural county, and we expect some difference between an urban residence and a country cottage even though we implicitly categorize both as domiciles. But such variations in expectation are built into the notion of type. In speaking of type, we include the formal organization of buildings and building elements, much as reflected in the statement by Cicero about the necessity of temples having symmetrical roofs with pedimented ends. In present-day circumstances his observation might translate to the desirability of a triangular, symmetrical sloping roof atop a residence or the form of an office building as a block with repetitive, evenly spaced windows as a logical reflection of the repetitive offices and work spaces within. A child's drawing of a house, for instance, is often limited to those very elements that symbolize "home" to the child: a rectangular facade topped by a symmetrical triangular roof, out of which pokes a chimney, while on the facade are one or two windows with singular mullion and muntin bars crossing at the center and the all-important oversized door. This surfacing of that natural human proclivity in a child reflects a basic human need to typify, that is, to isolate the important characteristics of a thing so that we might always recognize and identify each instance of that thing when we come across it. At its most fundamental level the key to the notion of type in the rules of classical architecture is recognition and group memory.

A type is timeless; it does not of itself evolve or change. A type is the idea and never a physical reality. One cannot build a type; one can only build something that reflects a particular type. The idea of typology is very different, for instance, than the modern notion of style. Contemporary historiography, which sees the evolution of classifications of artifacts as continuous and essentially progressive, represents a different frame of mind. A classical building's type is timeless, while its style is temporal and progressive. A classical architect selects a type without respect to the historical sequence in which it was developed. A Greek or Roman architect might design one temple based on an archaic form of a particular order and another temple based on a later evolved form of the same order. The architect's choice would be relative to the appropriate expression for the god to whom the temple is dedicated and not to something we would call either old-fashioned or up-to-date. What is true for religious buildings is true for other buildings as well because the approach to the design of the temple is seen as paradigmatic to the approach to designing any building, whether it be residential, civic, commercial, or military. An ancient commercial warehouse, for instance, would be designed as a simple, unadorned rectangle without reference to an architectural order; while a civic building such as a *bouleuterion* (an assembly hall for the governing body of a *polis*) would manifest a dignified and restrained order, such as the Ionic or Corinthian, in keeping with the building's role in the community. In all cases the selection of building type and its expression is controlled by the immediate circumstances of the building and not necessarily by any idea of progress or history in the Hegelian way we are in the habit of thinking today.

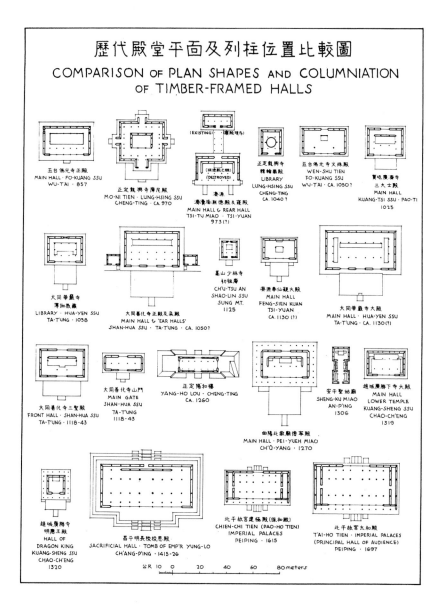

歷代殿堂平面及列柱位置比較圖

COMPARISON OF PLAN SHAPES AND COLUMNIATION
OF TIMBER-FRAMED HALLS

五台佛光寺正殿
MAIN HALL · FO-KUANG SSU
WU-T'AI · 857

正定龍興寺摩尼殿
MO-NI TIEN · LUNG-HSING SSU
CHENG-TING · CA. 970

·(EXISTING)·現存建築·

·(原建或已毀)·
·(DESTROYED)·

景縣開福寺修德殿及羅殿
MAIN HALL & REAR HALL
TSI-TU MIAO · TSI-YUAN
973(?)

正定龍興寺
轉輪藏殿
LIBRARY
LUNG-HSING SSU
CHENG-TING
CA. 1040?

五台佛光寺文殊殿
WEN-SHU TIEN
FO-KUANG SSU
WU-T'AI · CA. 1050?

寶坻廣濟寺
三大士殿
MAIN HALL
KUANG-TSI SSU · PAO-TI
1025

大同華嚴寺
薄伽教藏
LIBRARY · HUA-YEN SSU
TA-T'UNG · 1038

大同善化寺正殿及耳殿
MAIN HALL & 'EAR HALLS'
SHAN-HUA SSU · TA-T'UNG · CA. 1050?

嵩山少林寺
初祖庵
CH'U-TSU AN
SHAO-LIN SSU
SUNG MT.
1125

景縣奉仙觀大殿
MAIN HALL
FENG-SIEN KUAN
TSI-YUAN
CA. 1130 (?)

大同華嚴寺大殿
MAIN HALL · HUA-YEN SSU
TA-T'UNG · CA. 1130(?)

大同善化寺三聖殿
FRONT HALL · SHAN-HUA SSU
TA-T'UNG · 1118-43

大同善化寺山門
MAIN GATE
SHAN-HUA SSU
TA-T'UNG
1118-43

正定陽和樓
YANG-HO LOU · CHENG-TING
CA. 1260

曲陽北嶽廟德寧殿
MAIN HALL · PEI-YUEH MIAO
CH'Ü-YANG · 1270

安平聖姑廟
SHENG-KU MIAO
AN-P'ING
1306

趙城廣勝下寺大殿
MAIN HALL
LOWER TEMPLE
KUANG-SHENG SSU
CHAO-CH'ENG
1319

趙城廣勝寺
明應王殿
HALL OF
DRAGON KING
KUANG-SHENG SSU
CHAO-CH'ENG
1320

昌平明長陵祾恩殿
SACRIFICIAL HALL · TOMB OF EMP'R YUNG-LO
CH'ANG-P'ING · 1415-26

北平故宮建極殿(保和殿)
CHIEN-CHI TIEN (PAO-HO TIEN)
IMPERIAL PALACES
PEIPING · 1615

北平故宮太和殿
T'AI-HO TIEN · IMPERIAL PALACES
(PRINCIPAL HALL OF AUDIENCE)
PEIPING · 1697

公R 10 0   20   40   60   80meters

162

6.2

Left:

Building plans of classical Chinese "timber halls" based on the Sung Dynasty Building Standard which regulated civic architecture in China for several hundred years.

Bottom:

Building designs and plans by the sixteenth-century Italian architect Andrea Palladio, as depicted in J. N. L. Durand's once very popular Recueil et parallèle des édifices en tout genre published in 1801. These arrangements of building designs are typical of typologically based systems of design.

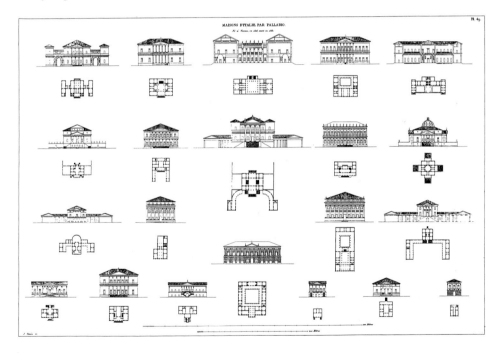

The notion of building type is widespread in the formal, visual range of classical architecture. Whether or not the orders of architecture are a constituent part of a building solution is itself a typological decision. Proportions, decorative embellishments, familiar functional elements, the basic form of the building, and so forth, are open to manipulation in a game of familiarity and expectation, surprise and innovation. But decisions regarding the building type—that is, recognition—precede all else in the planning of a classical building.

Finally, before leaving this discussion of types, it must be pointed out that numerous lengthy arguments have been launched on the appropriate applications of the idea of type as well as its relationship to archetypes and models, which are different but related concepts. The intention here is to suggest instead what has been the normative use of the concept of type so that we may sense something of the basis upon which invention, translation, innovation, and imitation ultimately rest.

Unity, or *Temenos*

At this point it is important to recall (from chapters 2 and 4) that the elements of Western classical architecture are derived from the process of construction, from the tectonics of building. This is the function of the myth of the primitive hut. The consistent application of decorative elements ensures that past constructional priorities are reflected in the building, sometimes directly and sometimes referentially as poetic recollections of earlier building forms. Together they tell the story of the architecture. All the constituent parts are manipulated by rules as well. They are proportioned by rules and adjusted by them in relation to one another and to the building as a whole. These rules hark back to the theoretical constructs embodied in the primitive hut and the universal man. Such constructs help to ensure that the building and all of its parts achieve unity.

In a metaphorical sense the rules that guide the planning of classical buildings to achieve unity, a *temenos*, enable the work to be complete unto itself, distinguished from all else by virtue of its own order, a kind of world within a world. The literal use of the word *temenos* refers to the sacred precinct surrounding a Greek temple. The concept of *temenos*, however, can be seen to reach beyond the literal meaning of the word. For instance, this is remarked

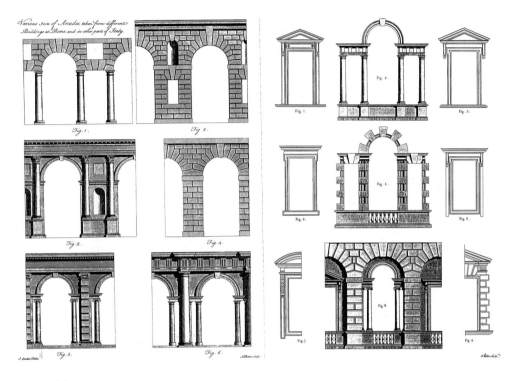

6.3

Topologically ordered building elements can be combined to produce an infinite variety of designs. Shown are trabeated elements (columns, pilasters, entablatures) combined with arches.

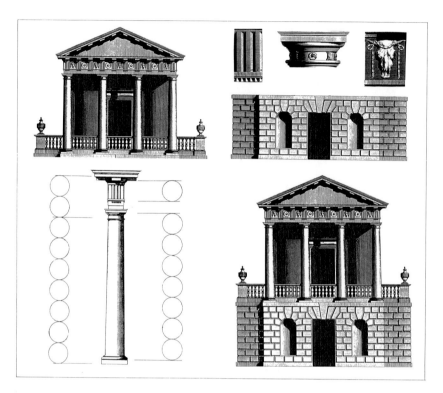

6.4

Constituent elements of a complete design, or
"temenos," from Chambers's 1759 treatise. The
"disassembly" illustrates how each element is a
complete design in itself. The column's diameter
(the circles besides the column indicating its pro-
portions) serves as a unit of measure for the
whole building.

on by Edith Hamilton when she described the Greek temple as a "shining marvel of white stone" set in sharp contrast against the wilderness. The Greek temple is complete. Its base, or *stylobate,* delineates a crisp edge against the earth just as its silhouette etches its distinct and familiar form against the sky. The line along the edge of the stylobate divides (but does not separate) the human creation from nature. But the distance between them is negligible. Upon seeing the temple from a three-quarter view one knows how it would appear from any other view. Its form is conceptually complete and fully apprehended from any direction.

Unity in a work of art such as architecture is seen as yet another reflection of nature's infinite paradigm. Aristotle, for instance, used the example of an animal as a model for the concept of compositional unity in a traditional Greek tragedy:

> *To be beautiful, a living creature, and every whole made up of parts, must not only present a certain order in its arrangement of parts, but also be of a certain definite magnitude. . . . Just in the same way, then, as a beautiful whole made up of parts, or a beautiful living creature, must be of some size, a size to be taken in by the eye, so a story or Plot must be of some length, but of a length to be taken in by the memory.*[7]

That is to say, the unity of the whole relies on the unity of its parts, its constituent elements one to another. Similarly Alberti described the artistic expression of any work of art such as architecture to be "that reasoned harmony of all the parts within a body, so that nothing may be added, taken away, or altered, but for the worse." Unity is seen as a requisite quality of each and every part of the building, the building itself, and even the city in which it resides. According to Alberti, "If (as the philosophers maintain) the city is like some large house, and the house is in turn like some small city, cannot the various parts of a house—atria, . . . dining rooms, porticoes, and so on—be considered miniature buildings?"[8] In other words, unity characterizes each step in a succession of scales of reference, from the smallest to the largest element of a building.

This raises an important question: If a building is so utterly complete and unified on its own, how can it be integrated into its environment so that it does not appear out of place in its setting? Perhaps the answer once again lies

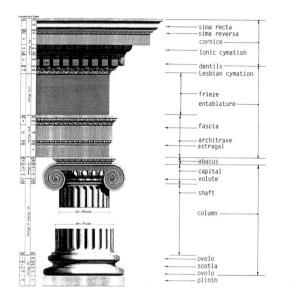

sima recta
sima reversa
cornice
Ionic cymation
dentils
Lesbian cymation
frieze
entablature
fascia
architrave
astragal
abacus
capital
volute
shaft
column
ovolo
scotia
ovolo
plinth

raking cornice
tympanum
pediment
entablature
capital
shaft
column
base
crepidoma
stylobate
stereobate

6.5

The names of elements of classical architecture reflect their typological basis. Although the arrangement and details of these elements may be varied from one design to another according to stipulated principles, each element remains a recognizable descendent of its prototype in the primitive hut.

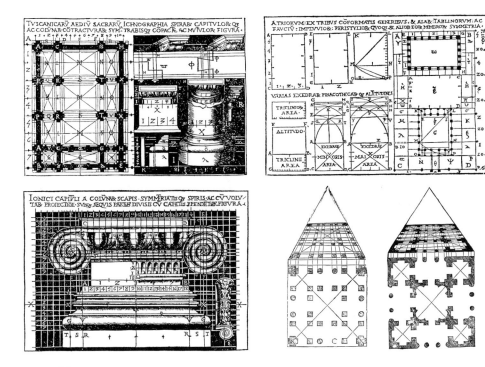

6.6

Proportioning systems and lineaments from Ser-
lio's treatise and from the 1521 illustrated edi-
tion of Vitruvius's Ten Books.

in the analogy of nature, in Aristotle's example of a "beautiful animal." Although morphologically complete, the animal's survival is nonetheless dependent on its environment. A polar bear would not live for long in the desert and an armadillo is similarly unequipped to live in the arctic. In the same sense a building's character, size, and shape are determined in relation to its place on earth and to other buildings around it—as well as with respect to requirements not associated with the setting.

Lineaments, or *Lineamenta*

With the ideas of type and unity firmly in place, other design operations can be established. Perhaps most important among them is the establishment of the controlling lines, or what Alberti called *lineamenta*.[9] This involves the creation of a matrix of lines in three-dimensional space for purposes of disciplining the overall form of the building and the relationships of its constituent elements with one another. The lineaments determine the thickness and position of walls, columns, piers, and the like; they set the requisite number and sizes of structural bays (the spaces between lines of bearing elements); they establish the proportions and positions of windows, doors, cornices, entablatures, engaged trabeation, and so forth. Major elements are subdivided so that the proportions of their constituent parts can be determined, such as the exact spirals of Ionic volutes, the delicate alternating egg-and-dart molding, the size, position, and shape of lettering on an inscription.

Beyond these purely practical properties of the *lineamenta,* it was sometimes seen to hold certain mystical qualities. For instance, while Alberti described the lineaments of a building in a comparatively matter of fact way, some treatise writers depicted it in Neoplatonic or Pythagorean terms. Thus, while viewed for practical purposes as a geometric matrix of lines within which the building and all its elements reside, the *lineamenta* could be seen at the same time as a device of Platonic purity and perfection, as an intellectual construct.[10] In this view a building is but the approximate visible, finite actualization of the infinitely perfect and invisible world that disciplines a creation in the material world. This dualistic attitude toward the lineaments could be seen to have come about, on the one hand, as a means to encourage a consistently careful design and, on the other, to strengthen the sacred connotation of such theoretical tenets as the primitive hut and the universal man.

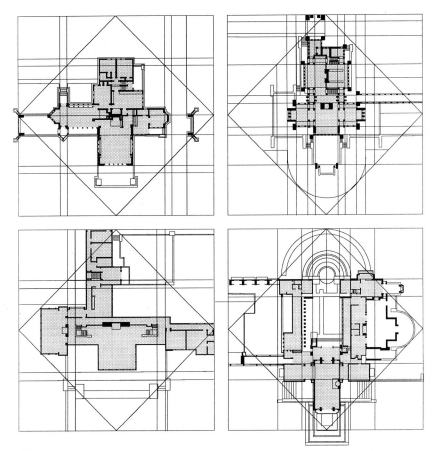

6.7

**Plans of four houses by Frank Lloyd Wright,
with lineaments. The use of lineaments is not exclusive to Western classical architecture. Equivalents can be found in some form in the
architectural practices of all cultures, including
all styles and eras.**

Composition

Once regulating lines of the lineaments are in place, the next task is to furnish the matrix of lines with the elements of architecture. The designer must now assemble a family of related architectural elements, having selected them on the basis of appropriate types. The rules for composing the elements of architecture are very complex, so here we will only touch on some of the more important ones. Most of this process is engaged in the laying out of lineaments, but here it has been extracted so we can better see how a classical building is planned.

The two most important considerations of composition are proportions and position. The positions of architectural elements, as noted earlier, have mainly to do with their relationships to the constructional priorities of building. These elements are systematically broken down into constituent parts so that the smallest unit can be designed with relation to the whole work of architecture. In this way everything is derived from the whole and not the other way around, and all characteristics are consistent with the selected building type. Were the approach to begin with a collection of elements and then to generate a building from them, the result would be merely an assemblage and not a unified whole. The prescribed approach is somewhat like deciding first of all what you want to say, then using appropriate grammar, syntax, and vocabulary of a language to communicate the intent. At this point it is instructive to return for a moment to the analogy of a language. Just as a language has a vocabulary, grammar, and syntax, the elements and parts of architecture must be brought together into their characteristic, conventionalized relationships in order for the design statement "to make sense." If an entablature, for instance, is omitted, out of proportion, or askew, it would seriously affect the character of the building, just as would a misplaced word in a sentence, or an incorrect grammatical construction, or an inept use of syntax.

The practice of determining proportional relationships based on repeated measurements is taken from the diameter of a column of the selected order. Then a column height, for instance, is said to be a certain number of diameters—say, eight diameters. The other elements of the building are described in similar terms: the entablature might be three column diameters in height, while the spaces between columns are equivalent to four diameters and the cornice above a half diameter in height, and so forth. There is a fixed standard

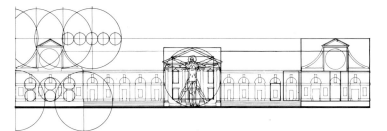

6.8

Composition and proportional relationships.

Top two panels:

An eighteenth-century house in Petersburg, Virginia, known as "Battersea." It was inspired by Palladio's Villa Maser, and employs related but simpler geometric proportioning and distribution of compositional elements.

Middle and bottom panels:

Front elevation of Villa Maser as it was designed by Palladio and a view of how it appears on the approach.

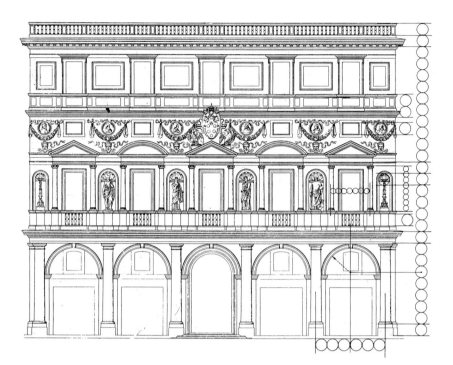

6.9

Proportions and positions of the principal ele-
ments of an Italian Renaissance palace. The cir-
cles indicate the column diameter, which was
used as the unit of measure.

of measure, of course, but it is applied only after the building's elements are measured according to the diameter of its columns. In this way a consistent dimensional and proportional relationship is maintained. If the building is very large, for instance, its constituent elements are proportionately larger so that they are kept in harmony with the size of the building.

Other means to compositional priorities include the repetition of like elements, namely windows, columns, moldings, and decorative features such as the alternating egg-and-dart motif or the squared and evenly spaced dentil course. Repetitive patterns of such elements are seen to produce a calming effect while contributing to the unity of the whole. The problem of composition also includes determining the customary number of subdivisions of constituent elements. Most elements are divided into three parts. For instance, a cornice is characteristically made up of the *cymatium,* the *corna,* and the *mutule,* a column consists of a base, shaft, and capital, and an entablature consists of the architrave, frieze, and cornice. A Doric frieze, however, is divided horizontally into alternating metopes and triglyphs, while the triglyphs themselves are divided again into thirds. In other words, characteristic subdivisions of major elements into minor ones, and minor ones into further subdivisions, are numerically consistent through the full hierarchical range of scales.

Working with the Rules and Beyond: Invention and Artifice
Before we leave this discussion of the rules of Western classical architecture, it is important to point out that these so-called rules are intended to be judiciously broken, manipulated, or modified as circumstances warrant. They are in no sense rigid rules but rather serve to guide and discipline the design process while allowing for regional variations, fundamental differences in an architect's ingenuity, and a certain latitude in the accommodation of a building to its site and use. The origin of these rules undoubtedly lies in the craft of building. The manipulation of the rules is at the behest of the architect, while their conventionality guides the work of the mason or carpenter. Their ultimate purpose is to produce pleasing results for the eye, and even trickery for the perspicacious mind. The kind of trickery this requires is not that which deceives, since we all agree to be tricked, but that which registers in our senses as "perfection," that is, a perfect solution. This is the function of artifice.

Artifice is employed to make the columns of a temple appear to stand perfectly upright in answer to the natural diminution of optical perspective, which would make them appear to lean together if they were truly vertical. So the stylobate of a temple is warped into a convex curve, thereby tilting the columns ever so slightly outward from one another. Or the elements high up on a building are proportioned so that they appear to be in their customary relationship with one another when seen from a steep angle up close, while in reality they are distorted to produce that effect. And the *entasis* of columns (the bulge and taper from top to bottom) tricks our subconscious into sensing the column's task of supporting a great weight. And there is the practice of creating perfect rooms within the reality of an imperfect building configuration. This is perhaps the most elaborate instance of artifice. Rooms conceived as volumes of space of Platonic purity—circles, ovals, cubes, rectangles, and the like— cleverly reside within buildings that must conform to the tortuous confines of an urban site. The skill with which architects have been able to manipulate the

6.10

Front and side views of a Greek temple drawn with the characteristic refinements exaggerated: the swelling of the columns (entasis) to express their carrying great weight, the curvature of the stylobate and entablature to counter the optical illusion of "sag" if it were perfectly level, the enlargement of the corner columns and the diminution of the adjoining space so that the corner columns do not appear thinner or more widely spaced than other columns, since in their corner position they are usually seen silhouetted against the sky.

6.11

Proportioning of the constituent elements of architecture to compensate for the effects of fore-shortening and the illusion of inclination when seen from close to the building, from the 1521 edition of Vitruvius's treatise.

ground plan of buildings to distinguish important rooms with geometric purity is no less than astounding. The idea of a man-made world in sharp distinction to nature is perhaps nowhere more apparent than in these perfectly formed rooms and their connections with one another—capable of transforming rugged nature into what we perceive as idealized geometry.

Still, beyond all these intricate manipulations of form, it is important to keep in mind that the idea of the classical is permanence. But in reality nothing is ever permanent, so the emphasis eventually must shift from the existence of something we would like to last forever to an assumed immutability of the principles and ideas that lie behind it. The mythical history of Greek classical architecture describes a transformation of an early trabeated architecture of timber into a permanent architecture of stone. To keep the newly transformed architecture consistent with its ancestral path, rules were devised to ensure that the memory of its timber predecessor would never be lost. In all traditions of classicism in architecture there must be reliable means for preserving the memory of the past, whether set down in written rules, through the ritualization of the act of designing, or by means of coupling architecture with another area of the culture, such as religion, that is seen to be more durable than architecture. A brief look at three other classical traditions in architecture, each a product of a distinctly different cultural setting, will demonstrate some of their commonalities.

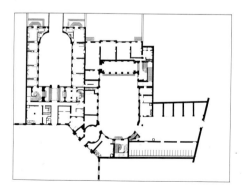

6.12

Plans for a pair of adjoining French hôtels from the early eighteenth century. Important rooms assume ideal shapes regardless of the constraints of the urban site to which the building's exterior shape must conform.

Classical Language of the Sung Dynasty Building Standards

The superintendent for construction under the Chinese Emperor Hui-tsung early in the twelfth century AD compiled a building code that was to guide the design and construction of monumental architecture in China for the next six centuries. The code, known as the *Ying-tsao Fa-shih,* or Sung Dynasty Building Standards, provided Chinese classical architecture with a coherent set of rules reminiscent of those in Vitruvius's treatise on Western classical architecture. The Sung Dynasty Building Standards, however, is more straightforward, more of a how-to manual without theoretical discussion. But if we read between the lines, we can discern the theoretical precepts that lie behind each stipulation, and the intentions appear to be remarkably similar.

The Building Standards are attributed to the authorship of one man, known as Li Chieh. This document consists of thirty-four chapters. Thirteen of the chapters are devoted to rules governing the design of various architectural elements, seventeen chapters are on the definitions of terms and methods for estimating materials and labor, and four chapters provide illustrations of typical building designs. While much of the content is on good building practices, implicit in all of the rules is a recognition of cultural priorities.

As in Japan, Chinese traditional monumental architecture did not make a full transition from a trabeated timber prototype to one of bearing stone masonry. There are, however, many other characteristics of Chinese classical architecture that are remarkably consistent with Western classical traditions. For instance, like Western architecture the Chinese classical tradition traversed an evolutionary past that generated archetypal models. These models appear to have emanated from a much earlier domestic building form as well as from a humble house now lost in time. And they feature a column-and-beam assembly that likewise helps to set the scale, proportions, and character of a building's details. The relationship between the building and surrounding nature is very similar in both traditions. A Chinese civic building built under the aegis of the Sung Dynasty Building Standards is not integrated into its natural site in the romantic sense but rather stands in sharp geometric contrast with all else in its immediate setting. And it presents itself as symmetrical, unified in much the same way as a Western classical building. As a result the building is understood in its entirety from any point of view.

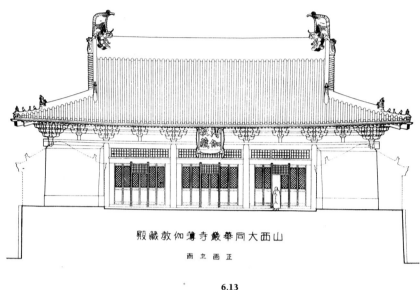

殿藏教伽導寺嚴華同大西山

正 立 面

6.13

Front view of the library in Hua-yen Ssu, Ta-
t'ung, Shasi Province, built in 1038.

At its inception the Sung Dynasty Building Standards undoubtedly picked up on ongoing aesthetic priorities and building practices, putting them into a succinct document for distribution and use across broad geographical and cultural distances. It was intended to ensure that the prevailing cultural and political authority would be recognized in places far from the center of power and authority, besides facilitating efficient building production without a loss of quality in either design or construction. Of interest with relation to Western practice is the use of specific techniques to establish unity in a building. For instance, the Sung Dynasty Standards describe a system of measurement and proportioning that employs a unit known as a *fen*, which like the column diameter in Western classicism varied systematically in length from one building to another to ensure consistency in proportional relationships for all the elements of a building regardless of the building's size. The *fen* is not based on the column's diameter as in the West but rather on the depth of a standardized column bracket arm known as a *ts'ai*. Coordination of a building's proportioning using the *fen* was accomplished as follows:

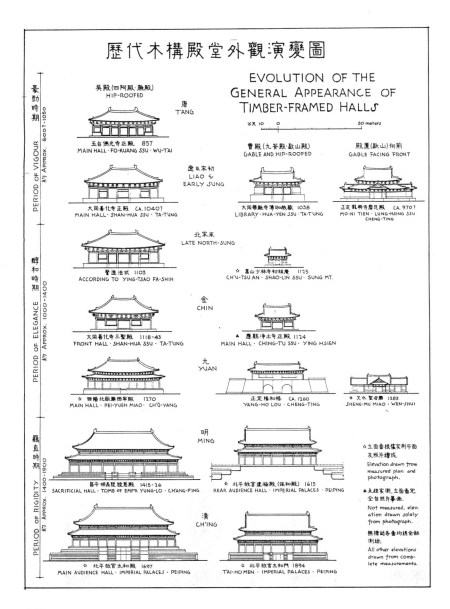

6.14

*Variations in the timber hall building design as
it evolved over hundreds of years under the aegis
of the Sung Dynasty Building Standards.*

The depth of each ts'ai is to be divided into 15 equal parts, called fen, *and the width of the ts'ai is to be ten* fen. *The height and breadth of every building, the dimensions of every member in the structure, the rise and curve of the roofline, in short, every measurement in the building, is to be measured in terms of* fen *of the grade of ts'ai used.*[11]

Although the depth of a *ts'ai* determined the unit of measure for a building, the corner column with its elaborate layers of cantilevered brackets set the conditions for the expressive character of a building. Subtleties of arrangement, color, and shape within the system of corner bracket assemblies varied from province to province, as well as among building types and from one historical epoch to another, ultimately reflecting regional, functional, and temporal priorities in a given building. Variations in the interpretation of the Sung Dynasty Standards, as well as modifications over time, accounted for changing taste and conditions. Still the memory of the most ancient Chinese civic building was preserved in the newest construction.

6.15

Column and bracket assembly in Chinese architecture.

Left:

Variations in the column and bracket assembly over time, as analogous with the evolution of Western classical orders.

Right:

The composition of a typical column and bracket assembly.

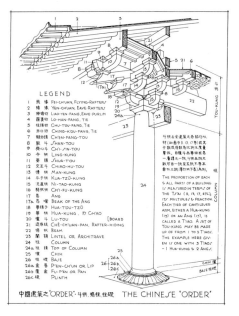

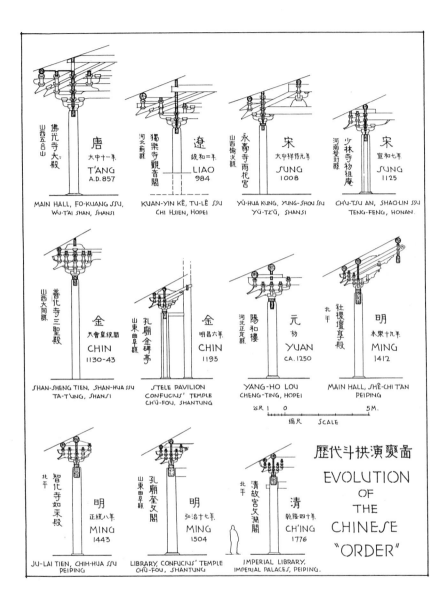

山西五台山
佛光寺大殿
唐
大中十一年
T'ANG
A.D. 857
MAIN HALL, FO-KUANG SSU,
WU-T'AI SHAN, SHANSI

河北薊縣
獨樂寺觀音閣
遼
統和二年
LIAO
984
KUAN-YIN KÊ, TU-LÊ SSU
CHI HSIEN, HOPEI

山西榆次縣
永壽寺雨花宮
宋
大中祥符元年
SUNG
1008
YÜ-HUA KUNG, YUNG-SHOU SSU
YÜ-TZ'Ŭ, SHANSI

河南登封縣
少林寺初祖庵
宋
宣和七年
SUNG
1125
CH'U-TSU AN, SHAO-LIN SSU
TENG-FENG, HONAN.

山西大同縣
善化寺三聖殿
金
天會皇統間
CHIN
1130-43
SHAN-SHENG TIEN, SHAN-HUA SSU
TA-T'UNG, SHANSI

山東曲阜縣
孔廟金碑亭
金
明昌六年
CHIN
1195
STELE PAVILION
CONFUCIUS' TEMPLE
CH'Ü-FOU, SHANTUNG

河北正定縣
陽和樓
元
CA. 1250
YANG-HO LOU
CHENG-TING, HOPEI

北平
社稷壇享殿
明
永樂十九年
MING
1412
MAIN HALL, SHÊ-CHI T'AN
PEIPING

公尺 1   0   5 M.
縮尺   SCALE

北平
智化寺如來殿
明
正統八年
MING
1443
JU-LAI TIEN, CHIH-HUA SSU
PEIPING

山東曲阜縣
孔廟奎文閣
明
弘治十七年
MING
1504
LIBRARY, CONFUCIUS' TEMPLE
CH'Ü-FOU, SHANTUNG

北平
清故宮文淵閣
清
乾隆四十年
CH'ING
1776
IMPERIAL LIBRARY,
IMPERIAL PALACES, PEIPING.

歷代斗拱演變圖
EVOLUTION
OF
THE
CHINESE
"ORDER"

Sukiya *Architecture of Japan*

Chinese classical architecture was imported into Japan along with Buddhism in the sixth century AD by way of Korea. Once ensconced in the Japanese tradition, Chinese architecture gradually took on characteristics distinctly Japanese. There were of course indigenous architectural traditions flourishing in Japan long before the Chinese models arrived on the scene. What distinguished the indigenous architectural traditions from the imported model was the elaboration of the latter as compared to the relative visual simplicity of the former. By the sixteenth century Chinese-inspired Buddhist architecture in Japan had reached greater heights in the elaboration of details and overall building form, with increasingly more pronounced curvatures in the roof line, more elaborate polychrome treatment especially as applied to the cantilevered corner brackets, and more ornamentation throughout the fabric of the building. Then, as a reaction to this increasing ostentation of official or civic architecture, and of the feudal lords in general, a new architecture was created in Japan, one that found its roots in ancestral traditions characterized by simplicity and humility. This architecture is known as *sukiya.*

The *sukiya* is seen to have taken inspiration from several sources. Among the sources were the ancient indigenous architecture of Shinto shrines, the Zen tradition of Buddhism, an indigenous residential architecture of the upper classes known as *shoin,* a particular style or "mood" of Japanese poetry, and the rustic hut of the hermit whose withdrawal from society is characterized by the cultivation of a heightened sensitivity to nature. The tea ceremony and its accommodation in the humble hut was integral to this tradition as well.[12] The Zen sect of Buddhism, with its characteristic appreciation of simplicity, humility, and closeness to nature, found a sympathetic reception among the Japanese whose indigenous religion, Shinto, involved the worship of nature. Although considered "the classical style" of Japanese architecture, *sukiya* is probably no more classical than those strains of Japanese architecture that descended from Chinese models, except that it was inspired primarily by ancient traditions in Japanese society and by a tradition of nature poetry and a special sensitivity to nature. In this sense the *sukiya* can be regarded as indigenous to the cultural forces of ancient Japan.

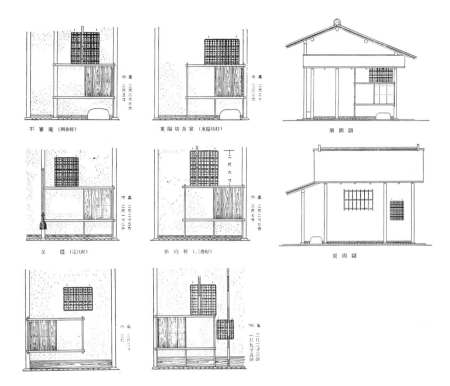

不 審 庵（利休好）　　　東 陽 坊 茶 室（東陽坊好）　　　南 面 圖

又 隱（宗旦好）　　　松 向 軒（三齋好）　　　東 面 圖

6.16
Various arrangements of panels, openings, and
structural forms of a humble Japanese sukiya.

Compared to Western classical architecture or Chinese civic architecture derived from the Sung Dynasty Building Standards, the rules that guide the *sukiya* remain curiously unformalized. No Japanese Vitruvius wrote them down for architects to interpret in succeeding ages. Instead, the design and construction of a *sukiya* building draws its constancy and consistency more from the ritual of a crafts tradition. Explanations of the process of creating a *sukiya* building stipulate the importance of a harmonious personal relationship between the owner, designer, and builder, namely the aesthetic sensitivity of the carpenters who will build it and the general frame of mind of everyone involved in the process. Unwritten procedures incorporated into the ritualized planning of a *sukiya* building have as much to do with the selection of materials, the geometry and proportions of rooms and walls, the choice of colors, the placement of characteristic elements, the determination of overall dimensions and building configuration, and so forth, as with any architectural tradition. But all of these decisions must be in direct relation to conventions, that is, to accepted stan-

6.17

Katsura Imperial Villa, the most sophisticated form of the Japanese shoin sukiya style of architecture.

dards and prototypical solutions, even though those standards and prototypical examples are not recorded in a code of practice.

"Planning" best expresses the nature of the design process of a *sukiya*
building. Unlike the Western practice of determining every part of the building
from the start, the *sukiya* building is planned in a more general way. It is the
task of the carpenter to sense the intention and complete the design as the
construction progresses. It is especially in the early stage that the reason for
the ritualized approach to the creation of a *sukiya* building is best understood.
The process from beginning to end is an organic one; each step must relate in
spirit as well as in fact to the preceding and following steps, all as integral parts
of an evolving event if the end result is to reach a certain level of refinement
that is characteristic of *sukiya* architecture. One writer with an intimate knowledge of the *sukiya* tradition put it this way: ". . . the act of creating a sukiya-
style building binds the client, the architect, and the master carpenter together
and constitutes a drama in which each plays a vital role. And in the harmony

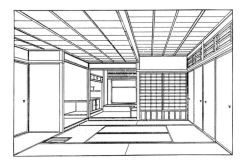

6.18

*An engawa (left), a continuous open porch, ex-
tending into an enclosed urban garden and separated from the interior by sliding screens.
Interior of a sukiya style residence (right) with
surfaces gridded by lines defining the edges of
building elements, separating and joining them
at the same time.*

among these three principals we see a reflection of the harmony that the tea ceremony creates among those who participate in it."[13] Thus the ritualized nature of the process is designed to ensure an outcome that is refined and unified, even though there is no individual overseeing all operations as is usual for an architect. At the same time the ritual ensures that the process of the building's creation is visible in the final building. It is because of this necessity to reflect the building process that *sukiya* buildings seem unfinished in the Western sense.

Sukiya carpentry is like that of no other architecture. Skillful joinery, for instance, is important to its construction, and it requires years of training for one to become an accomplished practitioner. The finishing has to be accomplished with special traditional hand tools that are unique to *sukiya* building. Each operation is integral with the creation process; each step proceeds according to tradition. Joints between beam and column are extremely complicated; each joint is an artful puzzle of perfectly fitting pieces held together by the friction of their precise fit.

As perplexing as the highly refined jointry is, *sukiya* architecture freely incorporates raw and unrefined materials, direct from nature and placed alongside materials and joinery of dazzling accuracy. A raw tree limb, for instance, may be found serving in a strategic position in the building as a column, while other columns in its vicinity are of processed cut-and-dressed lumber, secured in place with the finest jointry and rubbed to a dark quiet sheen. Occasionally, however, the coming together of a pair of beautifully shaped rails or battens will just miss where they are expected to intersect with the same perfection as all else around them. But, on reflection, we see that the juxtaposition of refined architectural details and overall geometric precision contrasts with these natural anomalies just as the human artifice of building contrasts with the natural landscape. One's awareness of the difference between the man-made and the natural is thereby enhanced—as with the boulder emerging ever so slightly through the floor in the living room of Frank Lloyd Wright's Fallingwater described in chapter 1. We are reminded of how the natural and the man-made intermingle and separate, set as the *sukiya* is in nature and created out of materials clearly supplied by nature.

Before leaving the discussion, it is important to point out that in its creation *sukiya* architecture encourages innovation in a number of ways. One important action of the designer-builder involves the incorporation of materials from the building's site. Whatever the innovation, however, the important controlling factor is not to alter the requisite mood of the whole. This mood comes largely from an expressive quality (known as *wabi*) of ancient poetry. As a result a new *sukiya* building and a much older one can be very different, but each is immediately recognizable as *sukiya*. Ultimately the poetic mood of the building is responsible for the harmonic resonance between the building and nature. Harmony, borrowed from poetry, is found in the *sukiya* where quiet eccentricities are played out—where the sound of water splashing on a stone nearby blends indistinguishably with the simmering of tea over a charcoal brazier. It is timeless nature experienced quietly and up close. The timelessness of a *sukiya* is not of itself but rather in a kind of dialogue between the man-made and the changing face of nature. The imparted sense of permanence, timelessness, and temporality is nature's allegory, a constant reminder that we, along with what we build, are a part of nature too. The idea is expressed in a line familiar to every Japanese, taken from the writings of a thirteenth-century hermit who built a rustic hut for himself in the forest and wrote about it in an essay entitled "Tale of the Ten-Foot-Square-Hut": "The river flows on without cease, yet its waters are never the same."

6.19

A twisted, rough hewen tree trunk is juxtaposed with highly finished wood as frame for a tokonoma.

The Sufi Tradition

Many of the rules that guide the Sufi tradition in Persian architecture, while integral to tenets of Islam, will appear similar to rules that guide Western classicism. Such consistencies should come as no surprise, since Western and Islamic civilizations share an intellectual and scientific history. Persian and Arabic contributions to mathematics and astronomy formed the basis for Western advances in these fields much later on, and Ionian science, especially the primacy of geometric and mathematical explanations for the cosmos, was likely indebted to the flow of scientific thought from East to West. Sufism is a philosophical and literary movement that began among Shiite Muslims in the late tenth century, and it directly incorporated ideas from Neoplatonism, Buddhism, and Christianity.

At the base of the Sufi tradition in architecture is the concept of the timelessness and temporality in all things. Tradition is regarded as having an existence outside of, or independent from, society. It resides in the cosmos, in the celestial realm in that when a tradition dies out on earth, it does not cease to exist but continues exclusively in the celestial realm. In this sense the Sufi tradition reminds us of Neoplatonism, with its belief in the perfection of generative forces in the cosmic realm while their progeny in the perceptual realm on earth are imperfect shadows of their celestial origins. In the Sufi tradition permanence and timelessness reside in a unity between the spiritual (religious) and the physical worlds, which includes both nature and things made by the human hand. So all things, natural and man-made, are sacred; it is only that some are more sacred than others. Therefore a building constructed in harmony with God's will becomes an integral part of the world that is itself sacred. Symbolic meanings conveyed by artifacts are not conventionalized in the Western sense; rather symbols are regarded as "theophanies of the absolute in the relative." "Man does not create symbols, he is transformed by them."[14] Thus the rules that guide the Sufi tradition in architecture cannot be separated from religious thought; the maintenance of the Sufi tradition in the concrete world of the present relies on a strict continuity of the religious faith of which it is a part. However, without going into the particulars of religious justification, the rules, directives, and procedures are still open to examination to see what they do in the way of conditioning built form.

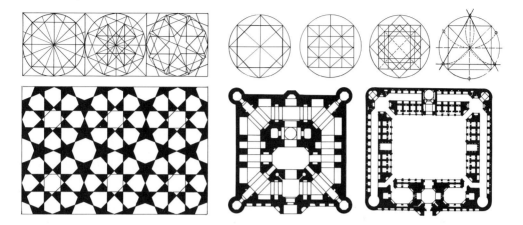

6.20

In the Sufi tradition of Islam, geometry is a sacred means to ordering all that is man-made. Circle and square are combined to produce an eight-point star (top, left). In repeating that figure, and in filling in some areas and leaving others open, a tile pattern is created (bottom, left). These same manipulations generate building forms as well (middle and right). The two buildings shown are fortified Persian caravanserai.

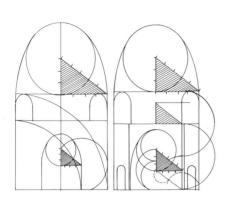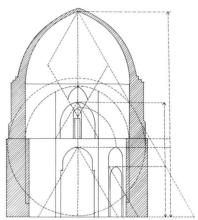

6.21

*The setting out of a Sassanian (pre-Islamic)
vaulted chamber. Harmonic diagrams and "Platonic" geometry disciplines and integrates the
form of the buildings.*

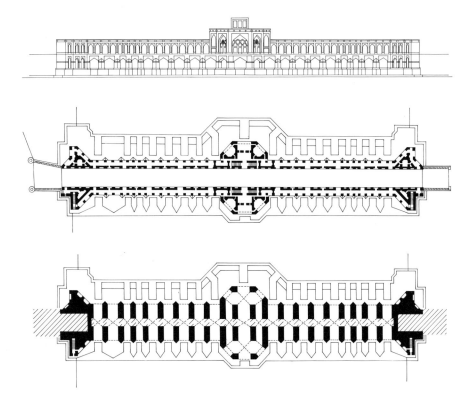

6.22

The sixteenth-century Khwaju Bridge in Isfahan.
The bridge is conceived as a building and gener-
ated by a complex geometry. It is set across a
wide river bed with pavilions, rooms, balconies,
connecting stairs and levels throughout.

Among the operational precepts that guide the creation of the physical form of buildings and urbanism is a strong preference for archetypal forms as the basis for important buildings. These archetypes are based on platonic geometric figures: squares, circles, triangles, pentagons, and "magic" rectangles—and their three-dimensional progeny in the form of cubes, spheres, cylinders, tetrahedrons, and certain rectilinear volumes. Pure geometries and their mathematical correspondences are important to the Sufi and other Islamic traditions. The Sufi tradition manipulates geometry in a way that captures the personality of numbers.[15] Two-dimensional platonic figures characteristically cover the planar surfaces of walls, floors, and ceilings, with a mathematical sophistication of dazzling intricacy and complexity. The patterns are rotated, transposed, transformed, overlapped, and interlaced, suggesting for the believer the universality, sacredness, and ultimate unity of nature. Each time a basic form is repeated in a different way, interlocking with other forms to create another perfect geometry, it reasserts the unity of the cosmos.

Like Western classical architecture, Sufi architecture incorporates complexity and simplicity in its geometric operations as evidence of the laws of nature, but it carries the transcendental character of geometric purity to much greater heights. As in the philosophical and religious language of Sufism, each operation, each form, and every part of the building possesses a meaning that is profoundly interconnected with all else in the world. Thus the sense of unity among all things is more strongly expressed in the animating ideas that lie behind the architecture in the Sufi tradition than it is in any of the other classical traditions discussed here. Once again, expressions of unity and harmony work to reconcile humankind's place on earth with a nature of cosmic dimensions and power.

Balancing the Timeless and the Temporal

It is important at this point to consider our present attitudes toward these classical traditions. Today dynamic change is championed in the name of progress. Most people find it difficult to understand a frame of mind that sets the idea of the preservation of things and ideas from long ago as a primary objective.

But we should recognize that the idea of the classic is never held to the exclusion of temporal values; it is rather a matter of preference or, more often, a matter of emphasis. The idea of the classic is an approach to the reality of time that sets constancy as its first priority, and it is selective as well. In a healthy classical tradition not only is the capacity for change built into the system, but the framework of classicism is selective in that it need not apply to all architecture or all areas of the society. The *sukiya* tradition, for instance, seeks to perpetuate a certain set of values; it was seen from the beginning to exist in parallel with other important cultural traditions quite outside its designated sphere of influence. Thus it is less comprehensive in its intent than the Western classical tradition discussed here. On the other hand, the *sukiya* tradition has indirectly influenced other architecture. The idea of the classic has always held the capacity to influence other areas of thought and practice outside its intended realm. In the West, Greek and Roman influence has been felt in law, government, literature, and science, to name just a few. The idea of the classic is then a way of thinking—an approach to understanding and to practice, implicit in the definition of ends as well as in the formulation of means to those ends.

A close-up look at the means for initiating change in Western classicial architecture will demonstrate how the tradition operated through time, permitting change while keeping its basic structure intact. Built into the structure of Western classical architecture and urbanism is a very refined means to accommodate temporality while conserving timeless things and values. The principle vehicle for this was in the form of the treatise on architecture.

The number of architectural treatises following on the heels of Leon Battista Alberti's first "modern" treatise on architecture written in the 1530s and 1540s reflects the importance placed on their production. Alberti's treatise, *De re aedificatoria* (or *On the Art of Building*), written in scholarly Latin in the style of Cicero, was a commentary on the validity, content, and meaning of Vitruvius's first-century BC *De architectura* (or *Ten Books on Architecture*). In effect *De re aedificatoria* brought Vitruvius up to date. It critiqued and interpreted the tenets presented by Vitruvius but held to the general spirit and format of the classical document that inspired it. Most treatises that followed Alberti's, however, were written in vernacular languages and printed for broad dissemination among architects, artists, and their patrons. Some were comprehensive and essentially theoretical as was Alberti's, but others focused on particular types of architecture such as military architecture or urban palaces, or on the theory and practice of newly perfected or lately refined techniques such as perspective drawing or stereotomy (the geometry of stone cutting), or on broadly practical aspects of design and construction such as timber truss design or the construction of city defensive works and the design of siege machinery—all subjects touched on in one way or another by Vitruvius. The many treatises produced after Alberti's may be seen as individual interpretations of, and expansions on, assumed rules for architecture and the design of cities. The whole enterprise might be thought of as not unlike the writing of legislation under the aegis of a constitution and a legal system that responds to a formalized treatment of precedents. Like Alberti, most treatise authors made direct reference to Vitruvius, and all addressed classical principles and then set about to expand on or reinterpret those principles for application to contemporary circumstances.

One of the most influential treatises was Andrea Palladio's *I quattro libri dell'architettura* (or *The Four Books of Architecture*). Its effectiveness arose from a mix of drawings of exemplary works of architecture accompanied by discussions relating them to the practice of architecture, with their theoretical basis explained in a decidedly nonabstract and straightforward way. In some respects this was a how-to book with theoretical arguments and explanations where they might be needed. Most drawings in the book are of buildings designed by Palladio himself, while others were taken from classical antiquity, and one describes a work by Bramante built only about eighty years earlier. But offering Palladio's own works as exemplary presented a problem of credibility. Contemporary work did not come with established credentials as did Roman examples. Obviously it was important for Palladio to square his personal designs with Vitruvian tenets and existing precedents (the available ruins of antique architecture) to ensure that his readers would accept his work as authoritative. His concern for convincing his readers of his faithful adherence to classical tenets is clearest in situations where it might appear he had taken unusual liberties with accepted tenets. For instance, Palladio's practice of putting temple porticoes on main facades of private dwellings runs counter to the statement by Vitruvius that temple porticoes are reserved for religious and public edifices. (The Pantheon, you will recall, provides a clear example of this practice.) So Palladio steps forward in this treatise with an explanation based on both precedent and rule:

In all the villas and also in some of the city houses I have put a frontispiece on the forward façade where the principal doors are because such frontispieces show the entrance of the house, and add very much to the grandeur and magnificence of the work, the front being thus made more eminent than the other parts. . . . The ancients also used them in their buildings, as may be seen in the remains of temples and of other public edifices. And, as I said in the preface to the first book, it is very likely that they got the invention and the concept from private buildings, that is, from houses. Vitruvius in the last chapter of his third book instructs us how to make them.[16]

Clearly he felt the necessity of pointing out that although he deviated from apparent ancient practice, his transgression was, in the end, not inconsistent with the spirit of antiquity. Palladio presented a similar logic for his practice of putting domes on private residences. This time he speculated on the etymology of the word "dome," suggesting that it arises from the Latin *domus*, which of course means "house" and therefore drawing a direct relationship between these words. He reasons that by putting a dome on a house, one is following a valid etymological precedent and thus a valid historical precedent.

Common Law and the Evolution of Custom

Palladio's argument recalls Western legal reasoning. The adaptability of classical precepts to changing cultural forces is not unlike that found in Anglo-American common law in its use of precedent. Anglo-American common law is inherently evolutionary, as legal scholar Munroe Smith notes:

In their effort to give to the social sense of justice articulate expression in rules and in principles, the method of the law-finding experts has always been experimental. The rules and principles of case law have never been treated as final truths, but as working hypotheses, continually retested in those great laboratories of the law, the courts of justice. Every new case is an experiment; and if the accepted rule which seems applicable yields a result which is felt to be unjust, the rule is reconsidered.[17]

Within each precedent is a latent principle, and the judicial process applies that principle to the case to be decided. Applying the principle is referred to as taking it "along the line of logical progression." If the principle is taken "along the line of the custom of the community," it is referred to as "the method of tradition." It is not at all difficult to find close parallels to these techniques in the operation of classical architectural design methods. One could elucidate the quotation by Smith as follows:

> *In their effort to give [contemporary logic and functional requirements] articulate expression in rules and in principles, the method of [classical architecture] has always been experimental. The rules and principles of [Western classicism] have never been [effective when they have been] treated as final truths, but as working hypotheses, continually restated in those great laboratories of [classicism, the architect's treatises and the ateliers of the practicing architects]. Every new [building] is an experiment; and if the accepted rule which seems applicable yields a result that is [inconsistent with contemporary requirements] the rule is reconsidered.*

To be sure, any analogy has its limits, but the application of precedent within the common law provides such a close parallel to the frame of mind of a practitioner of classical architecture that it is safe to assume these two otherwise disparate fields must certainly share many of the same objectives. In particular they share a recognition of the importance of cultural and social forces that animate the structures that lie behind their respective systems of rules. According to Benjamin N. Cardozo, a giant in American law, "Back of precedents are the basic juridicial conceptions . . . and farther back are the habits of life, the institutions of society, in which those conceptions had their origin, and which, by a process of interaction, they have modified in turn."[18] The body of law under which we live is in a sense an organic, evolving, and ever-adapting set of principles, ever sensitive to the human context in which the law functions. According to legal scholar Edward H. Levi, "[It is a pretense] that the law is a system of known rules applied by a judge. . . . In an important sense legal rules are never clear, and, if a rule had to be clear before it could be imposed, society would be impossible."[19] Likewise classical architecture, when practiced as an ever-evolving tradition, cannot become frozen in time, unresponsive to people and place. The rules of Western classical architecture, though sometimes vague, must be always open to challenge and interpretation, lest the architecture become a mere anachronism of a former golden age.

While not all great architects wrote treatises—or even read them for that matter—the presence of treatises and the influence of the architects who wrote and argued over them probably had a much broader effect than the frequency of their use might imply. Architectural treatises were as much barometers as they were instruments for determining architectural theory. They demonstrate how the practice of classical architecture continually revitalized its own theoretical underpinnings.

Many people no longer regard classical architecture an essential part of Western society, at least not to the extent that common law has become woven into the fabric of everyday life. That classical architecture has become estranged from our social order while common law has perservered is perhaps an indication of how our priorities and beliefs have changed in the face of modern science and developing technology. Classical architectural theory—and by extension, the arguments involving the imaginary evolutionary descendence of a primitive hut and the derivation of canonical proportions for buildings from the body of an adult man—was rendered antiquated by a different system of logic, despite its efficacy.

Classical Thought as the Means Rather than the End

The modern movement in architecture and urbanism sought to base a new architecture on immutable principles, objectively arrived at through a scientific frame of mind. At one level the intention was to arrive at a new concept of the classic. The attempt to set down principles objectively arrived at for all to agree upon, regardless of cultural or ethnic context, was a quest for universality and timeless principles like those which were once firmly seen to be the underpinnings of Western classical architecture. Thus the new architecture would be a truly international form of the classic. In fact it came to be referred to for a time as the International Style because of its presumed cross-cultural validity. Someday, it was reasoned, the man-made world will no longer be shaped by forces derived from one or another ethnic or cultural source but rather by forces derived from a logic that will transcend all that. It was much like parallel attempts to invent an international language, one that would be disassociated from any cultural origin and thereby neither favor nor offend any ethnic or national sensibilities. There were several attempts—including Esperanto, Interlingua, Novial, and Interglossa—each presumably without real roots in any community so that it could be used without prejudice in all communities. They all failed of course.[20] They failed because they had not arisen naturally in a community that generated a language out of human experience. While these invented languages were more logical—at least in a mechanical way—than natural languages with their idiosyncratic complexities from situations now lost from memory, they lacked the richness accrued naturally in a living community and so were unable to effectively change, adapt, and grow as they encountered the new or became immersed in yet another community with its own special requirements, biases, and flavors. If one of these languages had been adopted and then were to change over time by taking on local or regional characteristics, it would no longer be an international language of course, and so we would likely have to start over again. So it is with classical architecture. The four classical traditions in architecture discussed in this chapter reflect their cultural roots, while they share a sense of what it is that is timeless about them—that is to say, what is natural. Like languages, they came about "on their own," or "naturally"—they have the capacity to grow and adapt, to open themselves to invention and innovation while preserving a set of timeless principles and precepts.

What is especially important is that the classical system of rules, canons, and procedures does not operate in a cultural vacuum. It should be obvious that it is always a part of broader cultural attitudes, customs, beliefs, and practices. Further the resultant artifacts likely influence other areas of social and cultural life. Simply put, classicism is a way of thinking. As historians Alexander Tzonis and Liane Lefaivre expressed it, "in the end classical buildings through formal patterns embody abstract relations of quantity and space, out of which one can infer by analogy statements about many other facets of reality:

the reality of nature, the reality of thinking, the reality of human association, and the reality of future artifacts."[21] Classicism, as Tzonis and Lefaivre have expressed it, provides a perfect world within a world. Each piece—each building, each element of a building—is complete in itself, perfect in its own way as a kind of world unto itself. The whole is made up of the parts, but that whole is itself a part in a larger whole.

It has been said that in the classical tradition history corroborates natural law, while in the romantic tradition history evolves through a process of continual change. Polemical argument has often stressed these concepts as diametrically opposed and therefore mutually exclusive approaches to reality, but they may also be seen as two different lenses through which reality may be examined, leading to two different courses of action intended to produce equally valid but quite different results. Emphasis on the timeless illuminates those forces that tend to stabilize nature, society, and the built world, while stressing change shows us how they adapt. The lesson of nature is that there must be a balance between the temporal and the timeless—and the man-made world, just as the in world of nature, must do likewise.

Summary: The Timeless and the Idea of the Classical

This analysis of widely separated cultural settings points up the commonalties and the differences among classical traditions. But, if we set aside the differences, what we have left constitutes the essential qualities of classical traditions. In these contrasting classical traditions we have seen that the issue is not one of controlling the expressive characteristics of tectonic complexities, or of maintaining ideal proportions, or of perpetuating the orders of architecture. Rather it has to do with constructing a system for perpetuating what are regarded as timeless values and principles, ones that are seen as firmly embedded in a cultural setting and therefore as much a part of its fabric as its literature, mythologies, and rituals. Expressing tectonic complexities, or maintaining what are believed to be ideal proportions, or perpetuating the orders might well be components of a particular classical tradition, but they are not what classical architecture is all about. The architecture of the Pueblo tribes of the American Southwest, for instance, qualifies as a classical tradition just as much as Greek and Roman architecture if we see it as an expression of timeless values manifested in architecture and integral with the history of a people.

Why then do societies sometimes consciously reject their classical traditions? We needn't look far for an answer. It usually happens in response to the rejection of a particular group or to a political ideology that has appropriated the classical tradition as its own in order to establish its identity as timeless. For instance, Nazi Germany and Fascist Italy commandeered their own versions of classical architecture in their efforts to convince everyone that their ideologies were integral to Western culture and society, and especially that they were here to stay. In Renaissance and post-Renaissance Europe, with a new assertion of the centrality of authority of the Roman Catholic Church and the establishment of new merchant aristocracies over the formerly powerful guilds, there emerged plenty of individual and institutional interests that needed durable symbols to help ensure their continuity. In times of sweeping change the classical traditions identified with that which is being swept away or discredited are likely to be rejected as well. Occasionally, as exemplified by the architecture of Thomas Jefferson and the new federalist architecture of the emerging republic of the United States of America, the effort has been to change the classical tradition itself to reflect new ideologies firmly based on ancient roots. Jefferson's architecture took advantage of the broad latitude for visual expression inherent in classical architecture in order to differentiate a new American architecture from Great Britain's Georgian classicism. He championed an architecture that symbolized the idealism of the new country's fledgling democratic institutions, while the federalist architecture that followed asserted the authority of the new republic.

The idea of classicism, however, represents only one side of a balance in the man-made world and nature. Just as so-called classical thought affirms rationality and perfection, so-called romantic thought upholds the mysterious, spontaneous, and often spiritual side of nature and the man-made. It would be unfortunate indeed if this discussion were to lead to the conclusion that timelessness is the most important consideration; it must be seen as one side of a balanced equation, just as in the gestalt of figure-ground or the principle of balanced opposites of yin and yang. Whatever the structure of a classical tradition—be it encased in a definitive descriptive code as in the Sung dynasty's *Ying-tsao Fa-shih,* or in religious practice and dogma as in the Sufi tradition, or in treatises and exemplary practice as in Greek and Roman classicism, or in the rituals that guide the *sukiya*—its purpose is to convey what are regarded as the timeless qualities of forms and practice. The following chapter will bring this discussion to a close by examining the city, the ultimate expression of change and timelessness in what we build.

7.1
*An engraving of the seaport of Bordeaux in the
eighteenth century after a painting by Joseph
Vernet.*

7 NATURE AND THE CITY

Reflecting on an early fascination with some large paintings of eighteenth-century French seaports by Joseph Vernet, Claude Lévi-Strauss explained that for him, "their value lies in the fact that they allow me to relive the relationship between sea and land which still existed at that time; a port was a human settlement which did not completely destroy, but rather gave a pattern to, the natural relationships between geology, geography and vegetation, and thus offered an exceptional kind of reality, a dream-world in which we can find refuge."[1]

Lévi-Strauss's description of the seaport city may just as well have been of a Greek *polis*. The traditional European city, because of its small size and limited economy, occupied the land much as did the ancient Greek city long before it. The new industrial city did not begin to assert itself in the landscape until the nineteenth century. It is difficult for most of us today, especially North Americans, to grasp the idea of a city as did our ancestors before the industrial revolution. In medieval Europe and up to the industrial revolution even many of the farmers lived in fortified cities, where the daily ritual of their lives involved departing at daybreak through one of the city gates to tend their fields in the surrounding countryside, and then returning in the evening to their abodes, the center of their world within the safety of the city's enclosing wall. The times of day were marked by the city's church bells, giving time a place in the daily rituals of life.

7.2
The city of Urbino in Italy. Its surrounding walls
render it whole and complete as it sits in a land-
scape of orchards and vineyards.

The city, like every domicile within it, evoked a further sense of enclosure in the way it was situated in the landscape. Seen from afar it appeared as a monument on the horizon defined by its encircling wall. In some languages the word for "town" and the word denoting its defensive walls are the same thing. For instance, the character for the Chinese word *ch'eng* means both "city" and "wall," and the English word "town" originally meant "hedge" or "enclosure." The traditional city can be thought of as an entity unto itself, as "a kind of large house," as Alberti remarked in his *De re aedificatoria,* a bounded domain for all the enfranchised who dwelled within. Inside its defensive walls, houses blended one into the other, all facing onto enclosed courts or continuous corridors of streets that were broken only at the intersection of other streets and, in a less emphatic way, by openings into semiprivate entrance courts that mimicked the larger public squares, providing access to groups of houses within

7.3

The main street through the center of Dubrovnik in Croatia. The public area is crisply defined by this great corridor which is faced by a wall of closely spaced buildings with towers to mark the more important civic edifices along its length and at its termination.

each street-bound block. It was as though the city were as solid as a great stone and the corridor streets connecting public squares (each square a kind of outdoor room) were carved out of that stone after it had been set in place. The network of streets and public squares was joined by a few strategic monumental civic buildings—the town hall, churches, monastic institutions, monumental loggias, towers, and commemorative monuments. This was the traditional European city. Its form varied according to location and size of course, but essentially it was a solitary object in the landscape from without and a hierarchically ordered ensemble of houses, monuments, civic edifices, and public passages and gathering places from within.

The impression of a city's permanence was central to its citizens. The immutable city stood in fixed contrast to the mortality of its citizens. Hannah Arendt described the traditional city's affect of permanence as an important expression of human longing for immortality:

> *Nowhere else does the sheer durability of the world of things appear in such purity and clarity, nowhere else therefore does this thing-world reveal itself so spectacularly as in the non-mortal home for mortal beings. It is as though worldly stability had become transparent in the permanence of art, so that a premonition of immortality, not the immortality of the soul or of life but of something immortal achieved by mortal hands, has become tangibly present, to shine and to be seen, to sound and to be heard, to speak and to be read.*[2]

7.4

A map of Parma in northern Italy as the city appeared in the Renaissance. Southeast of the city the encircling wall connects to a fortress. Inside the walled enclosure are corridor streets, clearly defined public squares and civic edifices, and a dense configuration of buildings that combines housing with commerce.

7.5

The Appian Gate in Rome** (above) **and the Porta Nigra in Trier, Germany** (below). **Such grand and handsome city gates were designed as entrances to the city as well as being integral to a city's defense.

The quest for permanence is evident throughout the world in existing traditional settlements and in the remains of prehistoric settlements long abandoned. Prehistoric villagers saw it as a part of the function of their architecture "to create a sense of permanence and continuity, to build resources for their heirs and to commemorate their ancestors."[3] In this way the traditional city, along with religion and the continuity of the family, provided comfort and security for its community. Human artifice rendered the city as permanent as it could be, usually aided by the settlement's appearance as an integral part of the setting, in its compactness and its construction of "native" stone from the surrounding landscape. Thus, like as element of nature, the city appeared firmly rooted in its place. These are some of the qualities Lévi-Strauss must have seen in those paintings of eighteenth-century French seaports.

The embellishment of important civic buildings, bridges, wellheads, harbor works, defense accruements, and the like, as works of art evoked a strong sense of perfection, refinement, and beauty. Permanent monuments within the traditional city were seen as things that ought to manifest timelessness, permanence, and perfection—a stable armature upon which the common citizen's house, a structure more directly associated with human mortality, could rely.

The idea of an architecture with an evocative sense of permanence and perfection must have helped anchor the traditional city and its citizens both in the landscape and in time. The monumental and honorific architecture of the traditional city was of course the basis for its identity, and it helped to lay the foundations for its intellectual life. According to Peter J. Wilson, the intellectual properties of architecture—geometry, diagrams, and history—provided "people with the impetus, inspiration, and ambition to concentrate on the development of this human, cultural endeavor. So, considered objectively, one could argue that the evolution of domesticated society is typified by the striving toward the perfection of architecture, the geometry that is its abstract counterpart and foundation, the arts and sciences that spin off that geometry—music, sculpture, painting, mechanics—and the technologies that combine geometry and architecture, such as artillery, siege works, ballistics, plowing, formal gardening, and the theater."[4]

The traditional city comprised a man-made world in its totality. It was not just a practical replacement for nature but a reflection of the cosmic realm as well. Its unity permitted it to be sensed as a cosmos, a microcosm of the larger world around it now scaled to the community within. The traditional city was the penultimate expression of a man-made world set in nature and created as a "second nature" in the service of humankind alone.

The Transitory City of the Present

Early settlements and cities stand in stark contrast to the post-industrial city of today. The modern city's limits are lost in the ambiguities of streets that extend into the countryside to form sprawling suburbs and linear commercial strips, decreasing in building density the farther away they are from the center. There is no clear and definitive place where the city ends and the countryside begins. Important civic buildings, once dominant features in the urban fabric, now disappear among highrise office buildings, which present themselves as as monumental edifices, an expression once reserved for civic buildings alone. And to exacerbate the problem of identity, some civic buildings are designed to look more like commercial buildings than do some of the older commercial buildings. In this way the newer civic buildings suggest that they house bureacracies as efficient as those expected of private commercial operations. Finally, there is the appearance of temporality and impermanence in the modern city. Steel and glass buildings, set along streets as though they had been removed from a shelf and put there by a crane, present themselves very differently than do the stone walls and continuous fabric of the traditional city. It is especially this quality of the modern city—the disregard for permanence—that contrasts so sharply with its traditional counterpart.

Has human nature changed that much in the past hundred and fifty years or so to either cause or justify such an abrupt and dramatic change in the city? Or has our present idea of the city simply emerged from a market economy while our collective notion of the ideal way to live has shifted from the city to the countryside? Without much difficulty we can see how newly emerging forces have come together to create the modern city. As the city has changed, our concept of the city has changed with it. We have come to regard the late-twentieth-century city in different ways: We see it sometimes in relation to its consumptive role as "an energy system," sometimes as a concentration of economic activity, and sometimes as an efficient setting for what planners refer to as "functional specializations." When we choose to visualize the city as a formal entity, we tend to see it in response to the formal order imparted by its infrastructure—streets, underground utilities, railroad lines, subways, and freeways. The pre-industrial city dweller saw the city as something to be treasured; we see the city more as a dynamic repository of buildings on parcels of land known as real estate. We are prone to think of people who live in cities in objective demographic and economic terms or as nameless constituents of political and economic structures. Our idea of the city is as an aggregate of parts where the parts themselves take on more importance than the whole. One is reminded again of Archibald MacLeish's comment that we have come to replace our traditional way of thinking about the world with a "new precise, objective, dispassionate" way of thinking about it. Whatever the causes—the economy, the automobile, social mobility, racial and ethnic tensions, pollution, ideals of country living—the city's physical form has changed and our idea of what constitutes a city has changed with it.

By most *quantifiable* standards, the modern city is superior. We know that life expectancies, infant mortality rates, educational levels, and material wealth of the average citizen in the era of the modern city exceed that of the citizen of the pre-industrial city. But we also know that the traditional form of the city encouraged a frame of mind—although not so easily quantified—that only a fraction of the citizens of the modern city now enjoy. The density of the traditional city with its free mix of functions provided its citizens with an identity that could be reinforced through responsive community affiliations; a full array of daily amenities and necessities such as places to purchase food, places of entertainment, places of work and of commerce, were within walking distance. The desirability of living in a small New England or midwestern town, or on Boston's Beacon Hill, Chicago's Lincoln Park neighborhood, Washington's Georgetown, and other such communities of traditional urban form, attests to the tenacity of the attributes of the traditional city. These places provide very different ways of living from that of the new, open, functionally zoned, and automobile-oriented modern city. Recent successful efforts to launch a return to the traditional city form by architects Duane and Plater-Zyberk and Peter Calthorpe, among others, suggest that people are aware that something of considerable value has been lost and now must be regained. Their designs have attempted to restore the attributes of traditional communities, including lowered consumptions of energy resources and land, and considerably lowered levels of pollution and unrecyclable wastes.

The slow evolution of the city from the temporary hamlets of the Paleolithic period to the permanent ones of the Neolithic is believed to have taken place within about 1,000 years. The period of time since then, when the traditional city evolved, changed, and adapted throughout the world, spanned somewhere between 6,000 and 8,000 years. By contrast, the urban transition we appear to be in the midst of at the present time has been taking place over night; the time from the first stirring signs of what I have characterized here as "the modern city," to its full fledged dominance, is something like one hundred and fifty years. It is no wonder that the modern city is replete with problems despite its presumed advantages.

The speed with which the modern city has come about might suggest that the modern city is "unnatural" compared to the long evolutionary development of the traditional city. On the other hand, the modern city's extraordinary uncontrollable growth might suggest that it is in some way natural, evidenced by the city often appearing to have a life of its own, outside and beyond any citizen's or planner's intentions. Most major cities in the world today are larger than anyone wants them to be, and they continue to grow. At the moment Mexico City provides one of the most dramatic examples of the problems associated with unmanageable growth. Uncontrollable growth, however, is not exclusively a modern-day problem. In the sixteenth century Elizabeth I of England issued a series of proclamations to limit the growth of the city of London so that sanitary conditions, housing, and wagon and carriage traffic could keep pace with acceptable standards of the time.[5] Each successive proclamation tried a slightly different approach based on the failure of the proclamations before it, but each failed in about the same way. Some proclamations caused secondary conditions that rendered the treatments worse than the problems they sought to rectify. Although cities might be viewed as sufficiently teleological in their behavior for us to think of them as natural, their sizes and fortunes still depend on human decisions; that is, on private prerogatives in combination with the public will implemented by political systems. Since the aggregate effect of human decisions cannot be predicted, does this mean that the city is at least partly natural?

First of all we must establish a useful definition for "natural" in reference to the city. The classic definition of culture, as distinguished from "nature" by Lévi-Strauss, is "the sum total of the customs, beliefs, and institutions such as art, law, religion, and techniques for dealing with the material world, in short, all the habits or skills learnt by man as a member of a community."[6] Because the city and its architecture is an extension of culture, under this definition it cannot be considered natural. But, if the city is an extension of culture, does that rule out the involvement of human nature in its creation? Human nature is usually defined as "everything in our make-up that we owe to biological heredity."[7] By extension of these definitions, we should conclude that the city cannot be considered either strictly natural or wholly artificial because it is shaped by our biological natures as much as it is by our cultures—while our cultures are shaped in large part by our biological natures as well. So it remains a conundrum.

Perhaps returning to the evidence of the origin and evolution of the city will help answer the question. During the Neolithic Age the first permanent settlements were made possible by the domestication of animals, by the development of crops, and perhaps by the formation of trade.[8] Their stability allowed for a more effective accumulation of knowledge in agriculture; the year to year performance of crops could be monitored, experiments performed, and the results recorded for comparative use at a later time. The invention of writing is the likely link between these first tiny settlements and the growth of certain settlements among them into cities. A nomadic society had little use for keeping records of possessions, but once ensconced in a fixed settlement, the need to keep track of things, such as the storage of annual harvests, quickly extended beyond the reliability of memory. Evidence indicates that writing came about for the purposes of inventories, censuses, laws, and instructions. According to urban geographer Gideon Sjoberg, "once a community achieves or otherwise acquires the technological advance we call writing, a major transformation in the social order occurs; with a written tradition rather than an oral one it is possible to create more complex administrative and legal systems and more rigorous systems of thought. Writing is indispensable to the development of mathematics, astronomy, and other sciences; its existence thus implies . . . a number of significant specializations within the social order."[9] Just as our cultures evolved, with their characteristic components of language, myth, ritual, and art, followed by writing, philosophy, technology, and science, so did the city as integral to those cultures.

The evolutionary sequence of the city might be viewed as analogous to evolution in nature. Human artifice set the city in motion, then continually adapted it to change through time. Seen in this way, the city is like a living thing. Indeed it is not uncommon for urban geographers to view the city as though it were a biological organism. Consider the following description:

> *A city is an organism which evolves as all organisms do, in response to genetic*
> *signals—concepts of what a city should do and how it should interact in its*

parts—such as those which make all men and women basically "alike" but infi-
nitely different. . . . In the same way, city building responds to "genetic" signals
but never produces an identical product.[10]

One is reminded by this of Pascal's rhetorical question about nature and custom, and Cicero's observation that we have created a "second world" within
the world of nature. If the city is seen as a natural outgrowth of the human
capacity for ideas and invention, then, as noted by Aristotle, it mirrors a fundamental quality of human nature.

A related question to whether the city is natural is whether it is natural for
us to live in large permanently located communities in the first place. Biological
evidence tends to suggest an answer in the negative. First, the situation of humans living close together in large numbers encourages the transmission of
disease from person to person, infecting large numbers with relative speed.
And there is the problem of living near to where we deposit our feces, which
can pollute the drinking water as well as encourage the accumulation of
disease-producing organisms. Before Neolithic times, when people moved
about in small groups, often no larger than the extended family, the transmission of disease was more easily avoided. A related problem arises in the food
supply when plants are grown side by side as crops, thereby permitting plant
diseases to move unimpeded from plant to plant and destroy a crop with ease;
while the same specie growing as part of a large and naturally varied ecosystem
would easily resist or avoid most diseases that attack it.[11] So it would appear,
at least from these examples, that we were not meant to live in cities.

We might also ask if the formation of cities "naturally" encouraged the
quest for progress in human rights. This time it is evidence of history that
suggests an answer in the negative. Coincident "with the appearance of writing
[was] the establishment of hierarchical societies, consisting of masters and
slaves, and where one part of the population is made to work for the other
part."[12] Even where slavery was absent, city formation encouraged vocational
specialization in general, which in turn supported a more elaborate hierarchical ordering of societies. In time the order of the tribe—with its chieftan who
took care of maintaining a functionally effective ordering of everyone so as to
preserve the tribal unit, and the shaman who looked after everyone's spiritual
welfare—gave way to the king and priest, both of whom assumed roles of

greater power over others than their chief and shaman counterparts. The larger-scale order of the city with its specialized roles for citizens might well have meant more wealth for everyone, but both the distribution of wealth and the exercise of each citizen's rights were entirely dependent on the character of the ruler or the type of rule imposed. As Lévi-Strauss maintained, "If, in order to establish his ascendancy over nature, man had to subjugate man and treat one section of mankind as an object, we can no longer give a simple and unequivocal answer to the questions raised by the concept of progress."[13] Once again, it would appear that we were not intended to live in cities.

Clearly we must approach this question from a different direction. After all, we chose to live in cities for the advantages we found them to provide, and we have demonstrated a capacity to invent ways to bypass or eliminate the problems that arise from such practices as monoculture and of living together in large numbers in a fixed place. We have in fact approached the development of the city in a similar way to how we dealt with the design and evolution of primitive domiciles described in chapter 2. You may recall that each domicile was attuned to its setting through a continual process of trial and error, change and adaptation, always with the aim toward sustainability and the provision of security and comfort for those who dwell within. While human ingenuity operated to assure success, it was time that provided ingenuity the luxury of being able to err and then profit from the knowledge the error imparted. For the traditional city we might also assume that each error, like each successive step in the evolutionary development of the domicile, was sufficiently small so that disaster would not ensue. Such as evolutionary sequence was in a sense "natural" in that human ingenuity established the artifact, be it city or domicile, in the first place, then continually adapted it to changing conditions and desires over time. Seen in this way, the city might be regarded as a living thing, its existence and survival a product of a collective human intellect.

The City as a House

The city is not just a physical, formal, and morphological entity; it comprises human institutions that render it a desirable place in which to live. These institutions mediate and adjust relationships between individuals, groups, and the physical environment that accommodates them. But there are no reliable and comprehensive constructs in place for guiding the growth of the city, like those that guide the design of a classical building. Although the city's evolution is much more complicated than that of architecture, the principles that govern its physical growth and change over time could be much the same. We will examine some of the more important characteristics of the traditional city that have sustained its viability over time.

The Tectonics of Urban Order

Just as classical architecture incorporates a poetic expression of its tectonic origin, a city bears traces of each stage of its physical evolution. As its buildings fall and are replaced, the city adapts and remains. We easily accept the idea of an eternal city, but we flinch at the idea of an eternal building or an eternal country. Even if destroyed, a city is usually rebuilt; examples abound: London after the fire of 1666, Chicago after its fire of 1871, Rotterdam, Warsaw, Dresden and Berlin, Hiroshima and Nagasaki after the Second World War—the list goes on. Whole civilizations have come and gone, but cities have lived on as, for instance, Roman cities built on Etruscan foundations, medieval cities on Roman foundations, and modern cities on medieval and Renaissance foundations. Of course some cities have perished forever—like the world's first cities, the cities of Mesopotamia along the Tigris and Euphrates rivers—but many ancient cities which are far older than any buildings they contain today are still with us.

In the past once a city's settlement pattern was established, that pattern continued as the city grew. Chicago's incessant grid, Paris's powerful center and subsequent circular rings of growth, Turin's and Florence's foursquare Roman castrum, and Beijing's imperial center are a few of the more dramatic examples.[14] Today, however, wrecking balls, bulldozers, and clamshell excavators have the capacity to change a city completely, to easily erase patterns of the past and any sense of place that might have been. In the past the city was understood by its citizens in very human terms. Its history was often associated with the descendance of one's family, that likely would have survived a succession of changes in the city's political and military fortunes over time. The city was a place of continuity beyond that associated with a particular political ide-

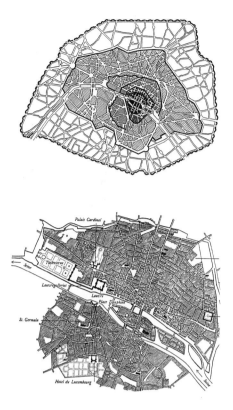

7.6

Paris began as an island in the Seine River. As the city expanded outward, successive, concentric bands of defensive walls constrained its growth (above), and they date from c.1180, 1370, 1676, 1784–1791, and 1841–1845. A closer view of the city center (below) shows that the most important and sacred civic monuments are to be found near the place of the city's origin.

ology or regime. The city could be experienced directly; it had historical meanings and associations, and it preserved those meanings and associations in its visage. The ancient practice of inventing stories about prominent places in the landscape—a flat place in uneven terrain, a prominent hill in flat country, a straight stretch of a meandering river, a lone tree on the steppes—reflects a basic human need to know the landscape. To "know" one's physical environment is as necessary as to know the people with whom one associates regularly. Assuming that the city was created to take the place of nature, certain places in it have reflected our ancestors' experiences with nature. Just as the mountain or the predictable cycles of the heavens assured them of the continuity of the natural world, the permanence of certain places in the urban landscape assured them that the city would remain forever.

The history of cities provides plenty of evidence of measures to retain the memory of the city's past through the reiteration of essential geometries. The city of Turin, for instance, was carefully guided through an elaborate expansion from its Roman core so that each stage in its growth would appear as entirely consistent with the founding core. In the sixteenth century, as newly created patterns of larger squares, blocks, and wider streets were needed to accommodate larger buildings, subsequent additions to the original castrum continued to respect the historic pattern. The medieval fabric of the centers of Paris and Rome were modified in later centuries by the introduction of new streets and boulevards to connect historic monuments, reordering the historic fabric while respecting its essential pattern and important monuments. Large palaces and government buildings were inserted into the delicate medieval fabric of Munich and Vienna in such a way that they would appear as having been there from the beginning. In all these cities, growth responded to an established pattern, reflecting what existed while adapting the new to unprecedented requirements for size and scale.

Monuments and public squares also serve to retain the memory of the city's history. Rome's Piazza Navona, for instance, one of the city's most frequented public square, reflects the form of an imperial Roman circus whose ancient spina is marked by a large public fountain. A line of buildings on the foundations of the stands for viewing the chariot races follows the line of the ancient race track and provides for churches, shops, cafes, restaurants, and houses. Once it came to be accepted as a public square, the Piazza Navona became a prominent feature in the minds of the community as well as in the form of the city. When in the seventeenth century it was learned that a design for the church of Sant'Agnese-in-Agone would project the facade forward of this line of buildings, there were public demonstrations. As a result the facade was redesigned so that it would not encroach upon this public space. The wall defining the piazza was clearly understood to connect the city with it's ancient past while providing for the public domain. No building, no matter how important, would be permitted to violate the imprint of the old circus. Each building bordering the piazza was primarily regarded as part of the greater entity of wall, and only secondarily as an independent building.

Another example of a city preserving the unity and identity of public space was medieval Siena. In the thirteenth century ordinances regulated the

7.7

The Piazza Navona, Rome.

Top:

The church of Sant'Agnese in Agone was designed to be the presiding force on the square but not to intrude on the public domain.

Bottom:

Detail from a map of Rome in 1748 drawn by Giovanni Battista Noli. The Piazza Navona (upper left) is the largest open space in the drawing. Approximately four streets to the right of it is the Pantheon, distinguishable by its round interior embedded in the fabric of the city. Noli's drawing gives equivalent treatment to interior as well as exterior public spaces by relating adjacent courtyards to piazzas and to interiors of churches, consistent with the notion of what is public and what is private space.

7.8
The Piazza del Campo in Siena. The city hall (Palazzo Pubblico) with its tower presides over the square.

heights, proportions, and placement of windows, the alignment of public facades, and the kind of ornamentation permitted on facades enclosing the piazza. The aim was to unify the public square so that the most important building, the *Palazzo Publico,* or city hall, would be emphasized. Although most of the buildings surrounding the piazza are the palaces of the city's nobility, emphasis on the figural space of the square, and the one civic building that presides over it, reflects the elevated status of the public domain as well as the city's merchant oligarchy over its entrenched aristocracy.

Memory and History

The retention of permanent monuments at strategic locations in the city works with its tectonic order to ensure a sense of stability across time. Meaning and history, a city's linear descendence, is preserved in important buildings, commemorative monuments, and significant works of civil and military engineering. Like the ornament and the orders of classical architecture, a city's monuments remain as symbolic reminders of past priorities. Architect Aldo Rossi refers to these fixed reminders of the past as "permanences." They are, according to Rossi, "parts of a past we are still experiencing." They frequently have stories to tell that connect them with important events in the life of the city. A castle is now a museum, the palace of a formerly powerful family the city hall, or the old railroad station a place for shops and restaurants. Rossi recounts that "When one visits a monument of this type, for example the Palazzo della Ragione in Padua, . . . one is struck by the multiplicity of functions that a building of this type can contain over time and how these functions are entirely independent of the form. At the same time, it is precisely the form that impresses us; we live it and experience it, and in turn it structures the city."[15]

The remarkably intact Pantheon makes ancient Rome seem a little more real, and its history less distant and abstract. Although the connection with the past is not always easy for dwellers of the modern city to grasp, it is not nostalgia that sustains the "permanence" of the Pantheon but rather its connection with the past. As historian Herbert Muller points out, "Nothing is more undignified than a past become quaint."[16] Another example is Verona's "Arena," a first-century AD Roman amphitheater that is still used today. Beneath the stands are modern television recording facilities for broadcasting the concerts and plays that are performed in this great oval on a regular basis. Restored to its function as an entertainment center, a nearly two-thousand year-old past is made more vivid by its continued use in the present.

However grand are the obvious connections to the past, even more effective are the countless incidental reminders throughout the fabric of a city: an old bridge over the river, a line of shops from a much earlier time than surrounding buildings, a piece of a former civic edifice now embedded in the new, columns from an ancient building reused in a more recent one. Such reminders help sustain the idea of the city as a permanent home for a stable community.

Size, Scale, and the Communities Within

The pre-industrial city was subdivided into distinct neighborhoods, quarters, and districts in such a way that a citizen could easily identify with the city through the neighborhood in which he or she lived. London, for instance, grew as small surrounding towns coalesced, yet each district retained a distinctive character inherited from the rural town it used to be. Similarly Stockholm grew by expanding from one island to the next, and each island, in response to the historical period in which it had become populated, acquired its own distinctive character. Paris, on the other hand, grew outward in a series of concentric urban expansions from its ancient core on the *Île de la Cité*. The city's circular form was made more emphatic by defensive walls erected at each stage of its growth. As a result citizens could identify their place within the city by the ring in which they lived, with the first ring starting at the city's center on the Seine.

7.9

The city of Turin, Italy, c. 1840. From this plan one can sense the scale of the city by the relative sizes of courtyards within the city blocks.

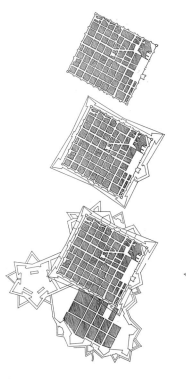
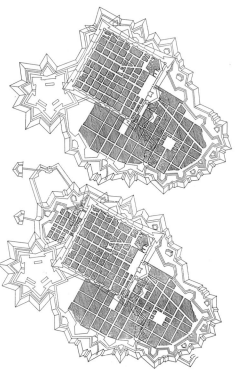

7.10

Five stages in the controlled growth of the city of Turin.

Left, top to bottom:
Roman town under Augustus, Turin at the close of the sixteenth century, Turin at the beginning of the seventeenth century.

Right, top to bottom:
Turin at the close of the seventeenth century and at the end of the eighteenth century.

When nineteenth-century Paris had grown so large and the narrow city streets so congested that it was beyond an average citizen's ability to travel efficiently in conducting daily affairs, a system of boulevards was introduced. Each boulevard cut across the medieval city, thereby creating new residential districts. These districts soon became designated as voting and administrative wards. Turin's conformity with its ancient Roman castrum plan, the natural multiple island configuration of Stockholm on the Baltic Sea, or any number of other instances that have preserved a conceptual order in cities as they grew beyond their walled enclosures were often not the result of someone's elaborate theoretical construct. City growth was charted in response to a conventional understanding of what constitutes a manageable community size and how that must relate to the city of which it is a part. While the examples cited here are the more dramatic ones of world famous cities, they are certainly not unique. We might see them today as abstract notions about the order of cities, but these measures were regarded by the wisdom of their times as appropriate ways to approach the problem of population growth.

Some scholars believe that the solutions to the growth of these European cities constituted a new understanding of the city, leading to the invention of a new city form, or the "classical city" as historian Carroll William Westfall called it. In Westfall's view, measures such as these went beyond the traditional city, whose adaptation to change might be considered more or less natural, to provide solutions to new needs without denying the city's long-evolved intrinsic form and character.[17] These were radical measures applied to the problems of urban growth, but in retrospect they appear to have gone relatively smoothly in comparison with later changes during the advanced stages of post-industrial urban growth and change.[18] In Paris, for instance, until the twentieth century the city remained essentially a pedestrian city, even though the new long straight boulevards provided for efficient carriage and wagon traffic. This "new" city still held onto its humanistic character, with neighborhoods, quarters, districts, civic monuments, identifiable building types, sundry "permanences" (to use Rossi's term), and its relationship with the adjoining countryside.

Today, in contrast, we often refer to the city in terms of vehicular transportation routes across it rather than pedestrian movement within it. We have factored the time and space dimension of the automobile into our intuitive understanding of urban form, size, scale, and order, but that does not eliminate our basic need to perceive the city in terms related to our bodies: the size of our bodies, our capacity for upright movement, our visual perception, our range of hearing. We are keenly aware of these faculties when we are not encapsulated in a car. Our body-related perception is as important in our understanding of the city as it is to our understanding of space and order in architecture. The invention of the motor vehicle, which has the capacity to travel effortlessly at high speeds across distances, has introduced a scale of reference that bears little relationship to human perception of urban space, detail, order, and scale. Twentieth-century solutions to problems of urban order have sometimes accommodated the automobile to the almost complete exclusion of our experiencing the city in a traditional way. They have destroyed the integrity of neighborhoods, distinctions of public and private domains, and symbols of a shared history that once had sustained a sense of community. In our enthusiasm for the automobile, we have often radically altered the city without regard to the individuals residing there.

7.11

The essential components of the traditional city, as illustrated by Leon Krier. The public realm consists in streets, squares, and civic edifices interposed by a private realm of houses and places of commerce and production to effect a civic expression of balance and clarity. This hierarchical ordering of urban elements is fundamental to traditional cities everywhere, regardless of culture and outward appearance.

RES PUBLICA

RES (ECONOMICA) PRIVATA

CIVITAS

Thus the modern city, with its characteristically low building and population densities and vast undifferentiated spaces, has become an incomprehensible entity. Long ago Gertrude Stein referred to Oakland as a place where "there isn't any there there." Today this epithet is characteristic of most American cities. Architect Leon Krier believes that part of the solution is to radically change the modern city from within. He suggests reconfiguring the city into "quarters" composed of traditional residential blocks and streets. The size of a quarter would be based on the length of time it takes a person to leisurely walk it; its periphery would be clearly defined. Krier sees the city quarters as essentially pedestrian areas with a balance of accommodations for living, working, and recreation. Each quarter would be a kind of *temenos* for those who live there, providing its inhabitants with a sense of unity and identity with the larger city. Krier's notion of city quarter size is derived from human body considerations rather than from mechanical calculations tied to the size of an efficient waste treatment facility, or to administrative convenience or convenient driving distances, or to some abstract economic measures that have nothing to do with the community settled in each quarter.[19] Others have suggested different rules for determining the characteristics of districts, quarters, and neighborhoods by basing them on the number of families it takes to support an elementary school or high school, or on so-called natural population size that permits everyone to recognize everyone else within the community. The details of such proposals are not important here; it is rather the recognition of a need to reconfigure the modern post-industrial city into divisions that are related to the traditional way we know and experience a city.

Time, Place, and the World Beyond

The automobile and the pedestrian represent two different scales of time and two different concepts of space. The automobile has radically changed the way the city and its outlying areas are perceived. It has changed our understanding of the city's form, space, order, and scale. We no longer huddle in cities for protection as our ancestors did because the city no longer is thought as sheltering its inhabitants from dangers that lurk outside it. We do not consider the

7.12

Village of Kastro on the island of Siphnos, Greece. The terracing of the agricultural hinterland—like the building of the village—is man-made, in contradistinction to surrounding nature. Human ingenuity has indeed taken possession of the land here and created, in the words of Cicero, "a second world within the world of nature."

city as a positive force in our lives to the extent our ancestors did; the city has become too large, too impersonal, and too dangerous from within. A city that no longer effectively shelters its inhabitants encourages them to seek refuge in the suburbs.

The suburbs, commercial strips, shopping centers, and the decaying inner city are the most recent and ubiquitous developments in the post-industrial city. Still the post-industrial city remains virtually the same worldwide no matter what the climatic zone, local culture, or surrounding natural (or agrarian) landscape. In the late twentieth-century we have created cities without identities, a remarkable international style of urbanism that is unlike any before it. By contrast, as the traditional city evolved, it produced a variety of forms, varying from one cultural setting to another and from one climatic and geographical setting to another, not unlike its architecture. But, while cities varied considerably, there remained certain constants among them. Those constants are the

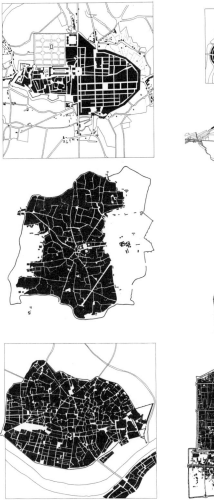

7.13
*Different settlement patterns of traditional
cities.*

Left, top to bottom:
*Nancy, France, eighteenth-century; Samarkand,
Uzbekistan, thirteenth-century Persian city; Se-
ville, Spain, twelfth-century Moslem city.*

Right, top to bottom:
*Ceske Budejovice, Bohemia, sixteenth-century;
Machu Pichu, Peru, sixteenth-century; Montpa-
zier, France, fourteenth-century; Aigues-Mortes,
France, fourteenth-century; Beijing, China, late
fifteenth-century.*

principle characteristics by which we recognize the traditional city: the clarity of public and private domain, the incorporation of monuments and important buildings as symbols of the polity and reminders of the community's shared history, and an evocation of timelessness and unity by the materials out of which the city is made and in its relation to the broader landscape. Along the way in their evolution, traditional cities generated variations on established themes of urban form that might be seen to act across the historical spectrum to achieve a sustainable balance like the biological proliferation of species. However, for today's "new world city," as it is sometimes called, one wonders at its unprecedented ubiguity and what the future holds for it.

Summary: Nature and the City

The city is the ultimate expression of artifice, a second nature built as an alternative to living exclusively within the natural world. In perfecting this second nature, we have progressively separated ourselves from real nature. The forces that shaped the pre-industrial city reponded to a natural sense of space and time that found expression in the unity of the city, in its monumental and permanent architecture, and in its clear matrix of public streets and squares. Regardless of what may be considered the traditional city's failings, it provided a balance between man, nature, and the built environment, and it ensured that changes taking place within were under human control. Our understanding of nature's complexity was manifested in an intelligible system of richness built into the traditional city's order.

Logic, meaning, and timelessness are intangible. We know that everything we build and everything in nature is subject to the limitations of human understanding and to time's destruction. But even though in quiet moments we know reality to be otherwise, we still seek consolation in the immutable: in the prospect of a snowcapped mountain, in the rhythm of the sea's tides, or in the discovery of an old bell tower or road through a town built by Roman legions long ago. Our need to sense the past is just as important in the relatively new North American city as it was to our ancestors in the traditional city. We anguish at the destruction of a neighborhood that "has outlived its usefulness," or we try to limit the expansion of suburbs into the countryside. We want a city that is both sheltering and eternal because it is integral with our lives. In erecting a permanent settlement, our ancestors came to understand these qualities of the natural landscape that was once their home. Whether we are conscious of it or not, we want to believe that the city, like nature, will continue through time.

CONCLUSION

At some point in our ancient past we began to extend our evolution beyond the limitations of biology by means of human culture. Over time the most elaborate expression of our culture came to be the city, an environment that replaced nature and would lead to our most profound achievements. But, while the man-made world of architecture, farmsteads, villages, towns, and cities is the result of conscious intervention in the natural order, it is shaped as well by evolutionary forces in response to natural human inclinations.

The use of geometry that characterizes our architecture and urbanism was present from the beginning. It emerged not as "a style" bestowed upon things as a passing fashion but with intrinsic meaning and in response to an awareness of our bodies in relation to the natural environment. By endeavoring to impart an order to the world of our own making as a kind of human counterpart to the order found in nature, there emerged something we might call "the idea of a man-made world." That "idea" continues to guide how we shape our world today and how we change nature to accommodate the presence of our world within it.

In our success in creating an effective equivalent to nature, we have tricked ourselves. Our man-made environment now desensitizes us to nature. From within our climate-controlled buildings or as we cross the city or the

landscape in the comfort of automobiles or airplanes, the natural world becomes detached from us, even abstract. Our ancestors were in awe of the regularity of the solstices, the expanse of the sea, and the frailty of life; we, however,
have come to consider these things as external to our affairs. Natural phenomena often are seen exclusively as subjects of scientific inquiry. Having perfected
the means for building our world, we find it increasingly difficult to adjust our
lives to it, and to adjust it to the natural world in which it resides. Nearly gone
are the evolutionary processes that once corrected our mistakes and ensured
that our architecture would continue to accommodate our spiritual and psychological needs. We need to pause and look back, to see where we have come
from to apprehend where we might be going.

Our natural quest for beauty in things—for order, unity, harmony, symmetry, balance, coherence, sense, and meaning—has compelled us to make a
world that like nature imparts a feeling of "correctness," of being guided by an
internal logic. Like any evolutionary process the forces that shaped our built
world were intended to ensure a kind of stability over time. That is to say, the
aesthetic impulse, as it has been demonstrated by Alexander Alland, George
Kubler, E. H. Gombrich, Karl Popper, Jacob Bronowski, Thomas S. Kuhn and
others, has been an important factor in disciplining the way we have shaped
our environment. Anthropology has pointed out how the aesthetic impulse of
"primitive peoples" is essential to their maintenance of a sustainable, balanced
world of man and nature. "The so-called primitive cultures . . . encourage us
to reject the divorce between the intelligible and the sensible declared by an
outmoded empiricism and mechanism, and to discover a secret harmony between humanity's everlasting quest for meaning and the world in which we
appeared and where we continue to live—a world made of shapes, colors, tex-
tures, flavors, and odors." For early man it was "better to love and respect nature
and the living beings who people it, by understanding that vegetables and animals, however humble they may be, did not supply man with sustenance only
but were, from the very beginning, the source of his most intense esthetic feelings and, in the intellectual and moral order, of his first and even then profound
speculations."[1] When we create, we are compelled to ensure that our creations
are in harmony with the natural order. An ancient Chinese myth recounts the
origin of the eight basic generative figures for Chinese calligraphy:

When Fú Xī governed everything under the sky, he looked upward and admired the splendid designs in the heavens, and looking down he observed the structure of the earth. He noted the elegance of the shapes of birds and animals and the balanced variety of their territories. He studied his own body and the distant realities and afterwards invented the eight trigrams in order to be able to reveal the transformations of nature and understand the essence of things.[2]

Has this sensibility failed us, and we no longer quest for harmony among things of our world and nature? How has it come to be that we now are confronted with a worldwide environmental crisis and that the modern city that has succeeded the traditional city is proving itself to be such a misadventure? The so-called Neolithic Revolution was driven by a search for a means to free humankind from nature's unpredictability. Now, many millennia later, we have returned to a place where we must deal with powerful forces that lie beyond our control, and this time it is not the forces of nature but forces we have created ourselves.

Today change takes place either too rapidly or too slowly—too rapidly as technological developments overtake human values, or too slowly with the disintegration of quality in the built environment progressing just beyond our capacity to intuit the loss and react accordingly. The modern notion that the man-made world must be reinvented, "free of the inhibiting constraints of the past," as it is often put, presumes that by scientific means we can account for all the subtle human factors that traditional processes have accommodated in the long evolutionary descendence of the man-made world—through trial and error, patient refinement, and subtle adjustments in response to unaccountable characteristics that are so important to the satisfactory lives of communities and individuals. This is not to say that we should now abandon science and submit to what might be regarded as teleological forces outside our control. If human intelligence, judgment, and conscious choice are factored into the nebulous thing we call cultural evolution, blind determinism is not an issue.

Biologists tell us that the most serious threat to an effectively sustainable worldwide ecosystem is a sharp diminution in the number of species on earth—that is, in biodiversity—and an equally extensive diminution in genetic diversity among those particular species we permit to exist. (The diminution in biodiversity has come about because expanding cities, agriculture, and industry are taking up more land and because industrial effluents are poisoning the environment; the diminution in genetic diversity has come about because of such agricultural practices as monoculture and the extensive hybridization of food plants.) Upon reflection, there might be a direct parallel to this in the world of cities and their human communities. While once the number of "types" of traditional cities continued to proliferate, they are now being replaced by the relatively ubiquitous and comparatively undifferentiated "world city." And while cultural differences around the world were once virtually endless, we are now moving toward a homogeneous world culture where ethnic diversity is celebrated more as a quaint vestige of a former time rather than the basis for living communities. Biologists Theodosius Dobzhansky and Ernest Boesiger suggested that if we were to see human culture from an evolutionary—that is, natural—perspective, we would be in a better position to guide it toward a more positive future. They recounted a series of human events that served to guide cultural evolution in positive directions. Their list included the Magna Charta of 1215, the fundamental English law of *habeas corpus* of 1679, the American Declaration of Independence of 1776, the Declaration of the Rights of Man and the Citizen in 1789, and other events that have become, in their words, "milestones marking progress in the legal basis of informed consent—progress made necessary by the frightful possibilities of destruction that cultural evolution has given man." They remarked that, "Other organisms undergo biological evolution according to laws and mechanisms that they do not understand; man alone understands evolution . . . both his own and that of other species. Not only is he able to act and to intervene in his evolution, but *he does so,* massively, for better or for worse—whether or not he wishes to do so." Or to put it more directly, because we are conscious of our cultural evolution, it is incumbent upon us to guide its course: "The survival of the species will be possible only if we dispose of ethics and altruisms that are limited to family, tribe, or those who hold the same religion or philosophy," they wrote. "We are no longer animals who submit passively to the laws of nature. We have foresight and can act accordingly." Their conclusion was that, "The cultural evolution of man must now create a truly humanistic ethic."[3]

At the center of "the cultural evolution of man," as Dobzhansky and Boesiger referred to it, lies the city. Its purpose is, as it always has been, for us to define. Aristotle said that, "Men come together in the city for security; they stay together for the good life." By "good life" he meant a life that strives to be consistent with our highest ideals, and not in the materialistic sense we usually take that phrase to mean today. We have come to view the city first as a marketplace and only remotely as a place for "the good life" in the Aristotelian sense. The ancient Greeks founded their cities on an *acropolis*—a "high place"—by the sea. Once they felt secure in their new place, they moved down from it to build a city at its base. But they continued to maintain the acropolis, for on it were their most important religious and civic monuments. Later, as they added new buildings, they always kept the acropolis's identity as the clearest symbolic expression of their *polis*—that is, of their community, and its physical embodiment in the form of the city which sheltered their lives and accommodated their polity. The acropolis stood for the intangible, exalted, idealized, timeless, and historic: for all those things that are so easily obscured in the practicalities of the day-to-day world. Especially in our own time we need an equivalent to the embodied memory of an acropolis to remind us that the man-made world is a thing of our own creation and its flaws and triumphs are directly accountable to human agency alone.

Notes

Chapter 1

1

Cicero, *De natura deorum,* trans. by H. Rackham, Loeb Classical Library (Cambridge: Harvard University Press, 1979), 2.60.

2

Vitruvius, *De architectura,* 6, intro 1.

3

Peter J. Wilson, *The Domestication of the Human Species* (New Haven: Yale University Press, 1988), xii.

4

Blaise Pascal, *Pensées,* trans. by W. F. Trotter (New York: Random House, 1941), 36.

5

J. B. Jackson, *The Necessity for Ruins and Other Topics* (Amherst: University of Massachusetts Press, 1980), 27.

6

Hannah Arendt, *The Human Condition* (Chicago: University of Chicago Press, 1958), 173.

7

Although not universally held, shades of this concept of "a great chain of being" can be found throughout Western philosophical, religious, and scientific traditions up through the eighteenth century. See Arthur O. Lovejoy, *The Great Chain of Being: A Study of the History of an Idea* (Cambridge: Harvard University Press, 1964).

8

Archibald MacLeish, To face the real crisis: Man himself, *New York Times Magazine,* 25 December 1960, 29.

9

Lynn White, Jr., The historical roots of our ecologic crisis, *Science,* 10 March 1967, 1203–1207. This now famous essay, some believe, overemphasizes the role of religion as contributing to the environmental crisis. It is cited here not to suggest that Judeo-Christian belief is necessarily at the root of the problem but rather that belief itself is as important a determinant of actions as objective facts revealed through science, and that systems of belief do not easily yield to abrupt revelations, no matter how convincing they might be.

10

James L. Peacock, *The Anthropological Lens: Harsh Light, Soft Focus* (Cambridge: Cambridge University Press, 1986), 92.

11

Jacob Bronowski, *The Origins of Knowledge and Imagination* (New Haven: Yale University Press, 1978), ix.

12

Jacob Bronowski, *Science and Human Values,* rev. ed., Perennial Library (New York: Harper and Row, 1972), 16.

Chapter 2

1

Christine Hugh-Jones, *From the Milk River: Spatial and Temporal Processes in Northwest Amazonia* (Cambridge: Cambridge University Press, 1979), 235.

2

For a discussion of the Roman family with relation to the larger political units that comprised its society, see Joseph Rykwert, *The Idea of a Town: The Anthropology of Urban*

Form in Rome, Italy and the Ancient World (Cambridge: MIT Press, 1988).

3

Émile Durkheim and Marcel Mauss, *Primitive Classification,* trans. and ed. by Rodney Needham (London: Cohen & West, 1963) 82–83; quoted in Jonathan Z. Smith, *To Take Place: Toward Theory in Ritual* (Chicago: University of Chicago Press, 1987), 37.

4

Peter J. Wilson, *The Domestication of the Human Species* (New Haven: Yale University Press, 1988), 71.

5

Frank Mitchell, *Navajo Blessingway Singer: The Autobiography of Frank Mitchell, 1881– 1967,* ed. by Charlotte J. Frisbie and David P. McAllester (Tucson: University of Arizona Press, 1978), 244; quoted in David P. McAllester and Susan W. McAllester, *Hogans: Navajo Houses and House Songs* (Middletown, CT: Wesleyan University Press, 1980), epigraph.

6

For a more detailed argument involving changes in cosmologies and consequent treatment of the natural world between Pre-Neolithic and Neolithic ages, see Calvin Luther Martin, *In the Spirit of the Earth: Rethinking History and Time* (Baltimore: Johns Hopkins University Press, 1992).

7

Martin Heidegger, *Poetry, Language, Thought,* trans. by Albert Hofstadter (New York: Harper and Row, 1971), 146–147.

8

Gaston Bachelard, *The Poetics of Space,* trans. by Maria Jolas (New York: Orion Press, 1964), 4, 7.

9

Mircea Eliade, *The Sacred and the Profane: The Nature of Religion,* trans. by Willard R. Trask (San Diego: Harcourt Brace Jovanovich, 1959), 56–57.

10

Hugh-Jones, *From Milk River,* 235.

11

Eliade, *Sacred and Profane,* 58.

12

Immanuel Kant, *Kant's Inaugural Dissertation and Early Writings on Space,* trans. by John Handyside (Chicago: Open Court Publishing, 1929), 23; as quoted in Jonathan Z. Smith, *To Take Place: Toward Theory in Ritual* (Chicago: University of Chicago Press, 1987), 27.

13

The Note Books and Drawings of Louis I. Kahn, 2d ed. (Cambridge: MIT Press, 1973). The "1959" date is supplied by Alexandra Tyng, *Beginnings: Louis I. Kahn's Philosophy of Architecture* (New York: Wiley, 1984), 68.

14

Demetri Porphyrios, Building and architecture, *Building and Rational Architecture* (London: Architectural Design AD Editions, Architectural Design Profile 53, 1984), 31.

15

Cicero, *De oratore,* 3.46 (as quoted by Demetri Porphyrios in ibid., 30).

16

This is not to imply that Japanese civilization never learned stone masonry bearing wall construction methods. Numerous Japanese castles stand upon battered walls of stone that present a potential enemy with an impenetrable and fireproof structure. But while there evolved a very refined aesthetic of stone construction for a few buildings, dwellings and important civic buildings alike reflect a preference for the open timber frame.

17

Such subtle observation of nature in Japanese culture evolved from Shintoism, the indigenous religion of Japan, and was subsequently reinforced by Buddhist monks of the Zen sect. Thus religious precedents figure into this aspect of Japanese culture as surely as do architectural preferences. But, since my focus is on the built environment, a discussion of nonphysical effects would be a major digression.

18

Wilson, *Domestication of the Human Species,* 71.

19

Ibid., 66, 73.

Chapter 3

1

See chapter 3, "Creating a Second Nature" in Clarence J. Glacken, *Traces on the Rhodian Shore: Nature and Culture in Western Thought from Ancient Times to the End of the Eighteenth Century* (Berkeley: University of California Press, 1967).

2

Eugene Victor Walter, *Placeways: A Theory of the Human Environment* (Chapel Hill: University of North Carolina Press, 1988), 204.

3

Ibid., 18–19.

4

Ibid., 15.

5

Ibid., 142.

6

The terms "place theory," "topistics," and "environmental memory" are not equivalent as my use of them might imply. Different writers have used them in their discussions of sense of place. I refer the reader interested in the concept of environmental memory to Malcolm Quantrill, *The Environmental Memory: Man and Architecture in the Landscape of Ideas* (New York: Schocken Books, 1987), and in the concept of topistics to Walter, *Placeways.* An area of philosophy that has dealt with the sense of place is phenomenology. For a broad-brush approach to phenomenology as it applies to place theory in relation to architecture and the urban environment, see Christian Norberg-Schulz, *Genius Loci: Towards a Phenomenology of Architecture* (New York: Rizzoli, 1980).

7

Auguste Choisy, *Histoire de l'architecture* (Paris, 1899), 1:14; as quoted by Reyner Banham in *Theory and Design in the First Machine Age,* 2d ed. (New York: Praeger, 1967), 26.

8

See E. J. Owens, *The City in the Greek and Roman World* (London: Routledge, 1992), 117, for "centuriation." See chapter 4, "The Problem of Meaning" in William L. MacDonald, *The Pantheon: Design, Meaning, and Progeny* (Cambridge: Harvard University Press, 1976) regarding symbolic and metaphorical intent.

9

Mircea Eliade, *The Myth of the Eternal Return or, Cosmos and History,* trans. by Willard R. Trask, Bollingen Series 46 (Princeton: Princeton University Press, 1971), 10.

Chapter 4

1

For a more complete explanation of classical harmonics and its sources for architecture, see Rudolf Wittkower, *Architectural Principles in the Age of Humanism,* 4th ed. (London: Academy Editions, 1988).

2

Leone Battista Alberti, *Ten Books on Architecture,* trans. by James Leoni (1755; reprint ed. by Joseph Rykwert, London: Alec Tiranti, 1955), 9.5.

3

Vitruvius, *The Ten Books on Architecture,* trans. by Morris Hicky Morgan (New York: Dover, 1960), 3.1.2, p. 72.

4

Wittkower, *Architectural Principles,* 18.

5

Alberti, *Ten Books on Architecture,* 9.5. Also see Dorothy Koenigsberger, *Renaissance Man and Creative Thinking: A History of Concepts of Harmony, 1400–1700* (Atlantic Highlands, NJ: Humanities Press, 1979), 18–19.

6

While currently somewhat out of fashion in anthropological investigation, structural analysis continues to provide a useful means for understanding ritual and myth.

7

Alexander Alland, Jr., *The Artistic Animal: An Inquiry into the Biological Roots of Art* (New York: Doubleday, 1977), 85.

8

Vitruvius, *Ten Books on Architecture,* 6.1.1, p. 170.

9

See Mircea Eliade, *The Myth of the Eternal Return or, Cosmos and History,* trans. by Willard R. Trask, Bollingen Series 46 (Princeton: Princeton University Press, 1971).

10

Edith Hamilton, *The Greek Way, The Roman Way* (1930–1932; reprint New York: Bonanza Books, 1986), 221.

11

Hannah Arendt, *The Human Condition* (Chicago: University of Chicago Press, 1958), 26.

12

Martin Heidegger, *An Introduction to Metaphysics,* trans. by Ralph Manheim (New Haven: Yale University Press, 1959), 152.

13

Robert Jan van Pelt and Carroll William Westfall, *Architectural Principles in the Age of Historicism* (New Haven: Yale University Press, 1991), 192.

14

Hamilton, *Greek Way,* 222.

15

Benoit B. Mandelbrot, *The Fractal Geometry of Nature,* rev. ed. (New York: Freeman, 1983).

16

Frank Lloyd Wright was quite familiar with classical design techniques, which he would have learned in his apprenticeship in the office of Louis H. Sullivan who reworked classical principles to the problems of new building types and expressive qualities, which he believed to be appropriate to the commercial and industrial needs of the North American city.

17

James Gleick, *Chaos: Making a New Science* (New York: Penguin Books, 1988), 117.

18

See Alberto Pérez-Gómez, *Architecture and the Crisis of Modern Science* (Cambridge: MIT Press, 1983).

Chapter 5

1

Marcus Aurelius, *Meditations,* trans. by Maxwell Staniforth (New York: Penguin, 1964), 6.15 (p. 93).

2

Leonardo da Vinci, *Codice Atlantico,* 71 r.a.; as quoted by Dorothy Koenigsberger, *Renaissance Man and Creative Thinking: A History of Concepts of Harmony, 1400–1700* (Atlantic Highlands, NJ: Humanities Press, 1979), 151.

3

See Indra Kagis McEwen, *Socrates' Ancestor: An Essay on Architectural Beginnings* (Cambridge: MIT Press, 1993), 32–38.

4

For a more detailed explanation of the philosophical and scientific impact of astrolobes and calendars, see J. T. Fraser, *Of Time, Passion, and Knowledge: Reflections on the Strategy of Existence,* 2d ed. (Princeton: Princeton University Press, 1990).

5

Vitruvius, *The Ten Books on Architecture,* trans. by Morris Hicky Morgan (1914; New York: Dover, 1960), 6.1.1.

6

Cicero, *Tusculan Disputations,* trans. by J. E. King, Loeb Classical Library (Cambridge: Harvard University Press, 1989), 1.25.

7

Lynn White, Jr., *Medieval Technology and Social Change* (Oxford: Oxford University Press, 1962), 124.

8

George Kubler, *The Shape of Time: Remarks on the History of Things* (New Haven: Yale University Press, 1962), 2.

9

See Thomas S. Kuhn, *The Structure of Scientific Revolutions* 2d ed. (Chicago: University of Chicago Press, 1970). Although important, it is not within the scope of this book to engage in a discussion of the place of invention in the evolution of things. Kuhn's now familiar essay considers the "paradigmatic shifts" that occur from time to time in scientific inquiry and alter the general direction of our understanding of nature and the sciences. Also see James Burk, *Connections* (Boston: Little, Brown, 1978), for a discussion of inventions and their antecedents.

10

As quoted in François Bucher, *Architector: The Lodge Books and Sketchbooks of Medieval Architects,* vol. 1 (New York: Abaris Books, 1979), 14.

11

Aldo Rossi, *The Architecture of the City,* trans. by Diane Ghirardo and Joan Ockman (Cambridge: MIT Press, 1982), 59.

12

The Ionian Greeks were a notable exception for reasons of their own history, as mentioned in chapter 3.

13

Vitruvius, *Ten Books on Architecture,* 2.1.3; preceding material from 2.1.1, 2, 6.

14

For a careful treatment of Aristotelian aesthetic principles as applied to architecture, and particularly the Greek concept of *mimesis,* see Demetri Porphyrios, *Classical Architecture: The Living Tradition* (New York: McGraw-Hill, 1992), especially the chapter, "Imitation in Architecture."

15

Vitruvius, *Ten Books on Architecture,* 2.1.4–5.

16

Ibid., 2.1.8.

17

Ibid., 4.2.5–6.

18

For more dteails on the concept of nature by Vitruvius and his contemporaries, see Frank E. Brown, Vitruvius and the liberal art of architecture, *Bucknell Review* 11, no. 4 (1963): 99–107.

19

Joseph Rykwert, *The Necessity of Artifice: Ideals in Architecture* (New York: Rizzoli, 1982), 41.

20

Gottfried Semper, Development of architectural style, trans. by John W. Root, *The Inland Architect and News Record* 14 (1889); 76.

21

Eugène-Emmanuel Viollet-le-Duc, *Dictionnaire raisonné de l'Architecture Française,* vol. 8, p. 495; as quoted in Philip Steadman, *The Evolution of Designs* (Cambridge: Cambridge University Press, 1979), 72.

22

Karl R. Popper, *Objective Knowledge: An Evolutionary Approach* (Oxford: Clarendon Press, 1972), 267.

23

Kubler, *Shape of Time,* 1962, 124.

24

Loren Eiseley, *The Firmament of Time* (New York: Atheneum, 1966), 56.

Chapter 6

1

Plato, *Timaeus,* trans. by Benjamin Jowett (New York: Bobbs-Merrill, 1949), 37–38.

2

For a more comprehensive discussion, see Demetri Porphyrios, *Classical Architecture: The Living Tradition* (New York: McGraw-Hill, 1992), especially the chapter, "Imitation in Architecture."

3

Alexander Alland, Jr., *The Artistic Animal: An Inquiry into the Biological Roots of Art* (New York: Doubleday, 1977), 41.

4

Ibid.

5

Ibid., 29.

6

Claude Lévi-Strauss, *The Savage Mind* (Chicago: University of Chicago Press, 1966), 30.

7

Aristotle on the Art of Poetry, trans. by Ingram Bywater, rev. ed. (Oxford: Clarendon Press, 1909), 23–25.

8

Leon Battista Alberti, *On the Art of Building in Ten Books,* trans. by Joseph Rykwert, Neil Leach, and Robert Tavernor (Cambridge: MIT Press, 1988), 156 (6.2) and 23 (1.9).

9

My use of the term *"lineaments"* for this matrix of lines reflects the Rykwert-Leach-Tavernor translation of Alberti's treatise. For a more comprehensive treatment of this, as well as other rules and procedures of designing classical architecture, see Alexander Tzonis and Liane Lefaivre, *Classical Architecture: The Poetics of Order* (Cambridge: MIT Press, 1986). Rather than "lineaments" or *"lineamenta,"* Tzonis and Lefaivre use terms from poetic traditions to more fully describe the subtleties of these operations which I have described very briefly. They use the term "taxis" for the matrix of lines that controls the composition of a work of architecture, and the term "scancion" to describe the process of analyzing a building design by using overlays, in effect, to re-create the lineaments, or "lines of taxis."

10

A somewhat mystical approach to the role of lineaments emerges in Sebastiano Serlio's tratise *Tutte l'opere d'architectura* written c. 1537–1553. For more on instances of Neo-platonic and Pythagorean magic in Italian Renaissance architecture, see G. L. Hersey, *Pythagorean Palaces: Magic and Architecture in the Italian Renaissance* (Ithaca, NY: Cornell University Press, 1976).

11

Liang Ssu-ch'eng, *A Pictorial History of Chinese Architecture: A Study of the Development of Its Structural System and the Evolution of Its Types,* ed. by Wilma Fairbank (Cambridge: MIT Press, 1984), 15.

12

Sukiya architecture is usually described as independent of other architectural traditions, though it manifests the influence of two residential architectural forms, *shoin* and *minka.* The architectural tradition with which it is most closely allied is the *shoin* tradition. A principle characteristic of the *shoin* is that it permits a full exploitation of the structural grid of posts and beams, a feature that translates directly to the *sukiya.* Sometimes the *sukiya* is referred to as *"sukiya shoin."* The rural architecture known as the *minka,* essentially a peasant house, employs a trussed roof structure in such a way as to more fully constrain the overall building form.

13

Teiji Itoh, *The Classic Tradition in Japanese Architecture: Modern Versions of the Sukiya Style,* trans. by Richard L. Gage (New York: Weatherhill, 1972), 26. The situation described here reflects the traditional planning of a residence "in the *sukiya* style." Recent civic buildings that are considered to be of this tradition are produced under the more strict guidance of an architect just as with other architectural commisions. It appears that in the case of complex modern public ownership, building codes, and the relative complexity of modern buildings with their mechanical and electrical systems, the quasi-ritualized approach to the planning of the building cannot be applied in the traditional way. See ibid., 26–28.

14

Nader Ardalan and Laleh Bakhtiar, *The Sense of Unity: The Sufi Tradition in Persian Architecture* (Chicago: University of Chicago Press, 1973), 5.

15

Ibid., 27.

16

Andrea Palladio, *Quattro Libri,* 2.16; as quoted in James S. Ackerman, *Palladio* (Baltimore, MD: Penguin, 1966), 65. I have used Ackerman's translation rather than the more familiar Issac Ware translation of 1738 because the language is more modern.

17

Munroe Smith, *Jurisprudence* (New York: Columbia University Press, 1909), 21; as quoted in Benjamin N. Cardozo, *The Nature of the Judicial Process* (New Haven: Yale University Press, 1949), 23.

18

Benjamin N. Cardozo, *Nature of the Judicial Process,* 19.

19

Edward H. Levi, *An Introduction to Legal Reasoning* (Chicago: University of Chicago Press, 1949), 1.

20

See Robert McCrum, William Cran, and Robert MacNeil, *The Story of English* (New York: Viking, 1986), 38.

21

Alexander Tzonis and Liane Lefaivre, *Classical Architecture: The Poetics of Order* (Cambridge: MIT Press, 1986), 275.

Chapter 7

1

G. Charbonnier, *Conversations with Claude Lévi-Strauss,* trans. by John and Doreen Weightman (London: Jonathan Cape, 1969), 97.

2

Hannah Arendt, *The Human Condition* (Chicago: University of Chicago Press, 1958), 167–168.

3

Peter J. Wilson, *The Domestication of the Human Species,* (New Haven: Yale University Press, 1988), 57.

4

Ibid., 155. "Domesticated society" is Wilson's term for communities that dwell within permanent settlements as opposed, for instance, to nomadic societies of hunter-gatherers, temporary (seasonal) villagers, or slash-and-burn farmers.

5

H. E. Priestley, *London: The Years of Change* (London: Fredrick Muller, 1966), 33.

6

The definition is from Charbonnier, *Conversations with Claude Lévi-Strauss,* 147.

7

Ibid.

8

Although the city arising after the establishment of agriculture is thought to be the usual sequence, there is also a convincing argument that cities made agriculture possible. This argument posits that cities arose beside some natural amenity such as a flint deposit. The city's inhabitants lived by trading either the raw flint or objects crafted from it (most likely arrow and spear heads), or both, for food gathered by passing hunter-gatherer groups. See Jane Jacobs, *The Economy of Cities* (New York: Random House, 1969).

9

Gideon Sjoberg, The origin and evolution of cities. In *Cities: Their Origin, Growth, and Human Impact.* Readings from *Scientific American* (San Francisco: W.H. Freeman, 1954–1973), 20.

10

James E. Vance, Jr., *This Scene of Man: The Role and Structure of the City in the Geography of Western Civilization* (New York: Harper and Row, 1977), 19.

11

See the discussion in William H. McNeill, ed., Microparasitism, macroparasitism, and the urban transmutation, *The Human Condition: An Ecological and Historical View* (Princeton: Princeton University Press, 1980).

12

Charbonnier, *Conversations with Claude Lévi-Strauss,* 30.

13

Ibid. 31.

14

For more on the relationship of initial settlement patterns to their growth and change as cities, see Vance, *This Scene of Man.*

15

Aldo Rossi, *The Architecture of the City,* trans. by Diane Ghirardo and Joan Ockman (Cambridge: MIT Press, 1982), 29.

16

Herbert J. Muller, *The Uses of the Past: Profiles of Former Societies* (Oxford: Oxford University Press, 1957), 22.

17

See the chapter by Westfall entitled "Cities" in Robert Jan van Pelt and Carroll William Westfall, *Architectural Principles in the Age of Historicism* (New Haven: Yale University Press, 1991).

18

This is not to say that such severe measures as cutting new boulevards through medieval Paris did not produce considerable pain and were not met with broadly based public resistance. But once each of these drastic measures was complete and finally absorbed into the social fabric of the city, life eventually returned to comparative tranquility based on more or less traditional social patterns.

19

See Leon Krier, What is an urban quarter? Form and legislation. In *Leon Krier: Houses, Palaces, Cities,* ed. by Demetri Porphyrios (London: AD Editions, Architectural Design Profile 54, 1984), 78–79.

Conclusion

1

Claude Lévi-Strauss, trans. by Joachim Neugroschel and Phoebe Hoss, *The View from Afar* (New York: Basic Books, 1985), 119–120.

2

Edoardo Fazzioli, *Chinese Calligraphy: From Pictograph to Ideogram: The History of 214 Essential Chinese/Japanese Characters* (New York: Abbeville Press, 1987), 13.

3

Theodosius Dobzhansky and Ernest Boesiger, *Human Culture: A Moment in Evolution,* ed. by Bruce Wallace (New York: Columbia University Press, 1983), 106–108.

Bibliography

Akurgal, Ekrem. *Ancient Civilizations and Ruins of Turkey: From Prehistoric Times until the End of the Roman Empire.* Trans. by John Whybrow and Mollie Emre. 6th ed. Istanbul: Haset Kitabevi, 1985.

Alberti, Leon Battista. *On the Art of Building in Ten Books.* Trans. by Joseph Rykwert, Neil Leach, and Robert Tavernor. Cambridge: MIT Press, 1988.

Alberti, Leone Battista, *Ten Books on Architecture.* Trans. by James Leoni. 1755. Reprint. Ed. by Joseph Rykwert. London: Alec Tiranti, 1955.

Alland, Alexander, Jr. *The Artistic Animal: An Inquiry into the Biological Roots of Art.* New York: Doubleday, 1977.

Ardalan, Nader, and Laleh Bakhtiar. *The Sense of Unity: The Sufi Tradition in Persian Architecture.* Chicago: University of Chicago Press, 1973.

Arendt, Hannah. *The Human Condition.* Chicago: University of Chicago Press, 1958.

Bachelard, Gaston. *The Poetics of Space.* Trans. by Maria Jolas. New York: Orion Press, 1964.

Balfour, Henry. *The Natural History of the Musical Bow: A Chapter in the Developmental History of Stringed Instruments of Music.* 1899. Reprint. Portland, ME: Longwood Press, 1976.

Barkan, Leonard. *Nature's Work of Art: The Human Body as Image of the World.* New Haven: Yale University Press, 1975.

Bloomer, Kent C., and Charles W. Moore. *Body, Memory, and Architecture.* New Haven: Yale University Press, 1977.

Bronowski, Jacob. *The Origins of Knowledge and Imagination.* New Haven: Yale University Press, 1978.

Bronowski, Jacob. *Science and Human Values.* Rev. ed. Perennial Library. New York: Harper and Row, 1972.

Brown, Frank E. Vitruvius and the liberal art of architecture. *Bucknell Review* 11, no. 4 (1963): 99–107.

Bucher, François. *Architector: The Lodge Books and Sketchbooks of Medieval Architects.* Vol. 1. New York: Abaris Books, 1979.

Cardozo, Benjamin N. *The Nature of the Judicial Process.* New Haven: Yale University Press, 1949.

Charbonnier, G. *Conversations with Claude Lévi-Strauss.* Trans. by John and Doreen Weightman. London: Jonathan Cape, 1969.

Clegg, Samuel, Jr., *Architecture of Machinery: An Essay on Propriety of Form and Proportion, with a View to Assist and Improve Design.* London: Architectural Library, 1842.

Collingwood, R. G. *The Idea of Nature.* Oxford: Oxford University Press, 1960.

Coulton, J. J. *Ancient Greek Architects at Work : Problems of Structure and Design.* Ithaca, NY: Cornell University Press, 1977.

Dobzhansky, Theodosius, and Ernest Boesiger. *Human Culture: A Moment in Evolution.* Ed. and comp. by Bruce Wallace. New York: Columbia University Press, 1983.

Eisley, Loren. *The Invisible Pyramid.* New York: Scribner's, 1970.

Eiseley, Loren. *The Firmament of Time.* New York: Atheneum, 1960.

Eliade, Mircea. *The Myth of the Eternal Return or, Cosmos and History.* Trans. by Willard R. Trask. Bollingen Series 46. Princeton: Princeton University Press, 1971.

Eliade, Mircea. *The Sacred and the Profane:The Nature of Religion.* Trans. by Willard R. Trask. San Diego: Harcourt Brace Jovanovich, 1959.

Elvee, Richard Q., ed. *Mind in Nature.* Nobel Conference 17. San Francisco: Harper and Row, 1982.

Fraser, J. T. *Of Time, Passion, and Knowledge: Reflections on the Strategy of Existence.* 2d ed. Princeton: Princeton University Press, 1990.

Gadol, Joan. *Leon Battista Alberti: Universal Man of the Early Renaissance.* Chicago: University of Chicago Press, 1969.

Gingerich, Owen, comp. *Scientific Genius and Creativity.* Readings from *Scientific American.* New York: W.H. Freeman, 1982.

Glacken, Clarence J. *Traces on the Rhodian Shore: Nature and Culture in Western Thought from Ancient Times to the End of the Eighteenth Century.* Berkeley: University of California Press, 1967.

Gleick, James. *Chaos: Making a New Science.* New York: Penguin Books, 1988.

Gombrich, E. H. *The Sense of Order: A Study in the Psychology of Decorative Art.* Ithaca, NY: Cornell University Press, 1979.

Haddon, Alfred C. *Evolution in Art: As Illustrated by the Life Histories of Designs.* 1895. Reprint. New York: AMS Press, 1979.

Hall, Edward T. *Beyond Culture.* New York: Doubleday, 1981.

Hall, Edward T. *The Hidden Dimension.* New York: Doubleday, 1982.

Hamilton, Edith. *The Greek Way, The Roman Way.* 1930–32. Reprint (2 vols. in 1). New York: Bonanza Books, 1986.

Haselberger, Lothar. The construction plans for the Temple of Apollo at Didyma. *Scientific American* 253 (December 1985): 126–132.

Heidegger, Martin. *Poetry, Language, Thought.* Trans. by Albert Hofstadter. New York: Harper and Row, 1971.

Herrmann, Wolfgang. *Gottfried Semper: In Search of Architecture.* Cambridge: MIT Press, 1984.

Hersey, G. L. *Pythagorean Palaces: Magic and Architecture in the Italian Renaissance.* Ithaca, NY: Cornell University Press, 1976.

Hill, Melvyn A., ed. *Hannah Arendt: The Recovery of the Public World.* New York: St. Martin's Press, 1979.

Itoh, Teiji. *The Classic Tradition in Japanese Architecture: Modern Versions of the Sukiya Style.* Trans. by Richard L. Gage. New York: John Weatherhill, 1972.

Jackson, J. B. *The Necessity for Ruins and Other Topics.* Amherst: University of Massachusetts Press, 1980.

Koenigsberger, Dorothy. *Renaissance Man and Creative Thinking: A History of Concepts of Harmony, 1400–1700.* Atlantic Highlands, NJ: Humanities Press, 1979.

Kostof, Spiro. *The City Assembled: The Elements of Urban Form through History.* Boston: Little, Brown/Bulfinch Press, 1992.

Kostof, Spiro. *The City Shaped: Urban Patterns and Meanings through History.* New York: Little, Brown/Bulfinch Press, 1991.

Kostof, Spiro. *A History of Architecture: Settings and Rituals.* Oxford: Oxford University Press, 1985.

Krier, Leon. *Leon Krier: Houses, Palaces, Cities.* Ed. by Demetri Porphyrios. Architectural Design Profile 54. London: Architectural Design AD Editions, 1984.

Kubler, George. *The Shape of Time: Remarks on the History of Things.* New Haven: Yale University Press, 1962.

Kuhn, Thomas S. *The Structure of Scientific Revolutions.* 2d ed. Chicago: University of Chicago Press, 1970.

Laugier, Marc-Antoine. *An Essay on Architecture.* Trans. by Wolfgang and Anni Herrmann. Los Angeles: Hennessey and Ingalls, 1977.

Lavin, Sylvia. *Quatremère de Quincy and the Invention of a Modern Language of Architecture.* Cambridge: MIT Press, 1992.

Lentz, Thomas W., and Glenn D. Lowry. *Timur and the Princely Vision: Persian Art and Culture in the Fifteenth Century.* Los Angeles: Los Angeles County Museum of Art, 1989.

Lethaby, W. R. *Architecture: An Introduction to the History and Theory of the Art of Building.* 3d ed. Oxford: Oxford University Press, 1955.

Lethaby, W. R. *Architecture, Nature and Magic.* New York: George Braziller, 1956.

Lethaby, W. R. *Form in Civilization: Collected Papers on Art and Labour.* Oxford: Oxford University Press, 1922.

Lethaby, W. R. *Londinium: Architecture and the Crafts.* London, 1923. Reprint. New York: Benjamin Blom, 1972.

Lévi-Strauss, Claude. *Structural Anthropology.* Translated by C. Jacobson and B. G. Schoepf. New York: Basic Books, 1963.

Lévi-Strauss, Claude. *The Savage Mind.* Chicago: University of Chicago Press, 1966.

Lévi-Strauss, Claude. *Tristes Tropiques.* Trans. by John and Doreen Weightman. New York: Atheneum, 1973.

Lévi-Strauss, Claude. *The View from Afar.* Trans. by Joachim Neugroschel and Phoebe Hoss. New York: Basic Books, 1985.

Liang Ssu-ch'eng. *A Pictorial History of Chinese Architecture: A Study of the Development of Its Structural System and the Evolution of Its Types.* Ed. by Wilma Fairbank. Cambridge: MIT Press, 1984.

Lovejoy, Arthur O. *The Great Chain of Being: A Study of the History of an Idea.* Cambridge: Harvard University Press, 1964.

MacDonald, William L. *The Pantheon: Design, Meaning, and Progeny.* Cambridge: Harvard University Press, 1976.

McEwen, Indra Kagis. *Socrates' Ancestor: An Essay on Architectural Beginnings.* Cambridge: MIT Press, 1993.

McNeill, William H. *The Human Condition: An Ecological and Historical View.* Princeton: Princeton University Press, 1980.

Macsai, John, and Paul Doukas. Expressed frame and the classical order in the transitional period of Italy, 1918–1939. *Journal of Architectural Education* 40, no. 4 (Summer 1987): 10–17.

Mandelbrot, Benoit B. *The Fractal Geometry of Nature.* Rev. ed. New York: W. H. Freeman, 1983.

Mander, Jerry. *In the Absence of the Sacred: The Failure of Technology and the Survival of the Indian Nations.* San Francisco: Sierra Club Books, 1991.

Martin, Calvin Luther. *In the Spirit of the Earth: Rethinking History and Time.* Baltimore: Johns Hopkins University Press, 1992.

Mitchell, Frank. *Navajo Blessingway Singer: The Autobiography of Frank Mitchell, 1881– 1967.* Ed. by Charlotte J. Frisbie and David P. McAllester. Tucson: University of Arizona Press, 1978.

Muller, Herbert J. *Freedom in the Ancient World.* New York: Harper, 1961.

Muller, Herbert J. *The Uses of the Past: Profiles of Former Societies.* Oxford: Oxford University Press, 1957.

Norberg-Schulz, Christian. *Genius Loci: Towards a Phenomenology of Architecture.* New York: Rizzoli, 1980.

Ortiz, Alfonso. *The Tewa World: Space, Time, Being, and Becoming in a Pueblo Society.* Chicago: University of Chicago Press, 1969.

Owens, E. J., *The City in the Greek and Roman World.* London: Routledge, 1992.

Papadakis, Andreas, and Harriet Watson, eds. *New Classicism: Omnibus Volume.* New York: Rizzoli, 1990.

Peacock, James L. *The Anthropological Lens: Harsh Light, Soft Focus.* Cambridge: Cambridge University Press, 1986.

Pérez-Gómez, Alberto. *Architecture and the Crisis of Modern Science.* Cambridge: MIT Press, 1983.

Plato. *Timaeus.* Trans. by Benjamin Jowett. New York: Bobbs-Merrill, 1949.

Popper, Karl R. *Objective Knowledge: An Evolutionary Approach.* Oxford: Clarendon Press, 1972.

Porphyrios, Demetri. *Classical Architecture: The Living Tradition.* New York: McGraw-Hill, 1992.

Quantrill, Malcolm. *The Environmental Memory: Man and Architecture in the Landscape of Ideas.* New York: Schocken Books, 1987.

Quantrill, Malcolm, and Bruce Webb, eds. *Constancy and Change in Architecture.* College Station, TX: Texas A&M University Press, 1991. Authors: Kenneth Frampton, Karsten Harries, Christian Norberg-Schulz, Alberto Pérez-Gómez, Joseph Rykwert, Marco Frascari and Claudio Sgarbi, Grey Gowrie, Stanford Anderson.

Rohr, René R. *Sundials: History, Theory, and Practice.* Toronto: University of Toronto Press, 1970.

Rossi, Aldo. *The Architecture of the City.* Trans. by Diane Ghirardo and Joan Ockman. Cambridge: MIT Press, 1982.

Rykwert, Joseph. *On Adam's House in Paradise: The Idea of the Primitive Hut in Architectural History.* 2d ed. Cambridge: MIT Press, 1981.

Rykwert, Joseph. *The Idea of a Town: The Anthropology of Urban Form in Rome, Italy and the Ancient World.* Cambridge: MIT Press, 1988.

Rykwert, Joseph. *The Necessity of Artifice: Ideals in Architecture*. New York: Rizzoli, 1982.

Scully, Vincent. *Architecture: The Natural and the Manmade*. New York: St. Martin's Press, 1991.

Scully, Vincent. *The Earth, The Temple, and the Gods: Greek Sacred Architecture*. Rev. ed. New Haven: Yale University Press, 1979.

Scully, Vincent. *Pueblo: Mountain, Village, Dance*. New York: Viking Press, 1975.

Semper, Gottfried. *The Four Elements of Architecture and Other Writings*. Trans. by H. F. Mallgrave and Wolfgang Herrmann. Cambridge: Cambridge University Press, 1989.

Sennett, Richard, ed. *Classic Essays on the Culture of Cities*. New York: Meredith Corporation, 1969.

Serlio, Sebastiano. *Tutte l'opere d'architettura*. 1611. Eng. ed. Lib. 1–5. New York: Benjamin Blom, 1970.

Simon, Herbert A. *The Sciences of the Artificial*. 2d ed. Cambridge: MIT Press, 1981.

Sjoberg, Gideon. The origin and evolution of cities. *Cities: Their Origin, Growth, and Human Impact*. Readings from *Scientific American*. Comp. by Kingsley Davis. San Francisco: W.H. Freeman, 1954–1973.

Sjoberg, Gideon. *The Preindustrial City: Past and Present*. New York: Macmillan, 1960.

Smith, Jonathan Z. *To Take Place: Toward Theory in Ritual*. Chicago: University of Chicago Press, 1987.

Smith, Peter F. *Architecture and the Principle of Harmony*. London: RIBA Publications, 1987.

Steadman, Philip. *The Evolution of Designs: Biological Analogy in Architecture and the Applied Arts*. Cambridge: Cambridge University Press, 1979.

Strauss, Leo. *Natural Right and History*. Chicago: University of Chicago Press, 1953.

Summerson, John. *The Classical Language of Architecture*. Cambridge: MIT Press, 1963.

Thompson, D'Arcy Wentworth. *On Growth and Form*. Abr. ed. Ed. by John T. Bonner. London: Cambridge University Press, 1961.

Tillyard, E. M. W. *The Elizabethan World Picture*. London: Chatto and Windus, 1943.

Toulmin, Stephen and June Goodfield. *The Discovery of Time*. Chicago: University of Chicago Press, 1982.

Tuan, Yi-Fu, *Topophilia: A Study of Environmental Perception, Attitudes, and Values*. Englewood Cliffs, NJ: Prentice-Hall, Inc., 1974.

Tzonis, Alexander, and Liane Lefaivre. *Classical Architecture: The Poetics of Order*. Cambridge: MIT Press, 1986.

Van Der Laan, Dom H. *Architectonic Space*. Trans. by Richard Padovin. Leiden: E. J. Brill, 1983.

Van Pelt, Robert Jan, and Carroll William Westfall. *Architectural Principles in the Age of Historicism*. New Haven: Yale University Press, 1991.

Vance, James E., Jr. *This Scene of Man: The Role and Structure of the City in the Geography of Western Civilization*. New York: Harper and Row, 1977.

Vernant, Jean-Pierre. *The Origins of Greek Thought*. Ithaca, NY: Cornell University Press, 1982.

Vidler, Anthony. *The Writing of the Walls.* Princeton: Princeton Architectural Press, 1987.

Vitruvius. *The Ten Books on Architecture.* Tran. by Morris Hicky Morgan. New York: Dover, 1960.

Walter, Eugene Victor. *Placeways: A Theory of the Human Environment.* Chapel Hill: University of North Carolina Press, 1988.

Wiebenson, Dora, ed. *Architectural Theory and Practice from Alberti to Ledoux.* Chicago: Architectural Publications, 1982.

Wilson, Peter J. *The Domestication of the Human Species.* New Haven: Yale University Press, 1988.

Wittkower, Rudolf. *Architectural Principles in the Age of Humanism.* 4th ed. London: Academy Editions, 1988.

Wycherley, R. E. *How the Greeks Built Cities.* New York: Doubleday, 1969.

Illustration Sources

Frontispiece:

From Vitruvio, *De architectura,* 1521 edition (facsimile edition with introductions in Italian and English, Milan: Edizioni Il Polifilo).

1.2

(c) Photo: James Tice.

1.4

Reprinted by permission of The New York Public Library, courtesy of Art and Architecture Collection, Wallach Division of Art, Prints and Photographs; Lenox and Tilden Foundations.

1.5

From E. Sommier, *Vaux-le-Vicomte: Notice Historique* (Paris: Edition Particulier, 1933).

1.6

Photo: Brian Crumlish.

2.1

Chinese ideogram from M. Silverstein, in *Dwelling, Seeing, and Designing: Toward a Phenomenological Ecology,* ed. by David Seaman (Albany: State University of New York Press, 1984). Petroglyph and village plan from M. Gimbutas, *The Civilization of the Goddess* (San Francisco: Harper, 1991).

2.4

Drawing: Christopher Placco.

2.5

(a) Drawing: Christopher Placco. (b) From J. N. L. Durand, *Recueil et parallele des edifices de tout genre, anciens et modernes* (Paris, 1801), courtesy Department of Special Collections, University Libraries of Notre Dame.

2.6

Drawing: Christopher Placco.

2.7

Drawing: Christopher Placco.

2.15

From Warner Blaser, *Japanese Temples and Tea Houses* (New York: F.W. Dodge, 1956).

2.16

After drawings in Franz Hart, *Kunst und Tecnik der Wölbung* (Munich: Verlag Georg D.W. Callwey, 1956).

2.17

After drawings in Franz Hart, *Kunst und Tecnik der Wölbung* (Munich: Verlag Georg D.W. Callwey, 1956).

2.18

(a) Drawing: Christopher Placco. (b) Drawing: Du Dong.

2.19

From Warner Blaser, *Japanese Temples and Tea Houses* (New York: F.W. Dodge, 1956).

3.1

Photo: Michael Lykoudis.

3.5

From Antoine Desgodets, *Les Édifices antiques de Rome, dessinès et mesurès trés exactement* (Paris, 1779), courtesy Department of Special Collections, University Libraries of Notre Dame.

4.1

The Winslow drawing is from Beneigus Winslow, *The Uncertainty of the Signs of Death and the Danger of Percepitale Intermentes and Dissection* (Dublin: George Faulkner, 1748).

4.2

From Vitruvio, *De architectura,* 1521 edition (facsimile edition with introductions in Italian and English, Milan: Edizioni Il Polifilo).

4.5

From Sebastiano Serlio, *Tutte l'opera d'archi-tettura* (Venezia, 1619), courtesy Department of Special Collections, University Libraries of Notre Dame.

4.6

Analysis and drawings: John Stanton.

4.7

Courtesy of the Rare Books Room and Manu-script Division, New York Public Library; As-tor, Lenox and Tilden Foundations.

5.1

From Steen Eiler Rasmussen, *Experiencing Architecture* (Cambridge: MIT Press, 1962).

5.5

From Vitruvio, *De architectura,* 1521 edition (facsimile edition with introductions in Ital-ian and English, Milan: Edizioni Il Polifilo).

5.8

From Sebastiano Serlio, *Tutte l'opere d'architet-tura* (Venezia: 1619), courtesy Department of Special Collections, University Libraries of Notre Dame, and Sir William Chambers, *A Treatise on Civil Architecture* (London: Harbe-korn, 1759).

5.9

From Eugène Viollet-le-Duc, *Discourses on Architecture,* vol. 2.

6.1

From Jules Gaihabaud, *Monuments anciens et modernes* (Paris: Librarie de Firmin Didot Fréres, Fils et Cie, 1857).

6.2

(*a*) From Liang Ssu-ch'eng, *A Pictorial His-tory of Chinese Architecture,* ed. by W. Fair-bank (Cambridge: MIT Press, 1984);

reproduced by permission. (*b*) From J. N. L. Durand, *Recueil et parallèle des édifices en tout genre* (Paris: 1801), courtesy Department of Special Collections, University Libraries of Notre Dame.

6.3

From Sir William Chambers, *A Treatise on Civil Architecture* (London: Harbekorn, 1759).

6.4

From Sir William Chambers, *A Treatise on Civil Architecture* (London: Harbekorn, 1759).

6.5

From Sir William Chambers, *A Treatise on Civil Architecture* (London: Harbekorn, 1759), and Nicholas Revett, *Antiquities of Ionia.*

6.6

From Vitruvio, *De architectura,* 1521 edition (facsimile edition with introductions in Ital-ian and English, Milan: Edizioni Il Polifilo), and Sebastiano Serlio, *Tutte l'opere d'architet-tura* (Venezia: 1619) courtesy Department of Special Collections, University Libraries of Notre Dame.

6.7

From Paul Laseau and James Tice, *Frank Lloyd Wright: Between Principle and Form* (New York: Van Nostrand Reinhold, 1991); reproduced with permission of the authors.

6.8

Drawing and analysis: Fritz Read.

6.9

Based on a drawing by Paul Marie Letarou-illy in *Le Vatican et la basilique de Saint-Pierre de Rome* (Paris: Vve A. Morel et Cie, 1882).

6.11
From Vitruvio, *De architectura,* 1521 edition (facsimile edition with introductions in Italian and English, Milan: Edizioni Il Polifilo).

6.12
From Jacques-François Blondel, *L'Architecture française,* vol. 3 (Paris: 1752–56).

6.13
From From Liang Ssu-ch'eng, *A Pictorial History of Chinese Architecture,* ed. by W. Fairbank (Cambridge: MIT Press, 1984); reproduced by permission.

6.14
From From Liang Ssu-ch'eng, *A Pictorial History of Chinese Architecture,* ed. by W. Fairbank (Cambridge: MIT Press, 1984); reproduced by permission.

6.15
From From Liang Ssu-ch'eng, *A Pictorial History of Chinese Architecture,* ed. by W. Fairbank (Cambridge: MIT Press, 1984); reproduced by permission.

6.16
From Harmuichi Kitao, *Cha-No-Yu Houses* (Tokyo: Shokokusha Publishing Co., 1953).

6.17
From Werner Blaser, *Japanese Temples and Tea-houses* (New York: F.W. Dodge, 1956).

6.18
From Edward S. Morse, *Japanese Homes and Their Surroundings* (New York: Dover, 1961), and Harumichi Kitao, *Cha-No-Yu Houses* (Toyko: Shokokusha Publishing Co., 1953).

6.19
From Edward S. Morse, *Japanese Homes and Their Surroundings* (New York: Dover, 1961).

6.20
After drawings in Keith Kritchlow, *Islamic Patterns: An Analytical and Cosmological Approach* (London; Thames and Hudson, 1976), and Arthur Upham Pope, *Persian Architecture: The Triumph of Form and Color* (New York: Braziller, 1965).

6.21
After drawings in Eric Schroeder, *A Survey of Persian Art,* ed. by Arthur Upham Pope, as reproduced in Nadar Ardalan and Laleh Bakhtiar, *The Sense of Unity: The Sufi Tradition in Persian Architecture* (Chicago: University of Chicago Press, 1973).

6.22
Drawing: Yu Wang.

7.1
From Pierre Auguste Marie Miger, *Les Ports de France: Peints par Joseph Vernet et Huë* (Paris: Chez l'Éditeur, 1812).

7.4
From Wayne W. Copper, The figure/ grounds, *The Cornell Journal of Architecture,* 1982; with permission, Wayne W. Copper, copyright 1967.

7.5
From Jim Harter, *Images of World Architecture* (New York: Bonanza Books, 1990).

7.6
From Steen Eiler Rasmussen, *Towns and Buildings: Described in Drawings and Words* (Liverpool: University of Liverpool, 1951).

7.7
Based on a map by Giovanni Battista Noli, 1784.

7.9

From Wayne W. Copper, The figure/
grounds, *The Cornell Journal of Architecture,*
1982; with permission, Wayne W. Copper,
copyright 1967.

7.10

From Steen Eiler Rasmussen, *Towns and
Buildings: Described in Drawings and Words*
(Liverpool: University of Liverpool, 1951).

7.11

After drawings in *Leon Krier, Houses, Palaces,
Cities,* ed. by Demetri Porphyrios, Architectural Design Profile 54 (London: Architectural Design AD Editions, 1984).

7.12

Photo: Michael Lykoudis.

7.13

From an unpublished work, courtesy of
Roger Sherwood. (Nancy: Nasser Al Hem-
iddi; Samarkand: Mohsen Heidari; Seville:
Antonio Gnisci; Ceske Budejovice: Saleh Al
Fouzon; Montpazier and Aigues-Mortes: Sa-
leh Al Fouzan; Bejing: Yu-Jen Kuo.)

Index

9.5.95   HENNESSEY   29.95   61851